LANDSCRIPT 4

Nature Modern

# LAN

# RIP

L A N D S C R I P T IS A PUBLICATION ON LANDSCAPE ÆSTHETICS INVITING AUTHORS FROM DIFFERENT DISCIPLINES TO INVEST THOUGHT ON ESTABLISHED MODES OF PERCEIVING, REPRESENTING, AND CONCEIVING NATURE. STEERED BY AN EDITORIAL BOARD COMPRISED OF INTERNATIONAL EXPERTS FROM VARIOUS FIELDS, WHICH WILL ENCOURAGE A CRITICAL AND CONTROVERSIAL DIALOGUE, ITS GOAL IS TO ACT AS A REVELATOR OF CONVENTIONAL PERCEPTIONS OF LANDSCAPE AND TO CULTIVATE THE DEBATE ON ÆSTHETICS AT A SCHOLARLY LEVEL. THIS DISCUSSION PLATFORM AIMS AT REKINDLING A THEORETICAL DEBATE, IN THE HOPE OF FOSTERING A BETTER UNDERSTANDING OF THE IMMANENCE OF LANDSCAPE ARCHITECTURE IN OUR CULTURE, FOCUSING CRITICALLY ON THE WAY WE THINK, LOOK, AND ACT UPON SITES.

Professor Christophe Girot, Albert Kirchengast (Editors-in-chief)
Institute of Landscape Architecture ILA, D–Arch, ETH Zürich

EDITORIAL BOARD



SUBMISSION GUIDELINES

Manuscript proposals are welcome in fields appropriate for *Landscript*. Scholarly submissions should be formatted in accordance with *The Chicago Manual of Style* and the spelling should follow American convention. The full manuscript must be submitted as a Microsoft Word document, on a CD or disk, accompanied by a hard copy of the text. Accompanying images should be sent as TIFF files with a resolution of at least 300 dpi at 8 × 9-inch print size. Figures should be numbered clearly in the text. Image captions and credits must be included with submissions. It is the responsibility of the author to secure permissions for image use and pay any reproduction fees. A brief letter of inquiry and author biography must also accompany the text.

Acceptance or rejection of submissions is at the discretion of the editors. Please do not send original materials, as submissions will not be returned.

Please direct submissions to this address:

*Landscript*
Chair of Professor Christophe Girot
Institute of Landscape Architecture ILA, ETH Zürich
Stefano-Franscini-Platz 5, HIL H 56.2
8093 Zurich, Switzerland

Questions about submissions can be emailed to:
kirchengast@arch.ethz.ch

Visit our website for further information:
www.girot.arch.ethz.ch

DSC

T 4

CHRISTOPHE GIROT
ALBERT KIRCHENGAST
(EDS.)

# NATURE MODERN

## THE PLACE OF LANDSCAPE IN THE MODERN MOVEMENT

# Foreword

Albert Kirchengast

When we set out to assemble this anthology, our premise was clear: we wanted to bring out the "knowledge" inherent in the modern house. We did not want to present a different take on the architecture of the Modern Movement (and its successors), or even to reframe it from the point of view of landscape architecture. What we intended instead was to explore the concept of the house as a cultural artifact, as a medium of ideas, a comprehensive "storage space," which, in and through its rooms and views, its constructive details, or its materiality, provides us with particular information about the human relationship with nature.

The relationship between architecture and nature inevitably manifests itself as a triangular one in which *we* interpose—as residents, builders, or interpreters. The seemingly clear polarity between nature and artifact instantly disappeares and gives rise to intellectual "complications." It is precisely these complications that became the subject of *Nature Modern*.

The first task of such an endeavor would be to convey what is expressed visually and structurally with and through architecture in conceptual language. This, then, was akin to the traditional procedure of interpretation as practiced in architectural criticism, where verbal statements are made in an abstract discussion about architectural qualities. A day-to-day affair, that turns out to encompass a second, deeper problem. If our understanding of nature is genuinely presented in architecture, it does not necessarily follow that architects themselves dispose of it in any other way than through their designs. Furthermore, if "nature" has played an *explicit* role in many buildings of the so-called "International Style," this platitude was not what we wanted to investigate. Our interest touches upon its *implicit*, hidden architectural "form;" an understanding of nature other disciplines, such as philosophy or the historical sciences, conceive in their own terms, constructing their own theories. Only if the "built object" opened up to our theoretical concerns, would it then be possible to position it in the broader context of the history of ideas. So the authors of this book had to stick closely to windows, columns, topographies, i.e., to concrete architectural manifestations—in order to *overcome* them.

*Nature Modern* looks at cultural phenomena through the lens of architecture. If our relationship to nature is considered as one of the key moments in the history of ideas, it surely reveals itself in various ways—evident in the examples from the wide range of locations and time spans that this anthology brings together. It is a diversity also present thanks to the individual approaches of our authors, who, for instance, do not always choose a single building to get closer to their subject. But most notably it is due to the subjects themselves: Richard Neutra demonstrates this breadth through his "scientific" *and* "esoteric"—so to speak—relationship with the nature of biology, while Adolf Loos seems to prefer to keep the views inside his richly adorned houses. His interiors literally take you on a geological journey through time or a trip into the heart of a tropical rainforest.

One thing is for sure: "nature" is the point of reference for all of theses thinkers and designers of architecture—and it moves. In a certain moment it comes closer to us, every once in a while it is given different names and theories, and then it moves off into the distance. Yet it always comes back and stays *virulent*.

Zurich and Vienna, July 2017

# Adolf Loos and Nature: America, Gardens, Science, and Matter

Marko Pogacnik

During the nineteenth century, the ancient idea of mimesis entered a critical phase due to the replacement of "the classical idea of constructing decoration with the post-classical one of decorating construction."—[1] Verisimilitude and analogy, two categories that had kept structure and decoration in a unified relationship until then, gradually lost effectiveness to construction methods that emphasized a greater independence between the building core and its envelope.

At the same time, the relationship between science and art became increasingly closer. For example, in *De l'abstraction*—a book published in 1864—the French chemist Chevreul—[2] demonstrated how in painting, the reproduction of a real model no longer entailed its exact copy; rather, it was the arrangement by the painter of colored matter on a flat surface following the law he called the "contraste simultané des couleurs"— i.e., the basis of Impressionist painting.—[3] The overcoming of the verisimilitude relationship between model and copy gave the image a kind of artistic autonomy from external reality. Thus it became possible to paint faces with three noses or purple trees, feel admiration for primitive art, or look at children's graphic expressions as another artistic practice. The American historian Neil Levine—taking the example of works by Labrouste, Viollet-le-Duc, Sulllivan, and Mies—described this phenomenon as an "erosion of

1 Neil Levine, *Modern Architecture. Representation and Reality* (New Haven: Yale University Press, 2009), 11.

2 Michel-Eugène Chevreul, *De l'abstraction considérée relativement aux Beaux-Arts et a la Litterature* (Dijon: J.-E. Rabutot, 1864). "le caractère d'abstraction de la peinture se monstre au plus haut degré dans la reproduction fidèle d'une forme colorée, qui n'est pas le modèle concrete, mais qui, au moyen des matières colorées habilment distribuées par l'arttiste sur une surface plane, offre à la vue la propriété inhérente au modèle d'avoir une figure déterminée que la lumière nous fait connaitre," 15.

3 See Paul Signac, *D'Eugène Delacroix au néo-impressionnisme* (Paris: Floury Libraire-Editeur, 1899). Signac anticipated Chevreul's arguments the previous year. Paul Signac, "Neo-impressionismus," *Pan* IV, nos. 1–2 (1898): 55–62.

representation."—[4] The influence of the classical idea of representation in architecture was gradually "eroded" by a concept of form, which in the nineteenth century had discovered the appeal of abstraction and the power of space itself.—[5]

The process of formal abstraction undermined the concept of representation, but not the relationship with nature, which remained an essential foundation of artistic activity. The work of Paul Klee, Wassily Kandinsky, Adolf Hölzel, and Piet Mondrian are emblematic examples. Klee stated, "The dialogue with nature remains for the artist a *conditio sine qua non*. The artist is a man, himself nature, and part of nature in natural space."—[6] Departing from the known statement that "Art does not reproduce the visible, but makes visible," Klee assigned to modern art the task of expanding the "art of optical seeing" through the "art of observing and of visualizing non-optical impressions." Klee was asking to enter the object in search for what eludes pure sensorial apperception: "Man dissects the thing and visualizes its inside with the help of plane sections …"—[7] Klee defined this particular understanding of an object as a "spatial" quality that emerges when the appearance of the object and its inner self are correlated. Space is distance, relational dimension that refers to the most abstract and mental part of the artist's work—that which in fact escapes the senses.

In the first two decades of the twentieth century, there was perhaps no other architect in Vienna than Adolf Loos whose work has been closer to the most radical contemporary art research. Loos regarded artists such as Kokoschka and Schoenberg as allies in fighting the hypocrisy towards the ornament; while Johannes Itten, supported by Loos, held in 1919 what is considered the first exhibition of abstract art in Vienna, a show that premiered in the same gallery where a year before the group of painters named "Bewegung" (Movement)

4 Levine, *Modern Architecture*, 178.

5 On the notion of mimesis see Walter Benjamin, "Ueber das mimetische Vermögen," in *Aufsätze, Essays, Vorträge*, GS. Vol. II.1, (Frankfurt am Main: Suhrkamp, 1977), 210, and the oeuvre of Roger Caillois, especially, *Meduse et Cie* (Paris: Gallimard, 1960).

6 Paul Klee, *Kunst-Lehre* (Leipzig: Reclam, 1987), 67. See also Wassily Kandinsky, *Punkt und Linie zu Fläche* (München: Langen, 1926).

7 Klee, *Kunst-Lehre*, 67.

showcased their art and were reviewed by Loos.—[8] "Non-philistine will, however, consider that all art is cubism. Cubism is simplification. Undoubtedly, the cubist also knows that man has a nose. But he omits it if it suits him."—[9] At the Internationale Kunstschau (International Art Show) in 1909, Loos bought the work of an unknown artist that impressed him: *Self-Portrait as a Warrior* by Oskar Kokoschka, a colored clay torso with the head in a contracted twist and the face marked by deep furrows where color thickened, strongly molded by fingermarks on its malleable clay mass—the same technique that Kokoschka used with colors on canvas.—[10]

8 Adolf Loos, "Bewegung. Eine neue Künstlerbewegung," in *Die Potemkinsche Stadt: Verschollene Schriften 1897–1933*, ed. Adolf Opel (Wien: Prachner, 1983), 137.

9 Ibid.
Loos had many critical texts on Cubism. See Herwarth Walden and Rudolf Blümner, *Der Geist des Kubismus und die Künste* (Berlin: Der Sturm, 1921) and Gabriele Koller, "Die Bücher aus der Bibliothek von Adolf Loos," in *Adolf Loos Exhibition Catalog*, ed. Graphische Sammlung Albertina (Wien: Seitenberg, 1989), 304.

10 On the continuity between Loos and visual arts see Joseph Masheck, *Adolf Loos: The Art of Architecture* (London: I.B. Tauris, 2013). On the relationship with Kokoschka see Oskar Kokoschka, *Mein Leben* (München: Bruckmann, 1971).

As for the classical notion of representation, Loos kept the idea of genres—the distinction between craftsmanship and art, house and palace, utilitarian object and monument—which allowed him to use the ornament or the column on the basis of convenience. The rigidly symmetrical, anthropomorphic composition that Loos applied to the main façades obeyed precise formal conventions, while only the side façades betrayed the complexity of the interior spaces. Loos's architectural sources refer constantly to the ancient past or to architects he regarded as having exemplary value: the Pantheon, Fischer von Erlach, and Schinkel. Nevertheless, we associate Loos with notions of space and abstraction, underlining the controversial amalgam that characterizes his ideas and architecture.

A commentary on the relationship between Loos and nature can but only highlight some key points of his research: the reference to American culture, the relationship with scientific thought, and the theme of the garden. Loos did not address all of these aspects in a systematic way, therefore our notes will have a fragmentary character.

Louis Sullivan, The Guaranty (now Prudential) Building, Buffalo, New York, 1894–95.

In modern times, the architect's social role changed radically, he was expected not only to deliver professional competence and humanistic knowledge, but also to be active in the public arena. The image that Loos created to introduce himself to the Viennese public is well exemplified by the synthetic portrait by Ludwig Hevesi: "On the extreme left of this line Loos stands by himself, having returned from America as a nihilistically leaning man of purpose …"—11 Thus it was not so much the English culture, but the New Continent and the direct contact with its architecture that were the key elements Loos used to mark the originality and uniqueness of his own view—primarily if we consider that the first major exhibition of Rennie Mackintosh's work was organized by the Secession in Vienna in 1900.

11 Ludvig Hevesi, *Österreichische Kunst im 19. Jahrhundert, Zweiter Teil 1848–1900* (Leipzig: Seemann, 1903), 285.

Most of all, Loos admired the balanced relationship that Americans had kept with nature, as well as between the countryside and the urban environment. Eduard Sekler described the scant documentary evidence about Loos's American journey: the house in Chestnut Street in Philadelphia where his uncle Frederik Loos worked, Sullivan's Auditorium in Chicago, the Fair Store by Le Baron Jenney, and the Fine Arts Building by Beman, both in Chicago.—12 Among these architects, it is definitely Sullivan who received the most attention by Loos, "even assuming they never met and Loos did not read his essays."—13

*Kindergarten Chats*—a book written by Sullivan in the early twentieth century, but published several years after Loos's *Ornament and Crime*—highlights the similarities and differences that characterize their intellectual approach: "Every building you see is the image of a man you do not see … the man is the reality, the building its offspring … the bricks, stones, steel and what not came into place in response to an impulse; and

12 Eduard F. Sekler, "Adolf Loos, Josef Hoffmann und die Vereinigten Staaten," in *Adolf Loos Exhibition Catalog*, 251–67.

13 Burkhardt Rukschcio and Roland Schachel, *Adolf Loos* (Salzburg: Residenz Verlag, 1987), 246 ff.

the cause at work behind that impulse was mental, not physical … Now if the mind of that man has departed from the normal and is more or less perverted, more or less degenerate, so will the building, which is its image, be more or less pervert or degenerate. I have told you that we must of necessity seek sanity by observing and noting the symptoms of insanity; that we must needs study disease [sic!], to discern the functions of health … Therefore, by this light, the critical study of architecture becomes not merely the direct study of an art …, but, *in extenso*, a study of the social conditions producing it; the study of a newly-shaping type of civilisation."—[14] Sullivan moved his gaze from the object to the man behind it and to the social conditions that allow its production.

14 Louis H. Sullivan, *Kindergarten Chats and Other Writings* (New York: Wittenborn, 1947); reprint 1976, 24. Writing on *Kindergarten Chats* began in 1901.

Similarly, what set Loos apart from the other artists of the Viennese Secession was his belief that the formal issue is not "merely" artistic, but a question about the conditions triggering the production of the artifact, which is civilization in its broadest sense. Pervert is the artist who focuses on creating teacups rather than caring about space as an organ of modern man's vital functions, the *Nervenmensch.*—[15] In this regard, Loos was the only one who understood Otto Wagner's criticism of nineteenth-century art: "It has appealed to artists to dissect the dead with a magnifying glass and lancet, rather than to grab the living at the pulse and alleviate their pain."—[16] The battle for the introduction of Western civilization in Austria was the fulcrum of Loos's intellectual project: he was fighting for the emancipation of farmers, women, and Jews, labeling degenerate anyone wasting time on drawing wallpaper patterns.

15 *Nervenmensch* (like *Nervenleben*, *Nervenkunst*) is the dweller of the modern metropolis who is in a constant state of nervous mental arousal.

16 Otto Wagner, *Moderne Architektur* 3rd ed. (Wien: Schroll, 1902), 59.

Sullivan's architecture featured an exuberant decoration covering the structural members, also invading the infill surfaces.—[17] According to Sullivan, structure and ornament can be separated only for analytical purposes, while a distinction between them is equivalent to the destruction of the work. Nevertheless, "I should say that it would

17 Louis H. Sullivan, "The tall office building artistically considered," *Lippincott's Magazine*, March 1896, 403–09; Louis H. Sullivan, "Ornament in Architecture," in *Engineering Magazine* (August 1892): 633–44.

be great for our aesthetic good if we should refrain entirely from the use of ornament for a period of years, in order that our thought might concentrate acutely upon the production of buildings well formed and comely in the nude."—[18] The nakedness Sullivan refers to was a transitory state, useful only to grasp an essential but not ultimate part of the building organism: "This step taken, we might safely inquire to what extent application of a decorative ornament would enhance the beauty of our structures—what new charm it would give them."—[19] Sullivan had a vast knowledge of the work of John Ruskin, Walt Whitman, and Ralph Waldo Emerson and he often used the image of nature to describe the essence of architecture: "… organisms in nature could be said to have style because each part was suited to the purpose and shape of the whole, both in form and function."—[20] According to Sullivan the reference to nature was the distinctive hallmark of the democratic organization of American society: "we must turn again to Nature,"—[21] a recommendation that Chicago, with its motto "Urbs in Horto" (City in a Garden) had transformed into an intelligent policy of public green areas to create an extensive urban park system.

18 Sullivan, *Kindergarten Chats*, 187.

19 Ibid.

20 Lauren Weingarden, *Louis H. Sullivan and 19th-Century Poetics of Naturalized Architecture* (Farnham: Ashgate Publishing, 2009), 249

21 Sullivan, *Kindergarten Chats*, 190. Sullivan was saying of himself: "… I am a gardener …", Ibid., 26.

"Wohnen lernen" (1921, Learning to Live) and "Die moderne Siedlung" (1926, The Modern Settlement) are the essays that outline Loos's program as Chief Architect of Vienna's Settlement Office, they are a synthesis of the civic program that Loos entrusted to architecture. Between 1919 and 1924—when his exile in Paris began—Loos enthusiastically shared the idea of the garden city, collaborating with landscape architects and economists such as Leberecht Migge—[22] and Hans Kampffmeyer. He developed his studies about the row house (the house with one wall) and the house with terraces. "The new movement, which has afflicted all of the residents of this city like a fever—the settlement movement—requires new people. People, who as Leberecht Migge the great

22 Leberecht Migge, *Die Gartenkultur des 20. Jahrhunderts* (Jena: Diederichs, 1913).

gardener rightly says, possess modern nerves."—[23] During those years, Loos designed what can be considered one of the finest master plans for a garden city, the Friedensstadt, which was to be built near Lainzer Tiergarten on the outskirts of Vienna.—[24] The principles for restoring a proper relationship to nature were the abolition of all picturesque romanticism, the subordination of the building to the landscape, and the replacement of the garden with the vegetable garden. The lifestyle Loos referred to was still the American one. "In the American, the city dwellers and the farmers are not as sharply separated as with us ... The American city dweller has not removed himself so far from nature ... For the Englander is also a real farmer."

23 Adolf Loos, "Wohnen lernen" (1921), in *Trotzdem*, ed. Adolf Opel (Wien: Prachner, 1982), 165. See also "Die moderne Siedlung" in the same book, 183.

24 Among his projects, one finds many diverse planimetric options: from very rigid schemes (*Verbauung am Laaerberg*) of row houses with an east-west orientation, to more complex schemes (*Gartenstadt Friedenstadt*, 1921) with the rows following the land.

Loos was aiming to involve the unemployed, the rootless worker, the soldier returning from the battlefront, in a process that—departing from the satisfaction of basic needs (vegetable garden as food support and self-built house)—was productive and not charitable. In contact with nature, the citizen discovers his noble origin because the gentleman comes from the rural world. "A gentleman is a person, who works only with the help of destruction. The gentleman is recruited from the farming community."—[25] When the mason picks up the pickaxe, the tailor his scissors or the farmer the hoe, their job assumes the most noble connotation as it becomes disruptive. The garden city, through the harmonious fusion between gentleman and peasant, between town and country, not only solved an immediate problem, the lack of housing, but also a serious political and social conflict that the war had exacerbated. Loos said: "The modern spirit is a social spirit and an antisocial spirit is an outmoded spirit." Therefore in the garden city, the contact with nature cannot be achieved through a private garden, but only with a park, a nursery, or an organized landscape. "Thus, possessing an individual garden is antisocial."—[26] The grounds of a house with terraces should not be a flower garden, but a garden to grow vegetables. In a

25 Adolf Loos, "Wohnen lernen" (1921), in *Trotzdem*, ed. Adolf Opel (Wien: Prachner, 1982), 165.

26 Ibid.

garden city, a tree is also antisocial and should be banned because it creates disagreement and contention among neighbors. Trees cast shadows on those who do not want them and reduce the amount of farming land.

Loos had a pragmatic and functional approach to nature when he considered it the transfiguration of a social relationship, while it became an emotional subject when contemplated as a live creature. Loos's love for nature—in the form of an animal, an insect, or a tree—was a sincere and deep feeling. His second wife, Elsie Altmann, recalls in her memoirs that he was once moved to tears by the movements of beetles that were feeding on manure: "You see how wise nature is, the instincts she has given her creations; the two are just insects and yet they know that by pushing the sphere uphill the friction and the pressure are stronger and thus more dung sticks. And they are not afraid of work. Just look how valiantly they push."—[27] After meeting Loos in 1917, Elsie saw him primarily reading Karl Kraus's magazine *Die Fackel* and works by Dostoyevsky, but his real passion was *Tierleben* (*Animal Life*) by Alfred Brehm, an encyclopedia in ten volumes whose first edition was released in 1869. Loos had empathy for the beauty of a tree threatened with pruning by real estate speculation. Claire Beck, his third wife, recalled his reaction when they were on the French Riviera and Loos heard that Juan-les-Pins pine trees might also be lost: "Loos buys a drawing board and ruler and is extremely busy for eight days. He designs a plan. He works feverishly. 'The pines, the pines,' he cries another time, 'they have to be saved!'"—[28]

Nevertheless, Loos had a controversial relationship with America. The statement by American philosopher and writer Ralph W. Emerson, "We go to Europe to be Americanised …,"—[29] could be easily applied to Loos's American experience. He traveled to America in search of a modernity that could answer his own questions: he went overseas to become Viennese.—[30] On March 11,

27 Elsie Altmann, *Mein Leben mit Adolf Loos* (Wien: Amalthea Verlag, 1994).

28 Claire Beck, *Adolf Loos. Un ritratto privato* (Roma: Castelvecchi, 2014), 102. Originally published as Claire Loos, *Adolf Loos privat* (Wien: Czernin, 2007).

29 Ralph Waldo Emerson, *The Conduct of Life* (London: J.M. Dent & Co; New York: Dutton, 1908).

30 Later Hevesi will comment that "Wien wird ihm [Loos] auf die Länge Chicago austreiben" (Vienna will drive Chicago out of him [Loos]). Ludvig Hevesi, "Kunst auf der Strasse," *Fremden-Blatt* (30 May 1899).

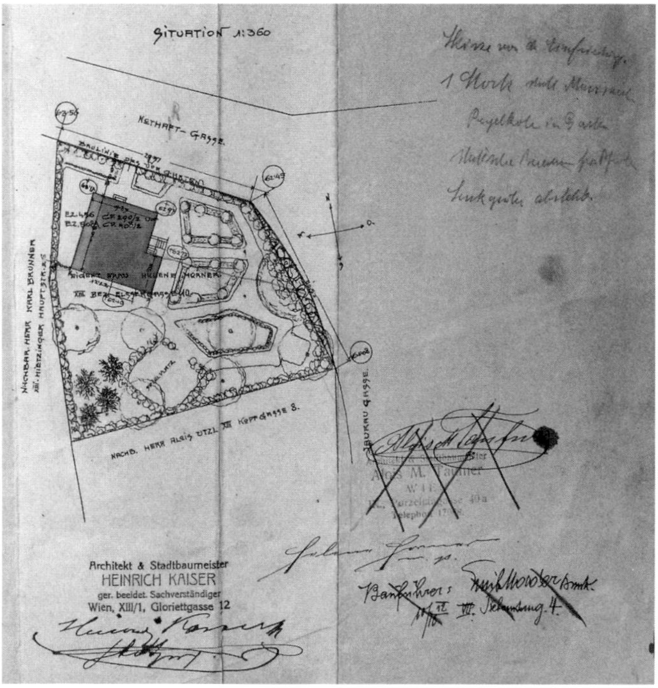


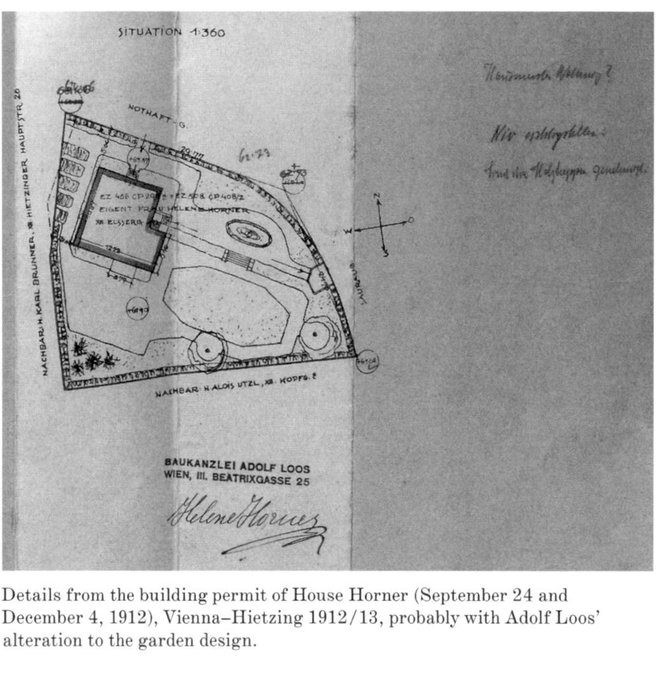


Details from the building permit of House Horner (September 24 and December 4, 1912), Vienna–Hietzing 1912/13, probably with Adolf Loos' alteration to the garden design.

1920, Rudolf Schindler sent Loos *Kindergarten Chats*, Sullivan's manuscript, with prayers to help the American master find a publisher because he had no economic resources.—31 Sullivan was later deeply disappointed by Loos's behavior, because Loos never answered Schindler's plea. When Baron Nicolai in Nice mentioned to Loos his plan to move to the US, Loos said: "America? No. I will remain here, the sun always shines here."—32

31 Rukschcio and Schachel, *Adolf Loos*, 246.

32 Altmann, *Mein Leben mit Adolf Loos*. See also Joseph Masheck, *Adolf Loos: The Art of Architecture*, 62.

## The Garden

Loos's architectural research developed during the First World War with a certain degree of systematic continuity. The Scheu House (1912) was the embryo for the later Terrassenhaus (1923); the "house with one wall" of 1921 proposes the same radical pragmatism one finds in House Steiner (1910) or House Horner (1912). The single-family houses built in the elegant suburbs of Vienna were devoid of any ornament, cornices, moldings, or columns; their simple, bare volumes have radical, abstract façades.—33 If owning a garden in the garden city was antisocial (because of space lost to farming), in the bourgeois house any kind of building decoration was unproductive and wasteful. Loos defined what was unproductive from the perspective of production, without giving any positive social function to the consumption and destruction of the excess, key issues in the Surrealist experience. Adorno writes that "art theory cannot resign to reflect on natural beauty" because "art is the refuge of mimetic behaviour"—34 and it is the artist's mimetic impulse that makes permeable any barrier established between fine art (autonomous) and applied art: "Only schematically can the moment of expression be relegated in art and split off from the things of use … Hardly a practical form, which—in addition to its appropriateness—would not also be a symbol."—35

33 See also David Leatherbarrow, "Interpretation and Abstraction in the Architecture of Adolf Loos," in *Journal of Architectural Education* no. 4 (Summer, 1987): 2–9. The chapter dedicated to Loos is not so convincing in Gevork Hartoonian, *Ontology of Construction: On Nihilism of Technology in Theories of Modern Architecture* (Cambridge: Cambridge University Press, 1994).

34 Theodor W. Adorno, *Ohne Leitbild: Parva Aesthetica* (Frankfurt am Main: Suhrkamp, 1967), 111.

35 Ibid.

What meaning does the garden have in Loos's villas?—[36] We know that in his library there were a few volumes by Adalbert Stifter, who rendered the garden in *Nachsommer* an epic space where man takes care of the world.—[37] However, the devoted kinship to nature described by Stifter does not appear in Loos's built work, surprisingly if one thinks how much attention was paid to this matter in the first decade of the twentieth century by authors such as Paul Schultze-Naumburg, Hermann Muthesius, Alfred Lichtwark, Fritz Schumacher, Peter Behrens, and Ludwig Mies van der Rohe.—[38] Loos's villas appear to touch the ground without establishing any relationship with it. This is quite peculiar considering that his architectural oeuvre consists mainly—aside from the house on Michaelerplatz—of single-family homes that must have been conceived and designed in relation with their gardens. Although the layout of the interior spaces is complex, the design of the outdoors appears almost banal. Some significant examples are the Horner, Duschnitz, Scheu, and Villa Karma houses.

During the construction of the Horner house in December 1912, Loos submitted a design review where the garden becomes the extension of the indoor spaces.—[39] The building, situated on a terraced plot, presents two-and-a-half stories on the side facing the street and three towards the courtyard located at a lower level. In the revised drawings, the two garden terraces are connected by a grassy embankment with a centrally located stairway corresponding to the interior staircase linking the basement to the main entry on the street side.

Even in the Duschnitz house, one can reconstruct the original garden layout from the construction files. In a 1962 drawing, submitted to build a swimming pool, one can see that the music room originally opened onto a terrace located on a slightly higher ground and was connected to the garden by three steps. With the revision

36 It was the architect Josef Frank, and his society "Haus und Garten," who first introduced in Vienna a true interest in gardens. See Iris Meder, "The Garden Determines the Interior," in *Josef Frank Against Design. The Architect's Anti-Formalist Oeuvre*, ed. Christoph Thun-Hohenstein, Hermann Czech, and Sebastian Hackenschmidt (Basel: Birkhäuser, 2015), 156–71.

37 Koller, "Die Bücher aus der Bibliothek von Adolf Loos," 305.

38 Paul Schultze-Naumburg, *Gärten*, vol. 2, *Kulturarbeiten* (München: Callwey, 1902); Hermann Muthesius, *Landhaus und Garten. Beispiele neuzeitlicher Landhäuser nebst Grundrissen, Innenräumen und Gärten* (München: Bruckmann, 1907); Alfred Lichtwark, *Park- und Gartenstudien* (Berlin: Cassirer, 1909); Fritz Schumacher and the urban projects for Köln and Hamburg; Peter Behrens, "Der moderne Garten," in *Berliner Tageblatt*, June 10, 1911, 9; Barry Bergdoll, "Das Wesen des Raums bei Ludwig Mies van der Rohe," in *Ludwig Mies van der Rohe. Die Berliner Jahre 1907–1938* (München: Prestel, 2001), 67–105.

39 First project September 1912; construction design review December 1912.

of the design, the garden was leveled off because the slight ground variations were seen to be an unnecessary obstacle.

Loos's houses always had basements, which created a discontinuity with the garden level. At the beginning of the twentieth century, it was common practice in Vienna to locate the kitchen and the staff quarters in the basement, while the dining room was above the kitchen and the food was catered upstairs with a small dumb waiter. This is the case, for example, in the Duschnitz and Stoessl houses. In fact, Loos favored a spatial organization originating from a more old-fashioned social structure, thus sacrificing the modern need for direct contact and a continuity between indoor spaces, and an outdoor natural garden as in English and American architecture. Loos, who could violently stigmatize a new decoration by Hoffmann, never opposed the practice of lodging the servants' quarters in wet basements, eventually commenting in *Wohnen lernen* that in America a woman is able to perform all domestic duties without personnel: "And this lack of domestic staff has brought with it the preparation of meals in the living area. Because the woman of the house has the right to spend her time in the living area, not in the kitchen."—[40] As Adorno had observed: "Even in Loos, the sworn enemy of the Viennese kitsch, one finds some remarkably bourgeois traces. Since the bourgeois structure had already permeated so many feudalistic and absolutist forms in his city …"—[41]

40 Loos, *Wohnen lernen*, 386.

41 Adorno, *Ohne Leitbild: Parva Aesthetica*, 110.

Continuing the analysis of the relationship between house and garden, in original photos of the time one also notices the peculiar presence of creeping plants that almost entirely cover the façades of Loos's houses. The presence of vines is not due to the owners' carelessness—vines are problematic inasmuch they attract bugs and damage the plaster—but because it had been a city requirement, as is clear in the Scheu house. In the building permit, the owners of the Scheu house had to commit to covering the building façade with creeping plants and were only allowed to choose between ivy or Virginia creeper. The building should have been completely covered by a green blanket. The façade of the house with its unadorned aspect and bareness was a social provocation for the quiet suburb of Hietzing, thus the green covering had the function of mitigating the radical nature of this linguistic approach. In the Goldman & Salatsch building, Loos decided to provide bronze planters to soften the façades, whose bareness seemed intolerable. Window boxes or creeping vegetation had the same function as the tiny decorative perforations on shoes—an ornament Loos accepted from social conventions he did not share, but out of respect towards those who did not have alternative aesthetic pleasures.—42

42 “Ich predige den aristokraten. Ich ertrage ornamente am eigenen körper, wenn sie die freude meiner mitmenschen ausmachen. Sie sind dann auch meine freude” (I preach to aristocrats. I can bear ornaments on my own body if they bring joy to my fellow human beings. Then they are also my joy) Adolf Loos, “Ornament und Verbrechen,” in *Trotzdem*, 287.

Nature however, was not transfigured by Loos in the form of ornamental plaster or ceramic floral tiles, this would have been the Wiener Werkstätte. Loos exposed nature in its material evidence, in the form of a flowering plant, a marble or wood vein, so that the most radical abstraction was presented in the most concrete and physical materiality. This dialectic opposition between the artifact’s bareness and the materiality of nature represented the exact opposite of the Wiener Werkstätte’s “stylization,” which Loos thought was derived from Japanese art: “Thus, Japanese is primarily the abandonment of symmetry. Added to this is the disembodiment of the objects to be represented. The Japanese portray flowers, but they are pressed flowers … A stylizing is created to decorate the surface. And in doing so, one can remain naturalistic. That is, above all, an embroidery technique that has to come in handy for anyone who takes pleasure in natural forms.”—43

43 Adolf Loos, “Kunstgewerbliche Rundschau” (1898), in *Ins Leere gesprochen* (Berlin: Verlag der Sturm, 1921), 24.

According to Adorno, Loos censored ornament as an erotic symbol because he believed that "unerfasste Natur" (uncurbed Nature) represented something regressive and painful, due to the degenerate aspect of exposing an erotic content.—[44] Holding his hand on the crotch of Elsie Altmann, his young lover, Loos confessed that "this was the most important thing on earth, the one which makes the world keep going; if it were not for the woman's sex no one would go to work."—[45] Loos admitted to being ashamed of the power of sexual desire, he felt a sense of guilt that forced the civilized man to remove a truth that for any primitive would be instead a source of happiness, a paradise.—[46] The removed entity emerges, however, in other forms of Loos's work: "The absence of ornament is not an absence of stirrings, but acts as a new allure, enlivened. The mill that does not rattle wakes the miller."—[47] Abstraction is a form of excitement of the senses whose effect could be compared to the contemplation of a naked body. Richard Schaukal, a critic who received some confidential comments from Loos on the Goldman & Salatsch building, noted that "his idea is strange: from the rich (perhaps too rich) garment, which slipped down from his hips, the naked body of the building rises."—[48] Schaukal compares the main façade to the image of a woman when the ribbon holding her dress loosens and slips to the floor thus revealing her naked body. Nudity enjoys an ambivalent status, because it may emerge as the beautiful, contemplative image of truth, or the projection of an indecent erotic desire.

In a text from 1923 entitled "Nacktheit" (Nudity), Loos debated the issue of how modernity changed the attitude towards the body: "The healthy person perceives every garment as erotic."—[49] It is a commentary that has great affinity with the statement by the art historian Ernst Grosse about primitive art: "… clothing to conceal the genitals … is in no way suited for detracting attention from the body parts concerned, but quite the opposite draws attention to them … All such costumes

44 Adorno, *Ohne Leitbild: Parva Aesthetica*, 111. "Loos führt die Ornamente auf erotische Symbole zurück … unerfasste Natur ist ihm rückständig und peinlich in eins" (Loos traces ornament back to erotic symbols … He finds uncurbed nature both regressive and embarrassing). Adorno refers the central question of Loos's architecture to the query "wie Kunst irgend noch möglich ist, der keine Ornamente mehr substanziell sind und die keine erfinden kann" (how art would be possible in any form if ornamentation were no longer a substantial element, if art itself could no longer invent any true ornaments), 112.

45 Altmann, *Mein Leben mit Adolf Loos*.

46 On the pedophilia charges against Loos, see the last work by Christopher Long, *Der Fall Loos* (Wien: Amalthea Signum Verlag, 2015).

47 Adolf Loos, "Ornament und Erziehung," in Adolf Loos, *Sämtliche Schriften: Trotzdem*, ed. Franz Glück (Wien/München: Herold, 1962), 393.

48 Richard Schaukal, "Ein Haus und seine Zeit," in *Konfrontationen. Schriften von und über Adolf Loos*, ed. Adolf Opel (Wien: Prachner, 1988), 46.

49 Adolf Loos, "Nacktheit," in Adolf Loos, *Gesammelte Schriften*, ed. Adolf Opel (Wien: Lesethek Verlag, 2010), 592.

Pillendreher bei der Arbeit.

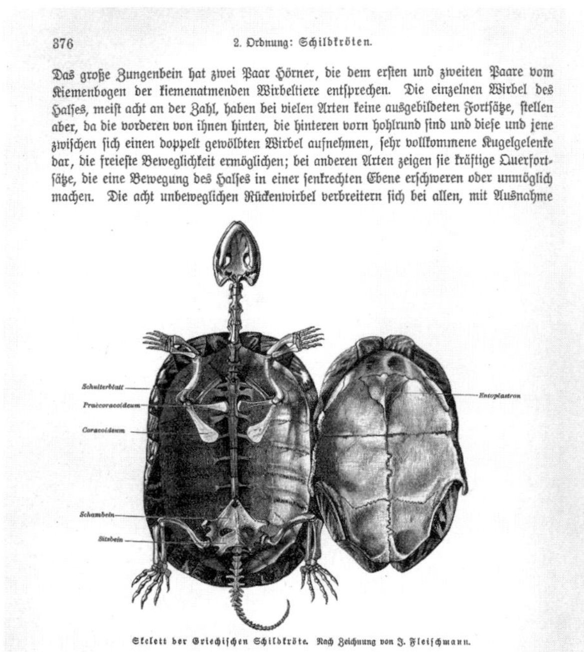

376 2. Ordnung: Schildkröten.

Das große Zungenbein hat zwei Paar Hörner, die dem ersten und zweiten Paare vom Kiemenbogen der kiemenatmenden Wirbeltiere entsprechen. Die einzelnen Wirbel des Halses, meist acht an der Zahl, haben bei vielen Arten keine ausgebildeten Fortsätze, stellen aber, da die vorderen von ihnen hinten, die hinteren vorn hohlrund sind und diese und jene zwischen sich einen doppelt gewölbten Wirbel aufnehmen, sehr vollkommene Kugelgelenke dar, die freieste Beweglichkeit ermöglichen; bei anderen Arten zeigen sie kräftige Querfortsätze, die eine Bewegung des Halses in einer senkrechten Ebene erschweren oder unmöglich machen. Die acht unbeweglichen Rückenwirbel verbreitern sich bei allen, mit Ausnahme



Skelett der Griechischen Schildkröte. Nach Zeichnung von J. Fleischmann.

einer einzigen Art, zu Knochenschilden, indem ihre Dornfortsätze zuerst mit Knochenplatten, die ursprünglich der Haut angehören, verwachsen; ebensolche Hautknochen, die anfänglich von den Rippen getrennt waren, verwachsen mit diesen, und sowohl die in der Mittellinie des Rückens hintereinander verlaufenden als auch die über den Rippen gelegenen Knochenplatten verbinden sich auch unter sich durch zackige Nähte miteinander und stellen so den Rückenpanzer dar; diesen überziehen wiederum äußerlich symmetrische Horntafeln, die sich in ihren Umrissen aber durchaus nicht mit den darunterliegenden Knochenschilden decken; nur bei den Weichschildkröten liegt eine dicke lederartige Haut über dem knöchernen Rückenpanzer. „Die Rippen“, sagt Vogt, „ziehen meist bis zum äußern Rande des Panzers hin; zuweilen aber sind sie als Platten nur in der Nähe der Wirbelsäule entwickelt, und nach außen hin stehen dann die Rippenenden gleichsam wie Radspeichen an dem Gerippe hervor,

Plates form Alfred Brehm’s book *Das Tierleben*, Edition of the “Bibliographisches Institut,” 1911–18.

do not prove the need to hide, but the obsession to show something."—[50] In Loos, the mere exposure of the body is not erotic, while the act of undressing, the dress that slides on the sides a moment before falling, is erotic.

## Science

In the nineteenth century, the development of scientific thinking radically changed the concept of nature. Seen until then as representation or mimesis, nature became a source of models whose high efficiency could be compared to the most advanced achievements in the technical field.—[51] Remaining in the field of construction, one can look at the bone structure analysis by English engineer William Fairbairn or at the "Victoria Regia" leaf morphology transposition in the roofing system of the Crystal Palace by Joseph Paxton. Nature astonished the engineer and the architect for the essential means and materials used to achieve formal solutions, which were not only highly efficient but also of rare beauty—evident in Ernst Haeckel's studies on diatoms and on radiolarians. The German zoologist—able to blend Goethe's notion of "metamorphosis of forms" with Darwin's theory of evolution—presented his observations on marine organisms with color drawings that influenced an entire generation of artists to develop a new artistic language.—[52]

Many esteemed scientists—[53] promoted the evolutionary theories of nature and the notion of a correspondence between phylogeny and ontogeny—[54] in the development of living organisms; Loos considered these theories valid in the field of culture and social relations: "The evolution of culture is equivalent to removing the ornament from the article of use."—[55] According to Loos, the concept of evolution—representing the peak of scientific research—was orienting the lifestyle of modernity—[56] and it also implied a political component.—[57] In the nineteenth century, the scientific world

50 Ernst Grosse, *Die Anfänge der Kunst* (Freiburg im Breisgau: Akademische Verlagsbuchhandlung, 1894), 113.

51 Jonathan Crary, *Techniques of the Observer: Vision and Modernity in theNineteenth Century* (Cambridge, MA: The MIT Press, 1990).

52 Robert Michael Brain, *The Pulse of Modernism: Physiological Aesthetics in Fin-de-Siècle Europe* (Seattle, WA: University of Washington Press, 2015).

53 See Hermann Helmholtz, *Vorträge und Reden* vol. 1 (Braunschweig: Vieweg, 1903), 288.

54 In his *Entwicklungsgeschichte* (history of development) Haeckel distinguished two parts: the ontogenesis (or embryology) and the phylogeny. The first addressed the development of single individuals, the second that of a species (through the study of paleontology). Ernst Haeckel, *Natur und Mensch* (Leipzig: Reclam, 1920), 35.

55 Adolf Loos, "Ornament und Verbrechen" (1910), in *Trotzdem, Sämtliche Schriften*, ed. Franz Glück, 304.

56 "Ich will gleich von vornherein sagen, daß ich für die wohnküche bin, aus rein evolutionistischen, modernen gesichtspunkten heraus" (I want to say from the outset that I am in favor of the open-plan kitchen, from purely evolutionist, modern perspectives). In Adolf Loos, "Die Moderne Siedlung," in *Sämtliche Schriften: Trotzdem*, 413.
→

discovered that, thanks to Charles Darwin, it could offer not only a new interpretation of natural phenomena, but also an overall view of the world to understand nature as well as man and his history—including art, which is the highest expression of mankind's history.—58 In addition to Charles Darwin (England), Michel-Eugene Chevreul—59 and Charles Henry—60 (France) and Hermann Helmholtz (Germany)—61 also developed studies that—departing from chemistry, optics, and physics—revolutionized science and the world of art. This particular scientific thought was also developed by exceptional protagonists in Austria, as witnessed by the work of Ernst Mach, which will be analyzed in the following paragraphs.

A place of incubation for modern art in Vienna was the salon of Berta Zuckerkandl and her husband Emil, a professor of anatomy at the University of Vienna.—62 Berta Zuckerkandl—art critic and passionate advocate of women's emancipation—had developed a close relationship with Gustav Klimt, Ludwig Hevesi, and Hermann Bahr, among the most active supporters of the new art, the Secession.—63 In her house—often also visited by the writer Arthur Schnitzler (laryngologist), by Otto Zuckerkandl (urologist), and the psychiatrists Richard Krafft-Ebing and Julius Wagner—scientific research and social commitment evolved alongside with innovative considerations on modern art. Klimt's work witnessed this mixture in an exemplary way.—64

Hermann Bahr, passionate critic of late nineteenth-century painting, described Impressionism as the latest manifestation of a classical pagan culture that selected nature as the basis of its vision of the world.—65 At the end of the nineteenth century, the parallel crisis of Naturalism and Impressionism led Bahr to talk about "an overcoming of Nature" itself. Reviving a statement by Huysmans, Bahr wrote categorically that "die Zeit

57 "Wer revolutionen vermeiden will, wie ich, wer evolutionist ist, soll ständig daran denken: der besitz eines gartens beim einzelnen muß aufreizend wirken" (Whoever wants to avoid revolutions, as I, whoever is evolutionist, should always remember: the possession of a garten must seem provocative). Ibid., 406.

58 Barbara Jean Larson and Fae Brauer, eds., *The Art of Evolution: Darwin, Darwinism and Visual Culture* (Lebanon, NH: University of New England Press, 2009); Linda Nochlin and Martha Lucy, eds., "The Darwin Effect: Evolution and Nineteenth-Century Visual Culture," *Nineteenth-Century Art Worldwide* 2 (2003): 2; David Kohn, "The Aesthetic Construction of Darwin's Theory," in *The Elusive Synthesis: Aesthetics and Science*, ed. Alfred I. Tauber (Dordrecht: Kluwer Academic Publishers, 1996), 13–48.

59 Michel-Eugène Chevreul, *De la loi du contraste simultané des couleurs …, considéré d'après cette loi dans ses rapports avec la peinture, les tapisseries des Gobelins …* (Paris: Pitois-Levrault), 1839.

60 Charles Henry, *Introduction à une esthétique scientifique* (Paris: La Revue contemporaine, 1885).

61 Hermann Helmholtz, *Handbuch der Physiologischen Optik* 2nd ed. (Hamburg/Leipzig: Leopold Voss, 1896).

62 Loos had a polemical discussion with Berta Zuckerkandl who was a supporter of the Secession. See Rukschcio and Schachel, *Adolf Loos*, 64. →

der Natur ist vorbei" (the time of Nature is over).—[66] Scientific knowledge, which provided Impressionism with studies on eye physiology and the laws on color perception, also laid the foundations for its overcoming by Expressionism through the studies by Ernst Mach on the relationship of sensations to external stimuli (*Empfindungen*). Impressionism was confined by Bahr to a purely technical aspect and its art to simple retinal experience.—[67] It is a transition that, according to Bahr, occurred in few years—from the 1898 publication—[68] in *Pan* magazine of Paul Signac's essay on Neo-Impressionism to the delayed reception of Ernst Mach's book on the *Analysis of Sensations* in 1900.—[69] In *Dialog vom Tragischen* (Dialogue on the Tragic) Bahr describes this transition in a chapter significantly entitled "Das unrettbare Ich" (the ego that cannot be saved).—[70] What Bahr derived from Mach's work was the idea that the ego's existence—like that of the world—is only nominalistic and that the "Thing" in itself (Ding) does not exist except for its function as "arrangement of our sensations." What we call "Thing" is nothing but a changing and mobile constellation influenced by the occurrence of diverse sensations that are chromatic, acoustic, and thermal all together. It is a concept Bahr shared with another author he quoted—Theodor Beer, who had just published in 1903 his *Weltanschauung eines modernen Naturforschers* (Worldview of a Natural Scientist), a work in which he publicly expressed his admiration for Ernst Mach.—[71]

Theodor Beer, professor of physiology at the University of Vienna, had a significant internship at the Zoological Station in Napoli, which was founded in 1872 by Anton Dohrn, a student of Ernst Haeckel and an advocate of Darwin's evolutionary theories. It is illuminating that Dohrn had called Hans von Marées—one of the greatest German painters of the late nineteenth century—to fresco the library of the Zoological Station in Napoli;

63 Bertha Zuckerkandl, *Österreich intim: Erinnerungen 1892–1942* (Frankfurt am Main: Ullstein, 1988).

64 Emily Braun, "Ornament as Evolution. Gustav Klimt and Berta Zuckerkandl," in *Gustav Klimt*, ed. Renée Rice (New York: Neue Galerie, 2007), 145–69.

65 Hermann Bahr, "Erste Kunstausstellung der Vereinigung bildender Künstler Oesterreichs (März–April 1898)," in *Secession* (Wien: Wiener Verlag, 1900), 20.

66 Hermann Bahr, "Die Décadence," in *Studien zur Kritik der Moderne* (Frankfurt: Literarische Anstalt Ruiten & Loening, 1894), 23.

67 Hermann Bahr, *Expressionismus* (München: Delphin Verlag, 1920), 60–64.

68 Paul Signac, "Neoimpressionismus," *Pan* vol. IV, nos. 1–2 (1898): 55–62. The book from the following year, Paul Signac, *D'Eugène Delacroix au néo-impressionnisme* (Paris: Floury Libraire-Editeur, 1899).

69 After fifteen years of silence, Mach's book suddenly entered the critics' spotlight at the beginning of the 1900s. Ernst Mach, *Beiträge zur Analyse der Empfindungen* (Jena: Fischer, 1886).

70 Hermann Bahr, *Dialog vom Tragischen* (Berlin: Fischer, 1904). Dedicated to Gustav Klimt.

71 Theodor Beer, *Weltanschuung eines modernen Naturforschers* (Dresden/Leipzig: Reissner, 1903).

Beer found himself in this innovative environment in the field of experimental research, where art and science contributed to shaping a culture that combined technical and scientific aspects with the humanities.

Theodor Beer was thus part of a reformative culture very close to that of Berta Zuckerkandl's circle, which was also significant for architectural patronage. Josef Hoffmann—[72] had Victor Zuckerkandl (Emil's brother) as a client, while Adolf Loos had Theodor Beer. At the turn of the twentieth century, both architects were perceived as part of the same idea of modernity. Hevesi had defined Loos by saying, "Adolf Loos behaves like a sincere non-Secessionist in his 'Café Museum'. Not as an enemy of the Viennese Secession, but as something different, because both are modern. The game room in his café is also furnished in the style of the Secessionists."—[73]

In 1903, Theodor Beer had commissioned Loos with the project for a villa on Lake Lemano, near Montreux;—[74] Villa Karma was a project that was only partially completed because Beer was accused of pedophilia and forced first to go abroad and then to serve three months in prison in Vienna, which was followed bankruptcy and suicide in 1919.—[75] The reference to the Buddhist notion of karma appears also in a note from Ernst Mach evidently known to Beer: "Buddhism comes to this conclusion [the dissolution of the ego] since millennia, departing from a practical point of view. … See also the wonderful novel: P. Carus, *Karma, a Story of Early Buddhism*, Chicago 1894."—[76]

The relationship between Beer and Loos cannot be described as a mere professional relationship between a client and his architect. Villa Karma was one of Loos's first major architectural commissions, though it was conditioned by the presence of an existing building. Loos established a relationship with Beer that shared aesthetic principles and lifestyle. Abroad because of his legal problems, Beer wrote to Loos from America: "I am sorry

72 The industrialist Victor Zuckerkandl commissioned Josef Hoffmann for the construction of the sanatorium in Purkersdorf, which can be considered one of his architectural masterpieces.

73 Ludvig Hevesi, "Kunst auf der Strasse," in *Acht Jahre Sezession (März 1897–Juni 1905). Kritik, Polemik, Chronik* (Wien: Verlagsbuchhandlung Carl Konegen, 1906), 174–75.

74 For the history of the project, see Rukschcio and Schachel, *Adolf Loos*, 92–94 and 425–29; Vera J. Behalova, "Adolf Loos: Villa Karma" (PhD diss., Universität Wien, 1974). About Theodor Beer, see W. Gerhard Pohl and Rudolf Werner Soukup, *Die wissenschaftliche Welt von gestern* (Wien: Böhlau, 2004), 89–96.

75 Florian Mildenberger, "'… als Conträrsexual und als Päderast verleumdet …'" – Der Prozess um den Naturforscher Theodor Beer (1866–1919) im Jahre 1905," in *Zeitschrift für Sexualforschung* 18 (2005), 332 ff; Christopher Long, *Der Fall Loos* (Salzburg: Muery Salzmann, 2014).

76 Ernst Mach, *Die Analyse der Empfindungen und das Verhältnis des Physischen zum Psychischen* (Jena: Fischer, 1903), 79. On p. 178 he quotes Beer's work on the vision structure of fish.

that … you are not in America; because you belong here and would be more recognized and busier as in our little Imperial-Royal Balkan country! You would have to aspire to become, for example, the first architect for Pullman and give the American touring car your seal—the absolute, dust-free, pure, practical, space-saving simplicity without any embellishment … I know hardly anyone whose taste appeals to me as much, and seems to be as honest, dignified and organically appropriate to our time, as yours."—[77] Beer shared with Loos—sent twice to England by him—the admiration for British culture as well as a contemptuous irony towards the small Balkan state.

Beer, however, was a difficult and very demanding client as seen in a letter dated December 1905, in which he severely reproached Loos for the construction of a bed that he criticized for "completely unnecessary ornament, which you have stuck me with."—[78] Loos, who a few years later would become the main opponent of ornamentation, shared with Beer the belief that any formal principle ought to be subjected to a radical exercise of coherence, which could not retreat—even when facing paradox and scandal.

Theodor Beer became known in 1903 after the publication of a series of articles about Ernst Mach in the *Neue Freie Presse*, the Viennese liberal daily paper that in previous years had also published some articles by Loos. Perhaps this is how they became acquainted. It is not clear whether Loos had read Ernst Mach,—[79] but the Beer case tells us that Mach's radical antimetaphysical position had affinities with a concept of architecture marked by the most rigorous functionality—plans, lighting, hygiene—[80]—the renunciation of all ornament, and, finally, the adherence to an image belonging to antiquity. "In front of the portico, a sarcophagus was to be placed as a fountain, not round pillars, but square pillars covered with marble slabs, the brass railings have to

77 Letter by Beer to Loos, July 1904. Behalova, "Adolf Loos: Villa Karma," 38. Beer returned from America in the summer of 1905 and in October he was sentenced to three months imprisonment.

78 Ibid., 43. Loos abandoned the project in 1907, and in 1908 the Viennese architect Hugo Ehrlich took over the design.

79 In Loos's library there is an uncompleted copy of Beer's book *Weltanschuung eines modernen Naturforschers*. See Rukschcio and Schachel, *Adolf Loos*, 92. About the relevance of Mach's theory for the Viennese culture see J. T. Blackmore, R. Itagaki, S. Tanaka, eds., *Ernst Mach's Vienna 1895-1930: Or Phenomenalism as Philosophy of Science*, Vienna: Springer, 2001. To Mach referred Schnitzler, Hofmannsthal, Roth and Musil who wrote his PhD-Thesis, *Beitrag zur Beurteilung der Lehren Machs*, discussed in 1908 in Berlin.

80 Behalova, "Adolf Loos: Villa Karma," 39: "Es handelt sich um die allereinfachste, aber saubere, auf Heizung, Canalisierung, Bad, Waschtische, Beleuchtung hygienischste und praktischste Ausgestaltung" (It is the simplest, yet clean, most hygienic and practical design for heating, canalization, sinks, and lighting).

Adolf Loos, Country House Khuner, Payerbach/Semmering, 1929/30.

be low, completely simple, somewhat antique-like."—[81] Simple forms, marble cladding and antique casings are architectural qualities that Beer shared with Loos, while, for the same functional reasons, he explicitly rejects the *Raumplan*: "The determination of the rooms remains … no differences in floor levels in the entire house. One should not stumble!"—[82]

Beer and Loos signed the contract for the design of the villa on February 10, 1904: the first five points accurately described the interior design development, while the sixth and last paragraph focused on the outdoors—garden, boathouse, and shed—which Loos would design at no charge.—[83] To client and architect, the design of the garden had a secondary importance despite being a villa with a park in a privileged position overlooking Lake Lemano.—[84] The relationship to the lake, the landscape, and the layout of the paths or the parterre did not seem to be of any design interest to Loos.

## Matter

"May I take you to the shores of a mountain lake? The sky is blue, the water green, and everywhere is profound tranquility. The clouds and mountains are mirrored in the lake, the houses, and chapels as well! They do not look as if they were fashioned by man, it is as if they came straight from God's workshop, like the mountains and the trees, the clouds and the blue sky. And everything exudes an air of beauty and peace … But what is this? A discordant note in the tranquility. Like an unnecessary screech. Among the locals' houses that were not built by them, but by God, stands a villa. Whether a good or a bad architect, I don't know. All I know is that the tranquility, peace, and beauty have vanished."—[85]

In the essay "Architektur" (Architecture)—probably written at the end of 1910 when the press campaign

81 Ibid., 35.

82 Ibid., S. 40–41.

83 From the contract dated 10.2.1904: "VI. Herr Loos verpflichtet sich die Zeichnungen für Gartenmauer, Gartentore u.a. Kleinigkeiten ausserhalb des Hauses, sowie für andere zum Garten gehörige Nebenräume in Karma und Chande ohne Honorar zu liefern." (VI. Mr. Loos undertakes the drawings for the garden wall, garden gates, among others. Small details beyond the house, as well as for other ancillary rooms in Karma and Chande are to be delivered without a fee). Ibid., 170.

84 In Behalova's dissertation, there is no information about the park, which must have had an extension of a few hectares.

85 Loos, *Architektur*, 90. English translation from: Adolf Loos, "Architecture" in *On architecture: studies in Austrian literature, culture and thought* (Riverside: Ariadne Press, 2007), 73–85.

against his building on Michaelerplatz was intensifying—Loos used the metaphor of a mountain village where the farms are reflected in the green waters of a lake, in order to describe the state of contemporary architecture. What presented itself to the observer was not the work of man, but of divine creation. The farms were built using the trees from the local forest and the stone of the surrounding mountains. Buildings and nature blended in an image of total continuity as if the houses had always existed—as long as the mountains, the woods, and the lake.

The house built by the contemporary architect introduced a dissonant note in such harmony. How could it be amended? The Landhaus Khuner is perhaps Loos's best answer to this question. The high base with slate stone slabs and the volume of the building in *Blockbau* (log construction)—with a large veranda towards the valley—reproduced Alpine architectural forms, although in original ways.

The base of the Khuner house deserves special attention. The slate slabs used by Loos come from the nearby area of Kreuzberg; it is a stone used in the construction of many functional buildings in the valley. When used for load-bearing walls, the rough-cut stone is typically laid in horizontal courses for better bearing. In the base of the Kuhner house, Loos instead placed many slabs vertically in the reinforced concrete cast. In this way, the slate slabs lose their load-bearing character and become more of a cladding. Whenever Loos utilizes the principle of constructive truth—as in the house on Michaelerplatz—this was applied to highlight the preeminence of the cladding on the structure, thus freeing its essence of every technical implication. One can appreciate the unique coloring of stone, the roughness of its surface, the colored reflection of the crystals characterizing its texture. Stripped of its technical and functional dimension a stone is just a stone; it assumes the canon that Martin Heidegger attributed to the object as "Thing"

(*Ding*). In one of the rare essays dedicated to the figure of Loos in the early twentieth century, Robert Scheu called Loos "der dinghafte Mann" wondering: "Who was this thing-ish man, who could get such magic from the most ordinary object and knew how to say so much brilliantly self-evident, childishly simple, immemorially new in such a charming manner? Adolf Loos dedicated his life's work that a chair should be a chair, a fork should be a fork, a house should be a house. A thing should be a thing … He is as intimate with glass, stone, copper, and leather, as some cosmic natures with the tides and the course of the stars."—[86]

86 Robert Scheu, "Adolf Loos," *Die Fackel* XI, H. 283–284 (June 26, 1909): 25.

The idea of *materialgerechtes Bauen* (material-compatible building) was far from Loos's concept; he considered it legitimate that a cladding metal sheet could simulate a steel beam, provided that the sheet ought to be made of the noblest material. In the case of the Goldman & Salatsch headquarters, the metal used for the flower boxes, lintel, portico ceiling, bases, and columns capitals was tombak—an alloy similar to bronze—a noble material that resembles the portico of the Roman Pantheon, which had also column bases and capitals clad with a bronze sheet.

On several occasions Loos had shared his debt to and admiration for Gottfried Semper. In the essay "Das prinzip der bekleidung" (The Principle of Cladding),—[87] in which he declares war on any material used as a surrogate, Loos radicalized his position until he was contradicting what had been one of the founding principles of the classical idea of representation as well as that of Semper's theory: the principle of imitation that allowed illustrating a stone monument based on the original forms of a wooden temple. "Our temples are no longer painted like the Parthenon, blue, red, green, and white. No, we have learned to perceive the beauty of naked stone."—[88] Of the "bare stone" Loos wrote: "The noble material is God's wonder. I would gladly give all the works of Lalique or all of the jewelry of the Viennese

87 Loos, "Das prinzip der bekleidung," in *Ins Leere gesprochen*, 108.

88 Loos, "Architektur," in *Sämtliche Schriften: Trotzdem*, 305.

89 Loos, "Hands off!" in ibid., 346.

90 Ibid.

workshops for a valuable string of pearls."—[89] Similarly he claimed that "today the most depraved person will refrain from decorating a noble wood surface with inlaid work, to engrave the extraordinary natural spectacle of a marble board, or to cut a beautiful silver fox into small squares..."—[90] The base of the house on Michaelerplatz presents as ornament the natural beauty of a precious material such as Greek Cipollino marble, whose veins and crystal reflections give the well-proportioned columns and entablature of Roman origin an almost transfigured dimension. One should not forget that Loos also saw in the splendor of that material the reflection of history. Cipollino marble immediately evokes Greek architecture and its monuments.

91 Friedrich Nietzsche, *Human, All Too Human*, Part 1 para. 218, trans. Helen Zimmern, https://en.wikisource.org/wiki/Human_All-Too-Human.

92 Ibid., 217.

The importance Loos assigned not to the use of the material, but to the manner with which he would emphasize the natural qualities, situates his thinking in continuity with certain considerations by Nietzsche. In one of his aphorisms in *Menschliches, Allzumenschliches* (*Human, All Too Human*) entitled, "The stone is more stone than before," Nietzsche discusses the meaning of architecture in modern times. A Greek or Christian temple meant the closeness to the deity, a deity perceived as something sublime and terrible. "... at the most beauty tempered horror—but this horror was everywhere presupposed. What is the beauty of a building now? The same thing as the beautiful face of a stupid woman, a kind of mask."—[91] Like music, of which Nietzsche speaks in the previous aphorism, even architecture has become more and more intellectual and abstract art—an art that speaks to the reason rather than to the senses. It's an art that bears witness to a "dulling of our senses" that are no longer called to ask if such a thing "exists," but rather what it "means." Nietzsche speaks of a "Desensualization of Higher Art,"—[92] a "coarsening" of our senses, a phenomenon that has led to an incredible expansion of the territory of art that from this moment will deal not only with the beautiful, but also with the ugly and banal. Architecture has lost the sublime veil that surrounded it and no longer lives in the spirit of god. The building is increasingly the subject of an abstraction, but paradoxically this has led to an ever greater exaltation of the physical nature of matter that, in fact, keeps all its mystery intact: "The stone is more stone than before." Tectonics is the first attempt to give architecture, now "desensualized," a meaning related to its technical, constructive, economic status. Fischer von Erlach was celebrated by Loos as "a king in the realm of materials,"—[93] for the appropriateness with which he uses them. The plaster and Cipollino marble possess the same dignity despite their substantial difference in tectonics: the first is processed into slabs and placed according to the rules of stereotomy, the second is closer to the skin and leatherwork that allow large surfaces without joints. Invoking the beauty of the stone or of the wood veins, the smoothness of metal or the transparency of glass betrays the increasing abstraction with which we enjoy art. In painting, the maximum abstraction is combined with the destruction of the object and its perception as pure color, painterly gesture. "It is not barbaric if we say that the sense of jewelry lies in the material. Thus, the artwork has to be content with showing off the material as much as possible."—[94] "The noble material is God's wonder."—[95]

93 Loos, "Die Baumaterialien," in *Ins Leere gesprochen*, 104.

94 Loos, "Kunstgewerbliche Kunstschau I," in ibid., 25.

95 Loos, "Hands off!," 346.

Nature in a Neutra house: Julius Shulman's iconic photograph of the Tremaine House, Montecito, California, 1950.

# Neutra's Nature

Sandy Isenstadt

*"Nature" as a system of interests and activities is one of the chief creations of the civilized man.*—[1]

1 Lewis Mumford, *The Brown Decades*, rev. ed. (1931; repr., New York: Dover, 1971), 26.

The violent spark that started architecture in the first place, as Vitruvius presumed; the sky-hook suspension conjured by Procopius; divine emanations reaching through lithic boughs to brighten Suger's spirit; God-granted inspiration pulsing in the veins of Renaissance Genius; the universality and constancy to principle that Laugier's Muse pointed toward; numbing vastness and unplumbed profundity for Boullée; fragility and resilience, rhythms in scale and across time, all admired by Ruskin; nineteenth-century glimpses of function, utility, healing virtue and commercial resource, autonomy and interdependence, dynamic formal complexity tempered by unvarying correspondences; its infallibility as paradigm and paragon despite mercurial metamorphoses and perpetual unfolding: nature, beneath it all. Upon which ever-changing aspect of never-changing nature did Neutra, in turn, rest his architecture?

In fact, although Neutra spoke often of it—*Nature Near* is the title of an essay collection, for example—nature is not quite onstage in his writings or, one might argue, even in his architecture. Despite countless references and all the green stuff pressed up against his walls of glass, Neutra is more interested in what he calls

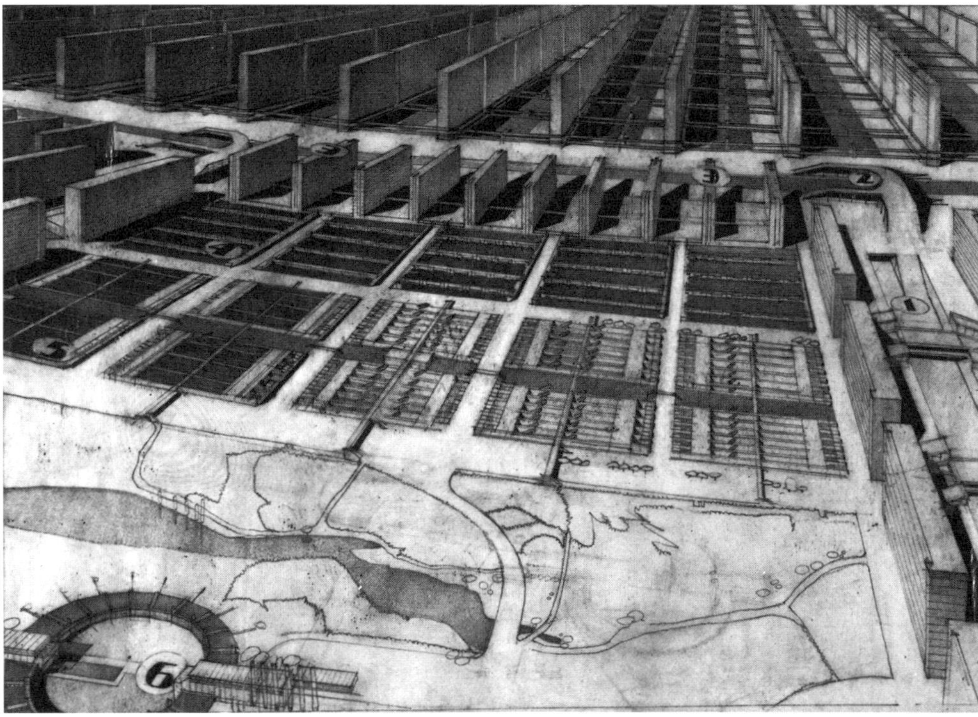

Rush City Reformed, circa 1924. Rush City, Neutra's version of the future metropolis, is organized around circulation and is lubricated by fluid transfers between modes of transportation. Nature is counterpoint to the well-organized, well-run city.

naturalism—"a return to nature, by the most up-to-date means," as he defined it—than in nature itself.—[2] To put it another way, Neutra is not interested in nature "out there" so much as he is concerned with the human perceptual organs that evolved in response to whatever is "out there." His own definition makes this emphasis explicit: "What we here may briefly call *nature* comprises all the requirements and characteristics of live organisms," with nature itself governed by a "'supreme plan'—that of biological consistency and requirement."—[3] Neutra's nature, then, is foremost a biological concept.

2 Variations abound in Neutra's writings, including: "Back-to-nature-by-scientific-method," said of Emile Zola for his realism, Richard Neutra, *Survival Through Design* (New York: Oxford University Press, 1954), 38. The long-standing tension between nature and technology in American thought is described by many, including Leo Marx, *The Machine in the Garden* (New York: Oxford University Press, 1964).

3 Neutra, *Survival*, 3.

Even this sharpened definition, however, is broader than his actual purview. He is fixed on the human senses in particular as mediating mechanisms between an outer world of physical phenomena and an inner world of mental functions that range from particles of sensation to cognitive chains. Architects, he argues, should direct their attention to the human body's "wonderful organic reactivity … responsive to all influences and stimuli."—[4] For Neutra, the most intimate of sciences—the physiology of sensation—should be the polestar of architectural design. Moreover, Neutra's interest in the senses is further confined to their laws of operation, following an Enlightenment-era conception of nature as a set of discoverable principles. But, whereas a central question during the Enlightenment was whether or not Man is a part of Nature or stands apart, Neutra is untroubled.—[5] Instead, he focuses directly on the membrane between: an electro-chemical interface between a physiological organism—rather than, say, a moral one—and an outer environment conceived largely as a source of stimuli and considered in terms of its effect on the organism. He wrote, "All objects can and must be considered as food for our nervous consumption."—[6] An intervening tissue, sandwiched between inside and out, is as much of nature as Neutra needs to propel his design thinking.

4 Richard Neutra, *Life and Human Habitat* (Stuttgart: Alexander Koch, 1956), 16–17.

5 Although he reviews the history of exactly this question from the *Upanishads* to modern science, he ends by suggesting we "lose our patience with all these speculations" and respond instead to the dire exigencies of the present. Neutra, *Survival*, 8–16.

6 Ibid., 263.

Neutra's best-known theoretical pronouncement, *Survival Through Design* (1954), concentrates on the mismatch between the novel material conditions wrought by modernity and humankind's obsolete organs of observation. Its first topic—indeed, its first word—is "nature." Simply put, the human perceptual apparatus evolved over millennia to accord with a natural, that is, a preindustrial and preurban, world, but the prior two centuries had produced "an entirely new environment … the man-made setting," which overwhelms and confounds our antique sensory equipment. Consequently, urban incongruities and modern dissonance jangled midcentury nerves and resulted in millions upon millions of "mental cases," in contrast with the gradual accommodations needed for non-man-made settings.—[7] Whereas in most interpretations of nature, mankind fits—comfortably or not—within a larger nature, for Neutra a vestige of nature in the form of the human body fits uncomfortably within a wholly man-made environment. Under these conditions, inner self and outer world—the product, respectively, of old biology and new technology—came unglued.

7 Ibid., 194.

Eventually, even the original operational principles of the human sensory apparatus could be superseded by dynamic, judiciously designed responses to changing conditions. Neutra believed that humanity would evolve to accord with the man-made environment, through processes of random mutation. Ultimately, technology would guide evolution itself to harmonize with an artificial world, as the scientific frontier shifted from manufacturing to human biology. One day, he mused, architects would play physiology like a keyboard, designing not buildings but stimulus-response chords to elicit specific somatic or psychic states.—[8] Just as the mechanical arts had earlier been rationalized to transform the built environment, so biology, if sufficiently understood, could transform the self, leading to a new and far more plastic understanding of architecture. Nature "out there" is replaceable, Neutra makes clear, but only when

8 The analogy is Neutra's own. Ibid., 201.

scientifically minded designers have learned how to artificially substitute for it, an inevitability still some time in the future. Neutra envisions, therefore, a new mandate for the architect: to shape and scale man-made external stimuli to suit nature-made human sensory capacities. Survival is the aim; Design is the means; Nature, in any sense of the larger organic world, is already lost. Only its residue—evident in physiological mechanisms forged by evolution for a setting that no longer existed and organisms ill-equipped to deal with a world of their own making—is left.

To be sure, the springs of Neutra's notions of nature are deep. He was employed in a nursery as a young man and worked for Gustav Ammann—a Swiss landscape architect and student of Carl Foerster, a German plant breeder. He fondly recalled reading Gottfried Keller's *Green Henry*, a semi-autobiographical *Bildungsroman* featuring a love of nature, retreat from the city, and a stint at landscape painting. He easily transferred his botanical observations to a sensitivity for humanity's "roots and blooms," and learned that the world's "natural physiognomy" was increasingly infused with a "cultural character."—[9] He carefully read Goethe's work in the natural sciences, including his color theory, and absorbed the poet's dynamic view of botany, particularly noting the importance of vision, both literal and aesthetic.—[10] In a convincing recent study, Volker Welter argues that Neutra's experience in the military before and during the First World War shaped his view of nature in a very specific way, leading him to the idea of an immersive environment that demanded, or at least rewarded vigilant attention. In the wartime setting, Neutra learned to read landscape closely, to interact with it intimately, to understand its spatial cues, to see it not as a scientist, but through an explicitly subjective set of concerns that, however specific to a given situation, is nonetheless a universal viewpoint. Indeed, "viewpoint" precisely captures the idea of an individual sensing him- or herself at the center of a larger environment.—[11]

9 Richard Neutra, *Life and Shape* (New York: Appleton-Century Crofts, 1961), 137–38.

10 In vol. 10, *Diaries*, n.d., Box 335, Richard and Dion Neutra Papers, Special Collections, University of California, Los Angeles, Library.

11 See Volker M. Welter, "From the Landscape of War to the Open Order of the Kaufmann House—Richard Neutra and the Experience of the Great War," in *THE GOOD GARDENER? Nature, Humanity, and the Garden*, ed. Annette Giesecke and Naomi Jacobs (London: Artifice Books on Architecture, 2014), 216–33.

However, as Raymond Williams wrote, "Nature is perhaps the most complex word in the language" and has meaning only in regard to other terms.—[12] The synchronic context of Neutra's nature is equally as important as its diachronic roots. Here, Neutra's views of nature will be set in relation to his views of society, the body, and architecture. These terms are crucial for Neutra, who, synthetic both by disposition and profession, aspired toward seeing the interrelationship of phenomena and, in this regard, ought to be noted in histories of holism, ecology, and "organic wholeness," which were just then emerging. For example, J.C. Smuts—who coined the term "holistic" in 1926—argued that the sciences of biology and physiology in particular were displacing classical physics and its mechanistic universe with complex new ideas of an interactive and "dynamic organic whole," concepts sympathetic with Neutra's own.—[13] Yet, even as Neutra insists on the interrelationship of the body, society, architecture, and nature, he retains the dichotomy of inner and outer worlds. Briefly, the inner world is congruent with the body and its perceptual equipment; the body evolved in response to an outer world that was once nature but is now society. Architecture, it almost goes without saying, is the bridge between the two.

12 Raymond Williams, *Keywords: A Vocabulary of Culture and Society* (New York: Oxford University Press, 1983), 219.

13 J. C. Smuts, "The Overthrow of the Mechanistic Theory," *Journal of the Royal Astronomical Society of Canada* vol. 25 (1931): 413–16.

## Society and the Body

In Neutra's analysis, modern society has a single outstanding trait, it induces stress: "In advanced situations of civilized life, such as a teeming metropolis with bewildering traffic and disharmonious neon lights, multitudes become nervous sufferers."—[14] Whereas in earlier works he admired modern society for an organization sophisticated enough to build skyscrapers and industrial complexes, his later writings emphasize little else about society than its enervating effects. In this context, paired with society, nature is complement and counterpoint.

14 Neutra, *Survival*, 194.

Neutra would have had ample opportunity in his life to absorb and internalize the basic structure of this opposition. Most immediately, popular, early twentieth-century, Central European trends—such as *Nacktkultur*, *Freikörperkultur*, or the *Lebensreform* movements—were premised on a tension between an overwrought, enfeebling civilization and a restorative countryside with occasion both for forest rambles or manual labor. In works ranging from the sociology of Ferdinand Tönnies to the fiction of Émile Zola, whom Neutra admired, to landscape photography and painting and urban planning, from regionalist revivals across Europe to the creation of an American national park system, nature contrasted with a city conceived as crowded, dirty, and bewildering. It was everything urban civilization was not: spacious, restful, and inspiriting, a vision of transcendent order that was all but impossible to achieve in the harried pace of modern life.—[15] In other words, this view of nature was the product of urban anxieties shared by many others; the opposition of nature and civilization comprised a single spectrum of cultural value. As Ralph Waldo Emerson put it in another context: "Our hunting for the picturesque is inseparable from our protest against false society."—[16] Mankind created society but came to encounter it as a threat and thus sought an ally in nature. Neutra would not have had to reach far for this moral dualism to consolidate all forms of Otherness under the sign of society—the institutions and relationships that organize a large population—in order to find restitution and redemption in nature.

15 As Raymond Williams notes, a full accounting of the term would constitute "a large part of the history of human thought." Williams, *Keywords*, 186.

16 Ralph Waldo Emerson, "Essays," in *The Complete Works of Ralph Waldo Emerson* III (New York: AMS Press, 1968), 171. Although Neutra learned much from Frank Lloyd Wright, he explicitly rejected Wright's own Emersonian views as too romantic and inauthentically rural. See, for example, Neutra, *Life and Shape*, 175.

Neutra gave this familiar critical dichotomy an American spin. The fount of urban chaos in his adoptive country was consumerism, which put profit ahead of everything else to the detriment of the environment and the injury to the individual. For Neutra, consumer society was especially vulnerable to the friction between what was technically possible and what was humanly tolerable, because manufacturers considered only the former. They reshaped the physical environment on the basis of nothing more than short-term margins. Neutra knew of building equipment manufacturers who conducted empirical studies of "subjective comfort, physiologically analyzed," but then let earnings growth override data showing, for example, the benefits of opening a windward window rather than switching on air conditioning because, after all, there was no profit in a breeze.—[17] At the same time, as Neutra saw it, consumerism was a factor in America's fundamental character, an element of its democracy, and distinguished it from European culture. Indeed, it was part of what attracted Neutra to emigrate in the first place.—[18] For an architect practicing in the United States (US), consumerism was as necessary a factor to acknowledge as gravity. Neutra underscores the point in his preface to *Survival Through Design*; it was addressed to the "consumer of physical design, of designed products, and of a planned and constructed environment as a whole," and was written with the aim of helping "with our consumer problems."—[19]

17 Neutra, *Survival*, 319–20.

18 Neutra, *Life and Shape*, 192.

19 Neutra, *Survival*, vii–ix. The consumer orientation of US culture was a long-standing theme for Neutra. See, for example, "Excerpts from lecture given by mr r neutra Sunday January 4th," box 194, clippings file 1932, Richard and Dion Neutra Papers, Special Collections, University of California, Los Angeles, Library.

What distinguished Neutra's view of consumer society in the US was his further concentration on the human body, the primary unit of nature remaining in the wake of widespread industrial urbanism. Above all else, modern urban consumer society presented a somatic challenge. As he put it: "The epitome of today's industrialized environment, as well as the grand problem in practical human biology, is our present city."—[20] Indeed, much of *Survival* tries to explain the urban triggers for the "nervous friction and wreckage [that] have multiplied in the metropolitan type of surroundings" and that left millions to languish in big cities across America.—[21] Although he notes issues raised by scientists, sociologists, cultural critics, and design professionals, he frames them not in terms of public policy, inequality, class tensions, racial relations, gender status, national character, history, and so on, but in terms of physiological, and therefore,

20 Neutra, *Survival*, 337.

21 Ibid., 24.

from his perspective, psychological effects. For example, Neutra had long been concerned with traffic congestion. When he addressed the matter in the late nineteen-twenties in "Rush City Reformed," his visionary scheme was a pointed critique of a national transportation system increasingly based on private automobiles.—[22] He addressed a problem arising in the public sphere with a proportionally public resolution.

22 See, for example, "Rush City Reformed," *La Cité*, 12:5 (May, 1934): 71–82.

Continuing the critique in 1954, Neutra describes congestion in US cities as a "monumental" problem that verged on "self-annihilation."—[23] Nonetheless, he implicitly accepts the automobile by this time and largely recommends natural vistas—available from the private home and distant from the urban workplace—to assuage nerves stripped raw in heavy traffic. There is no nostalgia here; Neutra's motivation is to compensate vexing nervous stimuli with restful sensations in order to make the city tolerable. Indeed, he is confident that even larger cities can be biologically livable.—[24] But, by framing frustrating social conditions in terms of their neurotic symptoms for the individual, Neutra effectively resolves those problems somatically and privately rather than politically. To be sure, neuroses were widely discussed in postwar popular culture as a kind of fallout of the early years of the nuclear age.—[25] Yet the society implied in Neutra's writings is comprised of asocial selves, however accurate his claims might be regarding individual physiological responses. His steady gaze on disturbances to the body's sensory organs is blind to intersubjective relations and consensual action.

23 Ibid., 357.

24 Ibid., 359–60.

25 For example: "Neurosis is the true epidemic of our time," wrote Ferdinand Lundberg and Marynia Farnham in *Modern Woman: The Lost Sex* (New York: Harper & Brothers, 1947), 47–48.

Correspondingly, Neutra's interest in mental experience, whether emotional or cognitive, is sharply circumscribed by his insistence on the physiological underpinnings of mind. He was clearly interested in psychological processes, having known the Freud family in Vienna, having taken copious notes on Freud's *Psychopathology of Everyday Life*, and evident in numerous references throughout his writing as well as his famous lengthy client interviews and questionnaires. Despite these factors, however, the mind is for Neutra plainly secondary to physiology. Talbot Hamlin noted as much in his review of *Survival* when it was published. According to Hamlin, despite Neutra's curiosity regarding mental functions, he left little room for psychological depth; his therapeutic viewpoint trivialized the unconscious.—[26] Neutra did follow the developing field of social psychology closely in the nineteen-thirties, (although curiously overlooking Wilhelm Wundt's own contemporaneous contribution, *Volkspsychologie*, despite having studied and been deeply influenced by the scientist's other works in his youth), but he disregarded their central question: how to relate individual and group psychology to cultural forms.—[27] Certainly, Neutra's vivid metaphor of "a digestible world picture," wherein the individual chews "an outer world in individual bites" or, conversely, the characterization of the built environment itself as a kind of discharge—"the shell which human society secretes through its manifold, system-controlled but often individually initiated, design activity"—are suggestive of later ideas of biophilia and ecological design, but they remain undeveloped in his own writings.—[28]

26 Talbot Hamlin, *The New York Times*, February 21, 1954, 7. Popular interest in psychology in this period is discussed in Ellen Herman, *The Romance of American Psychology: Political Culture in the Age of Experts* (Berkeley: University of California Press, 1995).

27 Gardner Murphy, for example, in a text Neutra cited, asserts early on that humans dwell at the intersection of biology and history. See Murphy, et. al., *Experimental Social Psychology* (New York: Harper & Brothers, 1937), 7–8.

28 Neutra, *Survival*, 123, 233. Neutra took copious notes when first reading Wundt and would continue to recommend to students Wundt's seminal *Principles of Physiological Psychology* more than a century after it was first published.

## Architecture and Nature

With the inner world a physiological system attuned by evolution for life on a vanished savannah and the outside world a cacophony of unnatural and unassimilable signals, architecture is left to generate stimuli sympathetic with outdated sensory equipment. It might do so in several ways. According to Sylvia Lavin, Neutra believed architecture can replicate conditions conducive to developmental processes from the womb through early childhood to assure that the individual's sensory and psychic mechanisms are commensurate with the man-made environment.

A properly designed house is a second chance in this regard, where natural developmental processes that prepared one for the preindustrial environment could be architecturally rehearsed for the man-made environment. Similarly, as Todd Cronan suggests, architecture can introduce a series of minor shocks to body and mind and thus gradually prod the self into acceptance of the new environment. Likewise, Michael Ostwald and Raeana Henderson detail Neutra's efforts to put Wundt's ideas into practice by concentrating on visual signals meant to induce reflex responses, carefully explaining the physiological benefit of doing so.—29

Alternatively, appropriate stimuli can be generated by an emphasis on private views of the landscape, which appear powerfully in representations of Neutra's postwar work, whether in his own writings or the photographs of Julius Shulman. Indeed, the visual argument of his 1951 book, *Mystery and Realities of the Site*—published while he worked on the manuscript for *Survival*—is that the architectural merit of a private home can be assessed by the scope of landscape afforded from it. Every image in the book has something to say about architecture's relationship to landscape, while the text brims with "sweeping views," "full views," a "view-commanding balcony," "a slatted view," "unobstructed views," a "panoramic view," a "far view," and an "agreeable outlook." Even the advertising for the book exploited the trope, claiming it "opens the windows of your home-building vision to the complete horizon of its setting."—30 In fact, landscape views usually do dominate the firsthand experience of many of his residential designs. A visit to a Neutra house—whether the modest VDL House, dating from 1932 and situated on a small site in Los Angeles, or the large 1962 Pitcairn House, on a ten-acre site in Pennsylvania—inevitably entails walls of glass opening on to green vistas.

29 Sylvia Lavin, *Form Follows Libido: Architecture and Richard Neutra in a Psychoanalytic Culture* (Cambridge, MA: MIT Press, 2004); Todd Cronan, "'Danger in the Smallest Dose': Richard Neutra's Design Theory," *Design and Culture* 3/2 (July 2011): 165–91; Michael Ostwald and Raeana Henderson, "The Modern Interior and the Excitation Response: Richard Neutra's Ocularcentric Phenomenology," *Architecture Research* 2/3 (2012): 27–35.

30 Richard Neutra, *Mystery and Realities of the Site* (Scarsdale, New York: Morgan and Morgan, 1951), throughout.

Neutra's emphasis on landscape views—in addition to the use of large flat surfaces, minimized ornament, and the

From left to right: Loring House, Los Angeles, California, 1960; Van der Leeuw Research House, Los Angeles, California, begun 1932; Pitcairn House, Bryn Athyn Pennsylvania, 1963; Cliff May House, West Covina, California, 1958. Julius Shulman, photographer.

rest of a modernist formal program—aligns neatly with similar sentiments expressed by his contemporaries. From theoretically minded writers to architects and window manufacturers, gazing through glazing at a natural scene was the keynote of modern domestic architecture at mid-century. Gyorgy Kepes, following a line of reasoning parallel to Neutra's own, argued that human senses had failed to keep pace with scientific and technological advances, leaving artists and architects to bridge the gap between old habits and new realities. He stressed the synthetic power of vision in particular as a means to maintain cultural progress: "Thus the control of nature includes the domestication of nature through the eye, the visual assimilation of space-time events." A private view of a distant landscape, in other words, was a didactic visualization of modern "space-time events" brought down to household scale.—31

Marcel Breuer, to take another example, was deemed an "architect's architect," and gained a special reputation for domesticating perspectives. He frequently placed the hearth directly in front of the view only to carve away at it, as he did in the 1949 Clark House, for instance. His designs were even likened to cameras positioned to frame a landscape: "His houses are observation posts from which to admire what no man can imitate," ran one review. "To Breuer, this aloofness is a very real way of paying your respects to the trees, the hills, the water and the changing skies."—32 In essence, the view replaced the hearth as the core of domestic representation. But the enthusiasm for nature pictorialized was surely at its highest among window and glass manufacturers who were thrilled by modernism's penchant for glass walls: "Instead of having a solid wall with a large picture on it, the post-war home will have a wall of glass that is in itself a natural, true-to-life picture."—33 Visual access to nature from the private home seems a simple, even naïve sentiment, yet therein dwells a commonly held philosophy of architecture, nature, and modernity.

31 Gyorgy Kepes, *language of vision* (Chicago: Paul Theobald, 1944), 66–79.

32 "Marcel Breuer, Teacher and Architect," *House and Home* 1 (May 1952): 104–15. See also, Marcel Breuer, *Sun and Shadow: Philosophy of an Architect* (New York: Dodge, Mead, 1955), 40. For more on the view's displacement of the hearth, see Sandy Isenstadt, "Four Views, Three of Them Through Glass," in *Sites Unseen: Essays on Landscape and Vision*, ed. Dianne Harris and J. Fairchild Ruggles (University Park, PA: Pennsylvania State University Press, 2007), 213–40. For more on the redemptive landscape view as the product of a materially advanced civilization, see Sandy Isenstadt, "The Ruler and the Eye: The Compensations of Spaciousness," in *The Modern American House* (New York: Cambridge University Press, 2006), 251–66.

33 A Preview of Tomorrow's 'House for Cheerful Living,'" a 1945 brochure describing an architectural competition sponsored by Pittsburgh Plate Glass, n.p.

Again, Neutra is unique in placing this popular formal program on a physiological foundation. He explicitly prized a distant view, which he believed had a particularly restful effect and therefore guaranteed the private home would fulfill its role as refuge from the dissonance of daily life. Distance, Neutra explained, has fewer salient visual details and, therefore, less optical variation; the eye sweeps the horizon without the impediment of arresting features or engaging facets. Ocular muscles move steadily rather than fitfully, in Neutra's telling, and visual stimuli file fluidly into the eye. The distinguishing minutiae of the black walnut and the blue oak, for instance, are submerged by distance, and therefore blend with other species to form broad horizontal sweeps of mottled green beneath a vault of blue. As Neutra puts it, the eye sails across a distant landscape and in so doing recalls to the mind an easy loping gait traversing level terrain or the frictionless feel of fingering a smooth surface:—[34] "Our eyes relax and rejoice in sweeping over distant vistas,"—[35] because "a minimum of neural energy" is expended."—[36] "Over an even surface, our tactile and our visual senses can move without abrupt changes in innervation, just as a skater glides over smooth ice."—[37] In short, distance is visually flat and thus, in Neutra's model, distributed sensory stimuli evenly with fewer maxima and minima of impressions. Hence, he surmises: "A person may look at large view windows of a living room with their unobstructed panoramic possibilities, and every time he does so he may feel like taking a breath of relaxation, gratification, and relief."—[38] In other words, linoleum and the horizon were similarly soothing for the singular reason that they diminished the need for the eye to shift focus. In contrast, episodic and uneven features, whether in view or underfoot, require sudden and potentially jarring adjustments of the sensory apparatus. Nature, at least in a distant view, was smooth; the city was jagged.

Neutra took these thoughts even further. Evolution, he asserted, inscribed the conservation of optical and somatic

34 Neutra, *Survival*, 91–96.

35 Richard Neutra, *Mystery and Realities of the Site*, 60–62.

36 Neutra, *Survival*, 127.

37 Ibid., 93.

38 Ibid., 219. Cleanliness and easy recall are similarly relaxing in physiological terms. Neutra explains the physiological structures underpinning these responses, in ibid., 197–201.

energy into the DNA of humankind. Throughout recorded history, "man has shown a certain preference for smooth and even surfaces,"—[39] an innate trait that explained why flint knives were polished beyond the requirements of utility alone. Likewise, the infant's predilection to put things in its mouth leads through the sensitivity of the tongue to a parallel preference for smooth surfaces. Our taste for smoothness is temporally and sensorially overdetermined by the long arc of evolution and the ingestive immediacy of infant development.—[40] In other words, the view through a glass wall is for Neutra less a matter of highlighting a site or accentuating a sense of place or even suggesting a realm innocent of human anxiety, than it is a means to cast comforting cyphers toward the eyes of viewers inside. The specific character of nature is foregone in favor of its psychic effects; nature is neither the world outside nor even the view of the outside, as much as it is a set of signals with fixed and predictable physiological responses. Although Neutra's emphasis on distant landscape views replicates eighteenth-century Picturesque predilections, he validates it on a different basis. Rather than, say, spark imagination or insinuate a spiritual realm, distance has a soothing, almost sedative effect. Decades before advances in neuroscience would empirically tackle the question, Neutra suggested that nature's transcendent beauty—he explicitly claimed that his is ultimately an argument about aesthetics—rests upon the dampening of innervation.—[41]

In this way, Neutra arrives at a new and powerful understanding of modernism's foundational functional credo. As he describes it, "functional integrity," "unimpeachable functionalism," "functional perfection," "functional appropriateness," and so on, are evident in nature as "fitness for assimiliation [sic] by our organic capacity."—[42] This principle must guide design if humanity is to survive a collective nervous breakdown. Whereas earlier modernist figures had suggested that form must express constructive principles or

39 Ibid., 93.

40 Ibid., 25.

41 Neutra's idea of aesthetic amortization embodies the notion that objects and environments are physiologically assimilated at different rates, and designers had necessarily to address these differential time horizons. Ibid., 120–21. For more on the aesthetic character of Neutra's thinking, see Sandy Isenstadt, "Richard Neutra and the Psychology of Architectural Consumption," in *Anxious Modernisms: Architectural Culture, 1945–1968*, ed. Sarah Goldhagen and Rejean Legault (Montreal: CCA, 2001), 97–118.

42 Neutral, *Survival*, 91.

programmatic requirements, Neutra posits a biological basis for modernist principles rather than a technical one. As Neutra put it, the modern world was "a biological situation without precedent … the early treatment through tradition … seems now out of the question."—[43] Modernist aesthetics had begun—Neutra mentions Louis Sullivan and Otto Wagner—with constructive expressionism, but in response to mid twentieth-century threats, it needed to move toward a biological rather than a structural basis.—[44] Architects arrived at modernism by trying to make aesthetic sense of new materials; now, in the mid twentieth century, they needed to understand how that material world was perceptually assimilated.

43 Ibid., 20.

44 Ibid., 45–47.

Notable in this formulation is Neutra's reconfiguration of modernist exceptionalism and his insistence, along with so many other architects, that modernism was not just another style destined to be eclipsed next season. He continues his sketch history of functional thought with the assimilation of the marketplace: "Thus the functional concept, the pragmatic concept of commercial values, gradually came into being—and the more mystical concept of quality faded away because it was too nebulous to offer security."—[45] Classical beauty, to which Neutra here refers, was "mystical" because it was believed to be innate and temporally transcendent. It was therefore ill-suited to the changeful pace of modern life. But the nineteenth-century notion of beauty was epiphenomenal, comprised of an intuition of the perfect integration of form and function. Attend to satisfying function foremost, and beauty—a new, modern beauty—will follow. To Neutra, the new function is psychic survival, achievable only by assuring that forms of everyday life will be agreeable—that is, that the physiological residue of nature residing in the human body will not be overstressed.

45 Ibid., 52.

Yet, despite removing modernism from cycles of style and fashion, Neutra roots his new functionalism precisely in the workings of a consumer society. He wrote that the US favorably distinguished itself from

Europe in large part through its commercial premise; it was something he admired.—[46] Despite his misgivings regarding unleashed consumerism's many dangers, it was in any event an inescapable context for American architecture. Modernism would assure its advantage over historical styles if it were to address the habits and expectations—as well as the physiological needs—of consumers. For example, the perceptual principle of "fatigue phenomena," Neutra explained, meant that people will seek greater levels of stimulation to reach increasingly higher thresholds of physiological response, a principle that was aggravated in modern cultures. He wrote that "*for the more highly developed human neuro-mental system a static changelessness seems especially unfit*," which was why fashion cycles could be seen only to accelerate and, again, why classicism, with its emphasis on balance and repose, was obsolete.—[47] Extensive in scope and dynamic in spirit, modern architecture was well positioned both to modulate and to satisfy the mental character of US consumers. Architecture can leverage "physiological purchasing power," Neutra's stunning phrase to describe the value added from the consumer's-eye view of physical things that produce therapeutic stimuli.—[48] Just as the suburban house lot might be said to have furthered the commodification of nature by parceling out bits of it into middle-class-sized portions, so does Neutra's proposal to segment and thereby satisfy physiological needs with manufactured goods and designed environments further extend the franchise of consumer society. Nature provided humankind with its physiological requirements; architecture meets those requirements with purchasable goods and designs optimized for sensory assimilation. Indeed, housing in general, Neutra once said, is in essence an "assimilation camp."—[49]

Nowhere is Neutra's closeness to consumer culture and his distance from nature—conceived as a primitive condition or the manifold of things and living processes—more evident than in his discussion of houses for "the masses

46 Neutra, *Life and Shape*, 192.

47 Neutra, *Survival*, 87. Emphasis in original.

48 Ibid., 20.

49 Interview with Richard Neutra in *Contact* vol. 1, no.10, June 4, 1958. Box 330, clippings file, Richard and Dion Neutra Papers, Special Collections, University of California, Los Angeles, Library.

of small consumers." He readily saw that therapeutic landscape vistas were unavailable on modest sites, and thus searched for alternatives that could provide the same restful stimuli. In a kind of architectural homeopathy, the shadow of a vine, for instance, conjured "an ideal landscape" and could therefore prove calm.—[50] "Even if there is not one shred of view,"—[51] insisted Neutra, the architect had other means to elicit soothing sensations, especially when architecture was reconfigured as a set of optical inputs that needed to reach sensory receptors. Indeed, he advised owners of small homes to "think of your house as a little visual empire,"—[52] rather than, say, a tectonic assembly or a crucible for the socialization of children. In this context then, leading features of his designs can be seen to reproduce the optical effects of distance, without the need for long dimensions. Smooth surfaces, so prominent in his designs, replicate the abstracting effect of distance that flattens texture, for example. His "outriggers," usually understood as an expression of structure, stand as literal diagrams of diminution, another key to deep perspectives, and his use of frosted glass can suggest the hazy effect of aerial perspective.

50 Neutra, *Mystery*, 55–56.

51 Ibid., 56.

52 Ibid., 62.

In this sense, Neutra creates an aesthetics of distance, an interior marked by visual mobility—with glass transoms, level changes that mark territory without impeding the eye, low partitions and, where appropriate, large windows—that is the optical correlate of a distant view.—[53] As he wrote, he tried in his designs to encourage "natural wholesomeness *as much as we can reproduce it or recreate it*."—[54] Regardless of whether they originated in nature or design, Neutra's "neurologically salubrious agents" yielded gently varying sensory stimuli whose therapeutic benefits were validated by the grand epic of human evolution.—[55] Uniform across divergent sources, restful stimuli were commodities in that nature was interchangeable with architectural design as the source

53 Discussed in more detail in Isenstadt, "Richard Neutra and the Psychology of Architectural Consumption."

54 Neutra, *Mystery*, 56. Emphasis added.

55 Neutra, *Survival*, 159.

From left to right: Wise House, Los Angeles, California, 1958; Kaufmann House, Palm Springs, California, circa 1947; Singleton House, Los Angeles, California, 1960; Loring House, Los Angeles, California, 1960; Pitcairn House, Bryn Athyn Pennsylvania, 1963. Julius Shulman, photographer.

of those stimuli. Through evolution, nature had created the physiological response to visual distance, but through design, architecture could induce that same response by technical means. False perceptions, such as imagined sounds, had long troubled physiological psychologists, but for Neutra they presented an opportunity to generate the therapeutic benefits of nature without the presence of nature by means of the optical reproduction of distance. Thus, with the effects of nature as fungible as currency, architecture was poised to replace the nature that had itself been displaced by the sprawling conurbations of modern society.

Neutra's neologism, "biorealism," best sums up his particular view of nature. He defines the term in *Building with Nature* (1971), as the "biological understanding of human existence and survival under the technically prevailing circumstances," or, more succinctly, "applied physiology," an idea that had preoccupied him since he had first picked up Wundt's *Physiological Psychology.*—[56] Biorealism is clearly anticipated in phrases such as "*ever better biological fitness of design*," "organic realism," "biological returns," or "natural logic," which already pepper *Survival.*—[57] It can be understood as a medicalization of earlier German modernists' discussions of *Sachlichkeit*. The notion synthesizes distinct factors into a coherent and architecturally productive idea of nature. It was prophetic in insisting on a holistic point of view and in anticipating advances in neuroscience, which are only just now affecting theories of architectural design. At the same time, it was considerably constrained, focusing only on those lost aspects of a displaced nature that might be replicated in architectural terms. Moreover, nature itself was conceived of as being fundamentally benevolent—most plainly evident in an unpopulated and, importantly, private view through glass—and was everything the city was not, a trope consonant with urban critiques stretching back to the nineteenth century. For Neutra, the historical process of self-estrangement was not the result of new

56 Richard Neutra, *Building with Nature* (New York: Universe Books, 1971), 222.

57 Neutra, *Survival*, 63–64, 341, 370–71, 374. Emphasis in original.

circumstances of labor under factory or corporate conditions, as much as it was aesthetic—the cumulative effect of the cacophonous sensory stimuli thrown off by the modern city. Nonetheless, biorealism is a virtuoso synthesis, fusing second-generation refinements to the modernist program in an effort to broaden its constituencies—in part by emphasizing its relevance to consumer society—into a single theory that aspired to explain the effect of the man-made environment on evolutionary biology, and argued to a large extent at an almost cellular level. The theory's scope is clearly impressive. Likewise, with biorealism, the goal of overcoming modern anomie leads neither to primitivism nor utopianism, the usual analeptic and proleptic poles of avant-garde cultural critiques. It leads, instead, to an observation that humankind has yet to leave the body it was born with—which, as a result, must be respected—and an extrapolation that someday it will. Neutra premised biorealism on the reality of the Anthropocene, a new age in which technology remakes the world at the largest and at the finest scales, a term that was still decades away when he wrote. Thus, to the long list of historically changing views of nature, Neutra adds a new twist: made by nature to make, *homo faber* has remade nature and is now poised to remake himself through architectural means.

# Le Corbusier Evergreen

Christophe Girot, Patrick Düblin

## Early Formation
## The Mountains, the Forest, and the Grid

Le Corbusier, whose real name was Charles-Edouard Jeanneret, grew up in a provincial bourgeois home at La Chaux-de-Fonds, a small town tucked away in a high valley of the Jura Mountains in Switzerland, not far from the French border. Le Corbusier's father was deeply committed to mountaineering and became an early member of the Swiss Alpine Club, for which he served as president of his subsection from 1887 to 1893. He was prone to depression and used to take the young Le Corbusier on long hikes to confer upon him a vision of nature that praised its fundamental laws and sublime aesthetics.—[1]

For Le Corbusier, these hikes up and down countless mountain valleys with his father were hard, but they profoundly marked his understanding of landscape, in that nature remained a daunting force to be contemplated beyond any form of manipulation. Le Corbusier later wrote that he disliked the nature hikes with his father because of the stress and hardship they entailed,—[2] and this probably explains in part the unfathomable distance that arose between architecture and landscape in his work, where these two realms were fundamentally juxtaposed: on one side, an object that could be crafted, sculpted, and controlled; and on the other, a space that was absolute,

1 H. Allen Brooks, *Le Corbusier's Formative Years* (Chicago: University of Chicago Press 1997), 10.

2 Stanislaus von Moos, *Le Corbusier: Elements of a Synthesis* (Rotterdam: 010 Publishers, 2009), 18.

reflecting some constant laws that were only there to be contemplated.

La Chaux-de-Fonds had a thriving watchmaking industry, which covered nearly half of the global demand at the beginning of the twentieth century.—3 After a devastating fire in 1794, the authorities—under the command of Moïse Perret-Gentil, a local watch engraver and self-taught architect—4—rebuilt the entire city following an orthogonal grid plan. This distinctive urban definition was quite unique in Switzerland. Given the orthogonal layout of the town, the grid not only negated the topographical features of the site, but also created a hard contrast between the urban framework and the mountains, meadows, and forests beyond. At a young age, Le Corbusier was already conscious of the flaws in the grid layout of La Chaux-de-Fonds, lamenting in his first unpublished urban critique that the initiators of this solution were officials from Neuchâtel who were unfamiliar with the high-altitude site they had planned. He remarked that the urban grid itself was the source of the permanent unpleasantness felt at La Chaux-de-Fonds: "It is generally known—and accepted by everyone—that the city is ugly … In the entire city plan one doesn't find a single street layout that creates a beautiful view."—5

3 Jacques Gubler and Geoffrey Baker, *Le Corbusier: Early Works of Charles-Edouard Jeanneret-Gris* (London: St. Martin's Press, 1987), 121.

4 Cf. Claire Piguet, "Perret-Gentil, Moïse," in *Dictionnaire historique de la Suisse* (DHS). http://www.hls-dhs-dss.ch/textes/f/F19411.php. Published on October 20, 2008.

5 Christoph Schnoor and Le Corbusier, *La construction des villes. Le Corbusiers erstes städtebauliches Traktat von 1910/11. Studien und Texte zur Geschichte der Architekturtheorie* (Zürich: GTA-Verlag, 2008), Lcdv 362–63, pp. 494–96. Translation by the authors.

Yet even more striking than just the absence of pleasant views at La Chaux-de-Fonds was the resulting dichotomy that prevailed between city fabric and the surrounding landscape, which was comprised of cow pastures and dark forests of conifers. There was no transition between city and landscape—only a hard border that resulted in an abrupt chasm between two distinct spheres. This hard contrast between architecture and nature manifested itself throughout Le Corbusier's oeuvre and may in fact be at the root of his persistently difficult and inhibited relationship to landscape. For instance, a sketch by Le Corbusier published in *La Maison des hommes* (1942), symbolically

The young Charles-Edouard Jeanneret (to the right) hiking above the tree line in the Swiss Alps with his mother and friends in August 1907.

Drawing of two fir trees standing at the edge of a forest by Le Corbusier, published in *La Maison des Hommes*, 1942.

View of the gridded town of La Chaux-de-Fonds around 1916 with the Maison Blanche on the top left.

The white architecture of the Maison Blanche (circa 1912–17) contrasting with the dark forest of fir trees.

View to the northeast, looking over the quarry towards the snow-covered fir forest from the antechamber of the Maison Blanche, 1912.

exemplifies how his approach—or rather non-approach—to landscape was determined by this notion of a sterile separation between the built environment and the natural world. The image literally reads as if there were no way to enter the forest and no connection whatsoever to nature. The sketched path literally swerves off in front of two fir trees placed at the center of the picture, and takes us either to the left or right of the scene along a forest edge, clearly marking a boundary of "unspoiled nature" beyond, while epitomizing a persistent segregation between architecture and landscape in the broadest sense.

The eradication of the town center at La Chaux-de-Fonds and the subsequent superimposition of an urban grid on the territory also created a "lack of a distinctive visual heritage"—[6] in the town, as William J. R. Curtis points out. Thus, its inhabitants had to search for symbols of identification outside the town, which they found in the omnipresent fir tree. Charles L'Eplattenier, Le Corbusier's teacher at the Ecole d'Art of La Chaux-de-Fonds and trusted father figure, was strongly influenced by the ideas of John Ruskin and proposed a form of regional traditionalism that consisted in the schematic transformation of vernacular forms of nature into art. With his keen interest in conifers, L'Eplattenier established his very own regional adaption of Art Nouveau—the *Style sapin*—a veritable folklore of the fir tree, which Le Corbusier embraced as a design student in the form of dark green stylized triangles on a stick.—[7]

6 William J. R. Curtis, *Le Corbusier: Ideas and Forms* (Oxford: Phaidon Press Ltd., 1986), 16.

7 Ibid., 18–19.

## The Enduring Cult of the Fir Tree
## Staging the Maison Blanche

As a young man, Le Corbusier had espoused his teacher's method and beliefs, as echoed in the following quote: "Whereas Parisians make a modeled leaf that imitates nature's forms, and the Germans do it on a square polished like a mirror, well, we will make a triangle studded with pinecones."—[8] While in the Maison Fallet, Le Corbusier's first known built project, the decorative usage of the fir and cone motif was obvious, the Villa Jeanneret-Perret, soon to be nicknamed Maison Blanche, is said to mark the first break with the Style sapin.—[9] The villa's garden was designed in the reform style that was very popular at the time, but whether or not Le Corbusier designed it remains a matter of speculation; some suggest that Le Corbusier's father, who himself was a passionate gardener, could have played a major role in its design.—[10] Concerning the architecture itself, the folklore of the fir tree persisted and transcended Le Corbusier's later work. This is particularly evident in the case of the Maison Blanche, albeit on an entirely different and much less figurative level. In an early letter written to Auguste Perret, he describes the indoor situation of the newly built house with a surprising number of references to the wintery woods:

8 Letter to Charles L'Eplattenier, February 26, 1908. Le Corbusier, Charles L'Eplatternier, and Marie-Jeanne Dumont. *Lettres à ses maîtres*. Volume 2: Lettres à Charles L'Eplattenier. (Paris: Editions du Linteau 2006). Translation by the authors.

9 Cf. Klaus Spechtenhauser and Arthur Rüegg, eds., *Maison Blanche. Charles-Edouard Jeanneret. Le Corbusier* (Basel: Birkhäuser, 2007).

10 Cf. Peter Wullschleger, "Der Garten der Villa Jeanneret-Perret," in *Maison Blanche. Charles-Edouard Jeanneret. Le Corbusier*, 147–69, here 157.

> The room where we dwell and converse, has its large window pane placed at the very navel of the home. This is where the armchairs, the large carpet and piano gather *in front of the tree fronds and the rolling horizon of snowdrifts*. Some windowpanes fall in place occasionally along a distance of fourteen meters, which terminates to the east with *an immense window hanging abruptly off the edge of a quarry, in which a majestic forest of firs sheltering us from the winds from the other side is framed* … In my room light comes from the ceiling through *a pane of frosted glass that prevents one from seeing the entire top of the big fir tree* that seemed so agitated last summer as we were building.—[11]

11 Letter to Auguste Perret, March 10, 1913. Le Corbusier, Auguste Perret, and Marie-Jeanne Dumont. *Lettres à ses maîtres*. Volume 1: Lettres à Auguste Perret. (Paris: Editions du Linteau 2002). Translation and emphasis by the authors.

In this short passage, Le Corbusier describes three views from different sets of windows at the Maison Blanche, always referring with great reverence to the forest of fir trees outside. Aside from aesthetic references to the branches, the forest as it is described obtains an almost sublime vibrancy while at the same time playing a protective role providing shelter from the inhospitable "Bise" wind that blows there. In the final sentence, the symbolic power of the fir tree is elevated to an almost mystical level as seen through a pane of frosted glass: even though the tall fir dematerializes through this view, its animated presence becomes even more tangible—the aura of the sapin in the Maison Blanche is ubiquitous and transcends every room.

A picture from the inside, most likely taken by Le Corbusier himself, depicts the "majestic forest of firs" framed by the "immense window" that he was referring to in his letter to Perret. Additionally, a drawing of the same northeast prospect shows the impenetrable forest edge indicated by a strong jagged line.—[12] The fact that the architect portrays his impression of fir trees repeatedly—in text, drawing, as well as photography—tends to prove that the actual framing of this looming dark forest embodied a significant presence in his early work. It is indeed very peculiar that Le Corbusier showed a marked preference for such confined views, halted abruptly by the dark dense coniferous forest of the Jura Mountains, a view that practically negated the presence of light and of the horizon itself. This deliberate choice was clearly aesthetic and was certainly not due to a lack of other prospects in the house, since the Maison Blanche was set at the top of a slope overlooking the entire gridded city to the southeast. Seen from the inside, the architecture provided a set of chosen views of firs close by, looked at from the outside, the white building as a whole stood out against a black wall of conifers. The contrast between the clarity of the architecture and the dark inertial density of the forest could not have been more emphatic.

12 FLC 30269, reproduced in Le Corbusier, *Early Buildings and Projects, 1912–1923* [The Le Corbusier Archive Volume 1] (New York, London, and Paris: Garland Publishing and Foundation Le Corbusier, 1982).

It may be also of relevance that the aforementioned woods were more than just an anonymous backdrop for his early architecture. Located at the rear of the Maison Blanche, the so-called Pouillerel forest, though seemingly impenetrable, used to be a place of refuge for Le Corbusier and his schoolmates. Together with L'Eplattenier, they "fled" the city of La Chaux-de-Fonds in a Rousseau-like escape, in order to experience the truth behind all the appearances of nature, in the form of rituals initiated by their teacher. For L'Eplattenier, the Pouillerel forest corresponded not only to a fleeting hideaway, but also to the place where he himself chose to set up his home—in the middle of a clearing, surrounded by this wilderness of sorts.—[13]

13 Gubler and Baker, *Early Works of Charles-Edouard Jeanneret-Gris,* 114, 122.

For L'Eplattenier, nature was something deeply original, a pure entity, and as such it stood beyond the reach and creation of man. It was not to be altered, but to be studied in awe. Through the observation of plants and rocks, he and his pupils derived a naturalistic geometric form of ornamentation, which they then implemented in watch-cases and on house façades. However, the model itself, Mother Nature, remained untouched and almost sacred to his disciples—including the young Le Corbusier:

> My master used to say: "Only Nature is inspiring and true; only Nature can be the support for human works. But do not render Nature as the landscapists do, showing only the outward aspect. Penetrate the cause of it, its form and vital development; make a synthesis from it by creating *ornaments*."—[14]

14 Quoted in Curtis, *Ideas and Forms,* 24.

Ten years after the zealous echoing of his master's approach towards nature, Le Corbusier then tried to dismiss it fiercely:

> Oh L'Eplattenier, your houses called for a fir tree to be made of stone, embroidered with pinecone and darts motifs. What a pig, this L'Eplattenier! But still he took me to bed with his ideas.—[15]

15 "Ô L'Eplattenier, tes maisons qui exigaient d'un sapin qu'il devienne pierre, avec des pives et des dentelles du dard. Cochon, va! Il m'a tout même encanaillé, L'Eplattenier." Letter to William Ritter, October 5, 1918. Le Corbusier, William Ritter, Marie-Jeanne Dumont. *Lettres à ses maîtres.* Volume 3: Lettres à William Ritter. (Paris: Editions du Linteau 2015). Translation by the authors.

But from the quote itself, and the fact that he admitted to having been *encanaillé* or blindly indoctrinated by his master, one can tell that he was still struggling with the education that he had received.

Some first impressions of Le Corbusier's early work can thus be drawn. First, the symbolic power of the evergreen sapin remained unchallenged. Indeed, while it disappeared as an ornamental motif from the façade of his buildings, the actual tree gained both in weight and meaning as a vital prop in the scenery in and around his buildings. Second, the aforementioned gap between city and landscape also applied to the scale of the single building: as taught by his father, nature was something almighty and to be juxtaposed as an absolute to the architecture of the city. This is underpinned by the choice of site for the Maison Blanche at the very edge of the forest. Moreover, the gaze through the windows of the Maison Blanche exemplifies what Dorothée Imbert observed with respect to most of Le Corbusier's early French villas: the primacy of the visual and the "denial of the physical … connection between architecture and landscape."—[16] By primarily relating to nature as vistas provided by the architectural frame, or vice versa, as a stage set accentuating the contrast with the building, it was reduced, not to say relegated, to a kind of two-dimensional backdrop.—[17]

One might object that the inventor of the *promenade architecturale* proved his mastery of spatial connection between the surroundings and the building with a dramatic sense of arrival set in a very sculptural act of scenography. However, the architectural promenade was always organized in a single direction: from the outside to the inside, and like a watch, it only worked clockwise. Going back or leaving the building was possible indeed, but the aesthetic experience was not in any way as pleasant or emphatic as on the intended way in—one would often encounter resistance through obstacles and a breakdown of the staged entry sequence when moving against the established architectural mechanism towards the outside.—[18]

16 Dorothée Imbert, *The Modernist Garden in France* (New Haven: Yale University Press, 1993), 178.

17 In his later projects, such as La petite maison (1923), views of wonderful natural scenery are incorporated in his architectural framing. However, Le Corbusier planted the immediate landscape around the house with ornamental trees—including weeping willows, pines, and paulownias—that grew unsatisfactorily; he ordered them to be cut down thirty years later. See ibid., 174–75.

18 This is best exemplified in the Salvation Army building in Paris (1929), where the dramatic main entrance sequence into the building does not compare in any way to the exit, where a lone evergreen yew tree stands haplessly beside the street as some feeble token of nature.

## Villa Stein-de Monzie
## Trial and Failure in the Landscape

Le Corbusier received the commission for the Villa Stein-de Monzie in Garches, near Paris, at a time when he had left home for good and was about to become more and more popular in influential Parisian circles. With his new pseudonym borrowed from his mother's Belgian lineage "Corbésier" meaning cobbler,—[19] which he then transformed into "Le Corbusier," he detached himself from his paternal origins, intending to leave no trace of his former small-town life.

19 Cf. Jean Haust, *Dictionnaire Liégeois* (Liège: Vaillant-Carmanne, 1933), 191.

The Villa Stein is set at the center of an oblong estate allowing for a generous forecourt that provides room for a dramatic perspectival mise-en-scène of the entrance driveway. On the north side, the tapering road emphasizes the access to the building, but the main door is shifted off the axis to the right, where it is framed by two evergreen firs. The trees were planted there intentionally, but they are completely out of context with the deciduous forest of the Paris region. The firs are the only two noticeable landscape elements composing this front elevation. Highlighted by the white façade of the Villa Stein, their distinct triangular silhouettes inevitably recall the scenery surrounding the Maison Blanche. The two conifers stand in contrast to the white walls of the house, yet they are awkwardly pushed to the side. Due to their isolation, they appear as though extracted out of a different environment—the Jura Mountains, maybe.

There are no drafts of the final landscape design project for the Villa Stein, but we do know that Le Corbusier originally tried to draw a garden in a rather conventional reform style, which he ultimately rejected. We also know that his landscape contractor, Lucien Crépin, began planting four months ahead of the construction work, mainly using a selection of evergreens.—[20] Hence, some scholars conclude that the clients and the architect had a special concern with regard to the landscape.—[21] Nevertheless, it may be that Le Corbusier was in fact unable to cope with an appropriate planting design scheme for the Paris region. The use of evergreens translates

20 The bill lists "11 firs, 4 Norway spruces, 11 false cypresses, 7 yews, 4 cedars, 6 pines, 1 larch, 1 cryptomeria, 1 auracaria, 3 junipers, 31 thujas, 150 aucubas, 130 eunymus, 78 privets, 299 laurels, 35 boxwoods, and 8 bamboos." See Imbert 1993, 156–58, here 158.

21 See, for instance, Tim Benton, *The Villas of Le Corbusier and Pierre Jeanneret. 1920–1930* (Basel: Birkhäuser, 2007), 164.

Front view of the Villa Stein-de Monzie, 1927–28, with the main driveway and two evergreen fir trees shifted to the right so as to frame the entrance, photographed by Charles Gérard.

An evergreen tree of the cypress family planted against the white architecture of the roof garden of the Beistegui apartment in Paris, 1930, photographed by Lucien Hervé.

Sketches by Charles L'Eplattenier showing the use of black triangles to represent the sapin as a decorative element.

Like a ship floating above a mixed forest and orchards, the Unité d'habitation at Firminy-Vert, 1965, dialogues with a few fir trees in the vicinity.

his architectural intent with respect to a given image of nature, one that recalls the sapins of La Chaux-de-Fonds as a constant presence, something invariable and timeless with the dark green needles of the fir precluding any notion of seasonal change.

The conifer remained a recurrent motif throughout Le Corbusier's early Parisian period; a prominent example of this is found in the Beistegui roof garden in Paris (1930), where a single conifer once again stands out on the rooftop against the white steps of the terrace. In this case, the choice of tree is an evergreen of the cypress family, which replaced a yew that had been planted there originally.—[22] With its dark aspect and inhospitable needles, the fir would not have been suited for nor have survived on a Paris rooftop. The fir tree in Le Corbusier's symbolic repertoire lacked any sort of sensuality, but embodied the raw, not to say hostile, qualities of a very rough form of primitive nature. Even though Le Corbusier strived to rid himself of any apparent link to his earlier formative years in the Jura Mountains, by writing that "the firs [were] about as friendly as a saw ready to cut you in two,"—[23] the evergreen conifer motif prevailed as a faithful companion in many of his subsequent projects. It is as though their threatening character had an actual impact on Le Corbusier's architecture—the evergreen tree often served as an easy symbol and pretext of his limitations in terms of actual landscape design. The planting arrangement of the Villa Stein front yard is just one example among many of a recurring stumbling block for him with respect to landscape design.—[24]

Three decades later, Le Corbusier returned to the Villa Stein site and romanticized the experience: "This week, I saw Garches again, after 32 years, white … behind the trees: an exquisite vision."—[25] The picturesque gaze on this evergreen landscape arrangement must have reminded him of his early childhood years. In this sense, the two

22 Imbert, *The Modernist Garden in France,* 170.

23 Le Corbusier quoted in Curtis, *Ideas and Forms,* 37.

24 Dorothée Imbert's thorough analysis of Le Corbusier's French villa gardens is a testimony to the architect's numerous failed attempts to create a correspondence between architecture and nature. Examples range from the Esprit Nouveau Pavilion, to the Villa Meyer, the Villa Church, and the Villa Savoye. See Imbert, 147–83.

25 Quoted in Imbert, *The Modernist Garden in France,* 158.

firs that stood there in the driveway in front of the house could be read symbolically as a reference to the primordial Jura nature of his childhood. The dark fir forests where he and his companions experienced nature firsthand, was just as idealized as the shepherds' life described in the texts of Virgil. In 1930, shortly after completion of the Villa Stein, Le Corbusier fantasized about an extensive modernist villa project in Argentina, where he sought to apply his own pastoral ideal of the cow meadows from the Jura Mountains, to some universal dogma about the relationship between nature and architecture on a global scale. Once again, the landscape was always meant to remain pastoral and intact:

> [W]e shall have twenty houses rising from the high grass of an orchard, where cows continue to graze ... Grass will grow along the edge of the roads, nothing will be disturbed, neither trees nor flowers nor herds. The inhabitants who came here because this countryside with its rural life was beautiful, will contemplate it, maintained intact, from their hanging gardens or through the four sides of the long windows. Their home life will be set in a Virgilian dream.—[26]

In a way, the cow symbolized the faunal equivalent of the sapin in Le Corbusier's recurring references to the rural environment of the Jura Mountains.—[27] It epitomized a permanent feature of the architect's basic vision of landscape, which culminated in his utopian urban vision: the wide, green open pastures of the Ville Radieuse. As already noted by Jan Woudstras, this idyllic Virgilian expanse of plain grass and trees amounted to almost everything in Le Corbusier's ideal landscape repertoire—[28]—mountains notwithstanding. Not surprisingly, this pragmatic functionalist attitude towards nature was further mirrored in his conception of the vast, green, gridded open spaces in his celebrated 1933 plan of the Ville Radieuse, where the word "zoning" appears in the subtitle.—[29] This vision of a zoned green expanse was propagated by the architects of the CIAM rather

26 Le Corbusier, *Precisions: On the Present State of Architecture and City Planning*, trans. by Edith Schreiber Aujame (Cambridge, MA: The MIT Press, 1991), 139.

27 See Gubler and Baker, *Early Works of Charles-Edouard Jeanneret-Gris*, 116–17.

28 See Jan Woudstras, "The Corbusian Landscape. Arcadia or No Man's Land?" in *Garden History* 28, no. 1 (Summer 2000): 135–51, here 138.

29 See Christophe Girot, *The Course of Landscape Architecture* (London: Thames & Hudson, 2016), 260–62.

uncritically. For Le Corbusier and the CIAM, the question of landscape was not central, but this was mainly because Le Corbusier was either unwilling or unable to design nature and incorporate it in his theories. His perception and enactment of nature can best be described as picturesque in the double sense of the term: *picture-like*, because he reduces landscape to a mere view; as well as *idyllic*, whereas his concept of a Virgilian idyll is either created by chance (Villa Stein) or remains wishful thinking (Ville Radieuse). The austere green spaces resemble the cow pastures of his hometown and are most likely more appropriate for grazing animals than for actual people.

## A Leap into Nothingness
### Corbusian Urbanism and the Unité d'habitation

Le Corbusier's difficulties with respect to landscape design reached their climax later in his career and more particularly in his larger urban projects. Whereas his earlier villa gardens were able to hide his incapacity to design a landscape, by filling the void with random evergreen plant arrangements, the leap in scale revealed a complete absence of ideas when dealing with the surroundings. The Ville Radieuse was originally intended to be a vast park, yet the austere unspecific gridded pastures of Le Corbusier's ideal city actually seem to be more suited to rapid transportation, parking, and sports than anything else. Through the Ville Radieuse's vast grid—a feature that he had severely criticized earlier in his own hometown for its lack of sensitivity to site—a new kind of mechanistic approach to the design of urban green spaces emerged. In contrast to the grid of La Chaux-de-Fonds, that of Ville Radieuse fenced in greenery instead of buildings. As a result, an enclosed yet undefined green vacuum prevailed in the heart of the modernist city.—[30] We are indeed far removed from the ideal motif of nature drawn from Le Corbusier's childhood surroundings.

30 The vast utopian landscape plan of the Punjabi capital Chandigarh does not escape this mechanistic rule. Built on a forty-five-degree skewed grid to catch a view of the mountains, it fails to perform its microclimatic functions well because of this orientation. Despite a phenomenal population growth in recent decades, there remains a problem with the scale and expanse of the designed landscapes interspersed between the poorly oriented city building blocks. Chandigarh, built essentially by Le Corbusier on a grid meant to frame some distant mountains, seems marooned in its territory, leaving most pedestrian visitors hapless and sweltering over long distances in the subtropical Punjab heat.

With the first Unité d'habitation in Marseilles, also named Cité Radieuse, the "Vertical Garden City" of Le Corbusier came into being, at least in part. Drawing on the technocratic ideas of Ebenezer Howard, landscape was primarily addressed in terms of its functions: vast green spaces detached from any context serve as areas for leisure activities, sports, entertainment, and relaxation.—[31] As the postulations of the Athens Charter demonstrate, the new dimension of Le Corbusier's imagined green spaces resulted in a blatant vagueness: he called for "broad verdant areas," liberated by high-rises, as well as "vast spaces" that consist of "forests and meadows, natural and artificial beaches."—[32] Thus, one could argue that, in lieu of an original landscape design concept, the unspecified green open spaces portrayed in Le Corbusier's writings and drawings remain completely open to interpretation by other capable designers and planners. However, many CIAM adherents took the architect's idea of a green plinth quite literally and defended it as something authentically Corbusian in style. Hence, the wide-open lawn sparsely planted with fast growing trees—like poplars, birch, and pine—became a generalized modernist paradigm.

31 Girot, *The Course of Landscape Architecture*, 260.

32 Le Corbusier, *The Athens Charter*, trans. by Anthony Eardley (New York: Harper Collins, 1973), 65, 70–71.

In the case of Firminy-Vert, one of Le Corbusier's last projects, the Unité d'habitation was set within a clearing on top of a green mound. A landscape architect named Michel Bourne was commissioned to design the environment around it, but one of Le Corbusier's chief architects, Charles Delfante, felt that the true spirit of modernist green space was in jeopardy. He dismissed Bourne's rather kitsch and rustic style as petty-minded and anachronistic, incompatible with the layout of the building and the precepts of modernist urbanism: "We find absolutely despicable, the log fences, wooden staircases and huts, which are not in any way in harmony with the architecture and the idea that one ought to have of the environment surrounding an Unité d'habitation."—[33] Thus, the Unité d'habitation of Firminy-Vert remained there

33 Quoted in Clarisse Lauras, *Firminy-Vert. De l'utopie municipale à l'icône patrimoniale* (Rennes: Presses universitaires de Rennes, 2014), 212. Translation by the authors.

on its original green plinth without any kind of landscape design, surrounded by a mixed forest that included some scattered conifers. The existing landscape produced a rather romantic form of non-interventionism that was quite removed from CIAM principles and more in keeping with Le Corbusier's earliest works, such as the Maison Blanche.

On a topological level, the form of the Unité d'habitation projects embodies a prevailing absence of correspondence between architecture and landscape. On the one hand, the elevated *pilotis* underline a strong detachment between the building and the ground; on the other hand, Le Corbusier often referred to his building as an ocean liner, a floating vessel that inspired the Unité d'habitation in many ways,—[34] reinforcing yet again the impression that the structure remained distant and out of touch with its surroundings. The only example with a distant visual link to the mountains and sea is the Marseilles example. There, landscape in the immediate surroundings is reinforced by a stand of evergreen Aleppo pines, which had probably been planted around the time of construction to screen off part of the neighborhood leading to the Prado Beach. Nevertheless, the views seen from the roof at Marseilles, which have been praised so often, should be put in perspective with the actual siting of all the other Unité d'habitation projects in and around France. Due to their inherent universality, these projects landed on various sites and became interchangeable; in most cases, the haphazard landscape context mattered so little, that it seemed to be the product of mere chance rather than intent. The boat-like *machine à habiter* could either cast anchor in the rather dense urban environment of the Prado in Marseilles, run aground in a desolate clearing on a green mound in Firminy-Vert, or be marooned like a shipwreck in the thickets of Briey-en-Forêt. The Unité d'habitation represents the best possible materialization of Le Corbusier's urban concepts in Europe and stands out as a striking example of non-engagement with context,

34 See von Moos, *Elements of a Synthesis*, 160–61.

leading to a complete absence of elementary landscape design considerations.

What can explain this recurring dichotomy between dwelling and terrain in Le Corbusier's oeuvre? Could it be that his extraordinary creative talent at inventing and manipulating built form was counterbalanced by a deep and persistent inability to design with nature? The key to this enigma undoubtedly lies in his formative years at La Chaux-de-Fonds, where he spent a good third of his life; a place where landscape was a considered to be the backdrop and mirror of a pastoral nature surrounded by evergreens never to be questioned or challenged.

Similar to L'Eplattenier's retreat in the Pouillerel forest, Le Corbusier sometimes spent some winter days in a farmhouse in the Jura Mountains during his teenage and young adult years. Impressed by the shape of the fireplace in that ordinary, vernacular abode, he repeatedly adapted it in his later designs, one of them being the Church at Firminy-Vert.—[35] But did the setting of the farmhouse itself, standing in a clearing surrounded by tall dark evergreen firs, also impact Le Corbusier's subsequent view on nature and the relation between his architecture and landscape? Why is it that the structures he created remain detached and adrift from the natural environment, not only symbolically but also physically? From the figure of the isolated building in the clearing like the Villa Savoye, to the more massive Unité d'habitation, the theme of the freestanding building in an unaltered natural environment recurs throughout his work; the direct implantation of an Unité d'habitation at Briey-en-Forêt at the very heart of a forest is probably the most radical and yet most dubious implementation of this modernist dwelling "concept." In this case, the juxtaposition between architecture and nature is blatant and results in an irreconcilable rift between building and landscape.

35 Brooks, *Le Corbusier's Formative Years*, 185–91.

Although Le Corbusier relentlessly strived to renounce his past, the characteristics of the terrain and the grid at La Chaux-de-Fonds prevailed in his mind. The same can be said of his indoctrination in the romanticist beliefs of both his teacher and father that haunted him all his life. His fetish for evergreens, which manifested itself throughout his work, persisted as the token of a form of nature that he knew best. This certainly suggests that Le Corbusier's incapacity to engage in landscape transformations and designs throughout his projects has to do with his early confrontation with the incredible forces of nature, which obviously transcended time, space, and architecture.

# Alvar Aalto's Villa Mairea: Between Nature and Culture

Richard Weston

Glimpsed through the surrounding trees, Alvar Aalto's Villa Mairea could easily be mistaken for an orthodox Modernist house, a white volume contrasting with the surrounding "nature."

As you enter the clearing of the informal garden, however, a very different picture unfolds. To the left, the composition culminates in an elevated, curved volume that appears to be clad in gray-brown weatherboarding. Below, large sheets of glass sit between a band of narrow teak boards and slabs of dark stone. And as you approach closer, you discover that what you took for white-painted render is in fact textured, lime-washed brickwork.

You enter under a two-level canopy. The stone paving and steps are irregular in profile—"crazy" as they are known in English—and to the right, the porch is contained by a line of closely spaced young saplings, stripped of their bark and suspended from the canopy, which is itself supported by angled, lashed-together, circular poles. The large, hardwood door has a large bronze handle, angled near its middle and swollen slightly at its ends and "joint."

On entering, you find yourself a few steps below the living spaces in a reception area screened by irregularly spaced vertical poles, refined versions of those that framed the entrance outside. You enter to the left, up a short flight of steps that open laterally, directing you towards the fireplace that is the focus of the intimate heart of the open-plan living space. Next to the fireplace, and sliding slightly past it, full-height glazing allows unbroken views out onto the private garden, around which the house is wrapped on three sides. At the farthest end, a flat-roofed wooden sauna is linked by an almost makeshift-looking gate and fence to a low earth mound that implies the fourth side of a courtyard.

Turn your back on the garden view and the interior opens diagonally into a large, more or less square space that seems—thanks to a properly modernist glazed corner—almost to "flow" into the surrounding forest. Throughout the living areas, you are struck by a succession of singular columns. They appear to be "lined up" as columns should be, but no two are the same. Some are single, black-painted steel tubes, others are paired, and one group is a cluster of three—and for no obvious structural reason. All are wrapped or clad. The wrapping is golden rattan that was, by all accounts, fiendishly difficult to apply. On some, it runs almost from top to bottom, while on others it forms a kind of skirt around a single column or, in one place, binds two together as a pair. Around the perimeter birch slats replace the rattan, and seen from a distance the reflection of the corner column appears to stand outside amongst the trees of the forest edge.

The change in "character" of the columns is reflected in changes in the floor finishes, while the main stair—one of Aalto's finest—echoes the sapling-framed entrance with a series of irregularly arranged poles acting as an enclosing balustrade. The first, broad, tapering tread is angled into the living room and in its "angling" recalls the first steps encountered under the entrance canopy.

As this brief description suggests, the interior of the Villa Mairea is even more "unorthodox" than hinted at by its exterior. This was in part a response to a seemingly contradictory brief. The clients were Maire and Harry Gullichsen: she, the heiress to Ahlström, one of Finland's major timber and paper companies; he, an astute Swedish businessman who, by marrying into the family, became the company's managing director. Two years before commissioning the house towards the end of 1937, Maire had become a co-founder of Artek, formed to make and sell the furniture, glass, and other designs by Aalto and his wife Aino. The Gullichsen family already had two properties on the estate, and what they asked Aalto to design was a summer house that was "both modern and Finnish" and combined the best of a progressive, industrial culture with respect for both Finnish traditions and the national love of nature. Spending time in "nature" remains an integral part of most Finns' lives, and the national culture that was defined in opposition to Russian rule in the nineteenth century celebrated the landscape—a seemingly endless network of forests and glacial lakes—as central to Finnish identity. Casting themselves as "the people of the forest," they set vernacular farmsteads against the "civilized" neoclassicism promoted by Russia. Akseli Gallen Kallela, the leading painter of the National Romantic period, led a "cultural retreat" into the forest, completing in 1895 his own home and studio, Kalela, on a lakeside site at Ruovesi, deep inland from Helsinki. Its rustic forms were based on Karelian vernacular houses and were eventually echoed in countless summerhouses and saunas.

In the Villa Mairea, Aalto explores the apparent opposition between vernacular and "high" style. Modernism takes the place of the previously normative neoclassicism—which, along with others of his generation, he had practiced briefly in the nineteen-twenties—but from overall conception to detail the design is suffused with ideas derived directly from, or intended to evoke, Finnish vernacular culture.

The courtyard-like plan, with its grouping of disparately sized and built elements, is intended to be a direct echo of a traditional farmstead. These began with the building of the sauna, where the family might well spend the first winter. Next came shelters for animals, and finally the family home—but the mother would always return to the sauna to give birth. In the Villa, the sauna can be seen as the symbolic "first building" of a composition that grows in size and sophistication of construction, until it culminates in Maire's lofty first-floor studio jauntily supported on a two-stemmed steel column.

Aalto's sauna has a grass roof with overlapping layers of birchbark as waterproofing, but is flat rather than pitched. Similarly, although the walls are of timber they are not of vernacular logs, but feel distinctly Japanese in character—a feeling confirmed by the woven panel on the door. Japanese influence on the design is, in fact, pervasive. While designing the Villa, one of Aalto's assistants recalled that he had a series of books on Japanese architecture opened to specific pages scattered around the office, where he occasionally appeared wearing a kimono given him by his friend, the Japanese ambassador. For the most part, the Japanese influence has been fully absorbed and it is only out of easy sight, on the roof, that Aalto dared almost to "quote," by treating the stone ballast for the covering as a *kare sansui* (dry garden).

Moving around from the sauna, one encounters a covered terrace framed in concrete, like a single story of Le Corbusier's Dom-Ino house, but, like the sauna, it is roofed with birchbark and grass. The roof runs on over the dining room, but is split at their junction to allow for access courtesy of decidedly rustic stone stair. The roof changes to timber boarding and above the dining room acquires a timber balustrade that is a direct echo of the intersecting logs of farm fences. But here the logs float in space supported by slender, white-painted steel uprights. This detail was, in fact, a late addition; early drawings showing a conventional "nautical" balustrade of the kind codified in the nineteen-twenties as part of what became known as the International Style.

One could point to many more such conjunctions of "vernacular" and "modern"—such as the timber trellis supported by concrete beams cantilevered out from the bedroom wing, or the symbolic "porch" made from poles adjacent to the side (staff) entrance—but these are far from the only "references" at play here. The lime-washed brickwork, for example, alludes to the vernacular not of Finland but of the Mediterranean, above all Italy's *architettura minore*, which had so delighted the young Nordic Classicists—Aalto among them—who made their first journeys to the cradle of Western civilization in the nineteen-twenties.

All of the "references" discussed thus far would potentially have been readily accessible to anyone in the Gullichsens' circle, but Maire's studio is something altogether more personal. What appears from a distance to be plain weatherboarding is found on close inspection to be subtly profiled. The shape recalls Classical moldings and is precisely the same profile Aalto used on the Finnish Pavilion at the 1937 Paris World's Fair—where, incidentally, he was impressed by African vernacular buildings with lashed-together posts, which may well have inspired the columns supporting the entrance canopy.

Maire Gullichsen had studied painting in Paris in the nineteen-twenties, where she began assembling one of the finest collections of modernist art in private hands in Finland, and in her new studio Aalto surrounded her with a cladding that was "both Finnish and modern." But the memories of Paris did not end there. Although the "flowing, interpenetrating space" of modern architecture and the "all-over" compositions of modernist painting are readily seen as interrelated expressions of similar formal ideas, rarely had the link between painting and architecture been as direct as it is in the Villa Mairea.

Aalto's model here is surely collage, which combined a broadly cubist formal syntax with "real world" materials or images designed to evoke specific memories, associations, or milieus. "Imported" from the forest and the vernacular, Aalto's logs (in variously refined states) and turf roofs play much the same role as the theater tickets, scraps of newspaper, and fragments of rattan encountered in early collages. Seen in this light, it is tempting to read—perhaps overread—every surface in Aalto's composition. For example, could the blue tiles that form a fragmented revetment to the end of the dining room be a reference to the Gullichsen family's Jugendstil house nearby? Although collage clearly offered Aalto a compositional model, his architectural collage is far less fragmentary than verbal description may suggest. The unifying idea behind the composition is his reinvention of modernist space as what his biographer Göran Schildt has called "forest space."

Let us return to the Villa's principal living space. There is a vernacular precedent for such a space in the *tupa* or main room of a traditional Finnish farmhouse, where areas for different activities were identified by changes of height or by hanging household items overhead. Aalto has melded this idea with modernist spatial continuity, articulating the flowing space into a series of milieus by changes in level, material, enclosure, and light, and by the use of the distinctive poles that screen the entrance and stairs. Yet what he has sought above all, through the presiding metaphor of the forest, is to give the interior the character of "nature."

Aalto's own statements accompanying publications of his work rarely went beyond the pragmatics of brief, site, and functional organization. Writing about the Villa, however, he said he wanted "to avoid all artificial architectural rhythms." To which one's immediate reaction might be to say that architecture rested on the geometric counterpoint between artifice and nature. What Aalto was attempting in the Villa was, for its time, unique, and the "naturalization" of the architecture pervades the design.

In the ground plan of the house, one could see that the columns are arranged on a "proper" grid—a "clear structure," as Mies van der Rohe famously observed, is the basis of the free plan. But as we noted earlier, experientially Aalto's structure is experienced episodically and anything but "clear." In a lecture in Stockholm given in 1944, just four years after he completed the Villa, Aalto proposed the branch of a flowering cherry tree as a model for housing: just as no two flowers were alike, differing according to their position on the stem, relationship to the sun and to neighboring flowers, so houses should vary to reflect varieties of terrain and occupation. It took Jørn Utzon, who was in the audience, to really fly with this idea in his courtyard houses but in the Villa, Aalto celebrated the never-repeating variety of nature in the clustering and wrapping of his columns. He even made one of concrete rather than steel: it is in Harry Gullichsen's library-cum-meeting room. The shutter left vertical striations that recall the flutes of Doric columns: could he really have intended this as an allusion to Culture, as opposed to the surrounding nature of his virtual forest?

The "forest" idea is reinforced by returning the columns to their putative origins as trees—e. g., Laugier's Primitive Hut—because not only do their wrappings serve to individualize them, but they also directly allude visually and texturally to the trees around. As they mature, pine trees generally shed a layer of black bark to reveal a golden layer below, and the height above the ground at which this begins and ends is variable. The color and variability are echoed directly in the columns at the heart of Aalto's interior, and the wrapping of rattan is designed both to make a visual connection to the surrounding trees and to mediate the industrial steel column by offering a surface that is texturally inviting and warm to the hand.

Along the edge of the fully glazed section of the living room, as noted above, the columns are clad with birch strips, while outside, hidden from internal view, is the double-column of white-painted steel supporting the studio. This had an interesting history. It appeared on Aalto's final drawings, only for his engineer to insist that the inclined section be removed; it had no structural function and would give him a bad name among his peers! When Maire Gullichsen saw the finished building she lamented the absence of the leaning column and an assistant was dispatched to find a suitable section—not an easy task with the Winter War with Russia in full spate. It was eventually found and fixed into place, but carries no load.

There is no question that, purely formally, the paired column is visually more satisfactory. But it also played its part in Aalto's "virtual forest": not only do similarly white birch trees often have just such twin stems, they are also found on the edges of pine forests, just as the double-columns appear here alongside its birch-clad counterparts, beyond which lie the rattan-clad "pines."

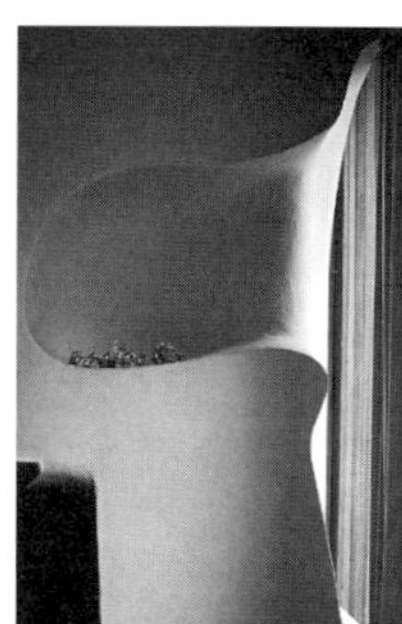

Another, exquisitely judged example of this process of "naturalization" is the fireplace. Similar plastered masonry "blocks" were a vital part of every Finnish farmhouse, and were frequently hollowed out and modeled to accommodate the fire and tools, and to act as a mantelpiece for display. A particularly famous sculptural interpretation of the vernacular form was created by the painter Akseli

Gallen-Kallela in his studio home on Lake Ruovesi, and Aalto, one suspects, was alluding to this Finnish icon in the shaping of what became known in the office as "Aalto's ear."

Visually, the modeled form mediates the junction between the fireplace block and the full-height glazing that runs a short distance past and behind it. It also recalls the gravestone Aalto designed for his brother-in-law, the architect Ahto Virtanen, which included the "negative" of half a classical banister along one edge. Those who knew Aalto's work well might have seen this as an "allusion" to the classical tradition, but what is surely not in doubt is that its final, flowing form vividly evokes the shapes of wind-sculpted snow and ice that would be seen through the adjacent glass during the long winter months. Such a reading seems consistent with the allusions to the forest and nature that pervade the Villa, but it is worth recalling that the lakelike profile of Aalto's celebrated Savoy Vase was, he said, inspired by the leather breeches of an Eskimo girl, not any direct reference to nature. In Freudian mode, it would be tempting to interpret the melting fireplace as a covert allusion to his intimate relationship with Maire: Aalto described the house as an *opus con amore* and his affair with Mrs. Gullichsen was not exactly the best kept secret.

Seen as an abstraction of the forest, the shifting relationships among the "individualized" columns, their absorption by the screens of poles into a vertically striated space, the changing floor/ground surfaces, and qualities of light and view, all make for a pervasive echo of the experience of walking through a pine forest. So, too, does the detailing of the glazed screen between library and living room. Harry Gullichsen demanded a separate room where he might hold private business meetings; Aalto was initially reluctant to concede to this, fearing that it would compromise the openness he sought. Early plans show a continuous open space; in the version Aalto published, the library is shown smaller than it was actually built. Framed by angled bookshelves, it is made to appear almost temporary or adjustable, and Aalto left the gap between these units and the ceiling open. When he discovered that his meetings could be overheard, Harry demanded that the gap be sealed. Rather than infill it with glazing alone—the obvious way to retain the desired openness—Aalto chose to devise a flowing, serpentine line formed of curved, concave and convex, solid elements and narrow strips of glass. With the lights on, radiating bands of light spill out across the ceiling, vividly recalling sunlight penetrating the edge of a forest. And to enrich our perception of this "slice" of forest, Aalto makes the panels white on the living room side and pale, golden brown facing into the library: viewed from the living room one looks out to metaphoric birches, from the library, into the "pine forest."

Villa Mairea is exceptional among Aalto's buildings in the vividness with which nature becomes a metaphorical model.

It was while designing this house that he produced a temporary interior of even greater intensity for the 1939 New York World's Fair. The ground had been laid in "Tsit Tsit Pum," the motto he gave to his second-prize-winning project for the 1937 Finnish Pavilion in Paris. A more radical design than the one the jury preferred, it was conceived as a terraced landscape with a small "lake" at one end, a "birch grove" of white flag poles and, most tellingly for his future work, an undulating balcony that might have been part of a lake shore traced from a map—his father, let us not forget, had been a land surveyor and Aalto famously wrote about the lessons learned at the "White Table" at which he worked.

In the New York pavilion, the undulating line becomes the project's leitmotif. It defines the edge of a shallow raised level for exhibits, while above it forms a three-level billowing curtain of wood, each layer defined by a subtly different curve and projecting slightly forwards and backwards of the layer below. Striated by projecting, tapering strips that frame large images of Finnish nature and culture, Aalto clearly intended the wooden "curtain" to evoke, abstractly, the texture of a forest edge, and thereby invites us to see the raised platform as the metaphoric shoreline of the reflective floor.

Aalto's motto for the project, however, does not allude to the landscape but to the sky: he called it "Aurora Borealis" and no one—including the present writer (in my monograph *Alvar Aalto*, London: Phaidon Press, 1995)—seems to have taken this very seriously. To the best of my knowledge, there are no surviving color pictures of what is arguably Aalto's finest interior, but his intentions were clear: the competition perspective shows a battery of lights in the ceiling, which he said would be used to bathe the timber screens in colored light. The pavilion's interior was calculated to evoke one of the most typical manifestations of the Northern Lights, familiar in numerous paintings and textbook illustrations, of an undulating curtain seemingly consisting of vertical "rods" of light. It remains a moot point whether this was Aalto's intention from the outset, or an inflection introduced when perspective studies suggested the analogy. We may never know, but the dialogue between a curved/broken line and a straight one, between the "variability" of nature and the "rationality" of construction would form the basis of countless future projects.

This dialogue was first worked out on the grand scale in the sinuous line of the Baker House dormitory at MIT, and later on a tiny scale in his own summerhouse on the island of Muuratsalo, where the square head of the courtyard house is joined to a tail of secondary volumes, each subtly angled to the terrain and supported by boulders on the site—a "site-specific" strategy comparable on the small scale with Wright's Fallingwater, which had incidentally been a catalyst for the design of the Villa Mairea.

Whitewashed brickwork outside and "crumbling" brickwork inside, the Muuratsalo courtyard is rendered as a piece of Italian *architettura minore* and brings to the fore another key aspect of Aalto's "naturalization" of architecture that was also hinted at in the Villa Mairea:

accelerating the "ravages" of time by "building in" the inevitability of weathering and decay. Although similar to De Stijl in their delicate balancing of textures and colors, the variously laid and pointed rectangular patches of brick and tile are driven by a narrative idea. The clue is the deep blue rectangle of tiles that comes complete with a (wholly redundant) timber lintel. Once understood as a metaphorical "window on the South," the artful patchwork of the walls becomes an abstraction of an Italian piazzetta, replete with "memories" of former door and window openings and mellowed by time and the elements.

In Aalto's public buildings, such references to nature, to the landscape, and to the passage of time, seem to me almost equally pervasive but are generally less overtly expressed. Most obvious, perhaps, is his preference for repeated vertical lines set against broad horizontal masses. Explaining the rounded tiles—like convex inversions of Greek flutings—that he designed for the ceramics company Arabia and used widely both inside and out, Aalto said that the low Finnish sun demanded vertical moldings as opposed to the horizontal ones found in the classical South. Seen en masse, the effect of these tiles varies depending on the light, with either the regular joints dividing the mass horizontally or the projecting tiles creating fine-grained vertical striations, which it is hard not to see as an echo of the endlessly repeated, and notably vertical trees of the Finnish landscape—which, in turn, are almost everywhere, set against broadly horizontal land or water.

The Seinäjoki Civic Centre provides a perfect illustration of Aalto's tactics of "naturalization" at work. Consider first the town hall. As a mark of its status, the volume containing the council chamber is clad all over in dark blue tiles, while the horizontal windows of the white-rendered offices are variously subdivided by timber panels, or overlain with mullion-like poles that rise beyond the windows to parapet level. On the library, the vertical security bars rhyme with the trunks of adjacent birch trees, and are thereby subsumed into an overall rhythmic articulation of the block. Inside, both plan and section are generated by the juxtaposition of straight and undulating lines. Both have straightforward functional justifications—the need for visual supervision of the radiating stacks and reflecting light into the interior—but it is hard not to see the two-level interior, with its "strata" of books and billowing "cloud" of a ceiling as an evocation of landscape.

For most people, one suspects, this operates at a subconscious level, and it would be vulgar if such associations asserted themselves too literally. However, in much of Aalto's work they seem to be inescapable and to arise not from a picturesque strategy of visually "harmonizing" with nature, but from an engagement with nature as a model for an architecture that could transcend, as Aalto put it, the "rootless technocratic constructivism" of the Machine Age. Today, the challenge remains and will not be met by the rootless digital biomorphism proffered by so many who are turning again to nature as a model.

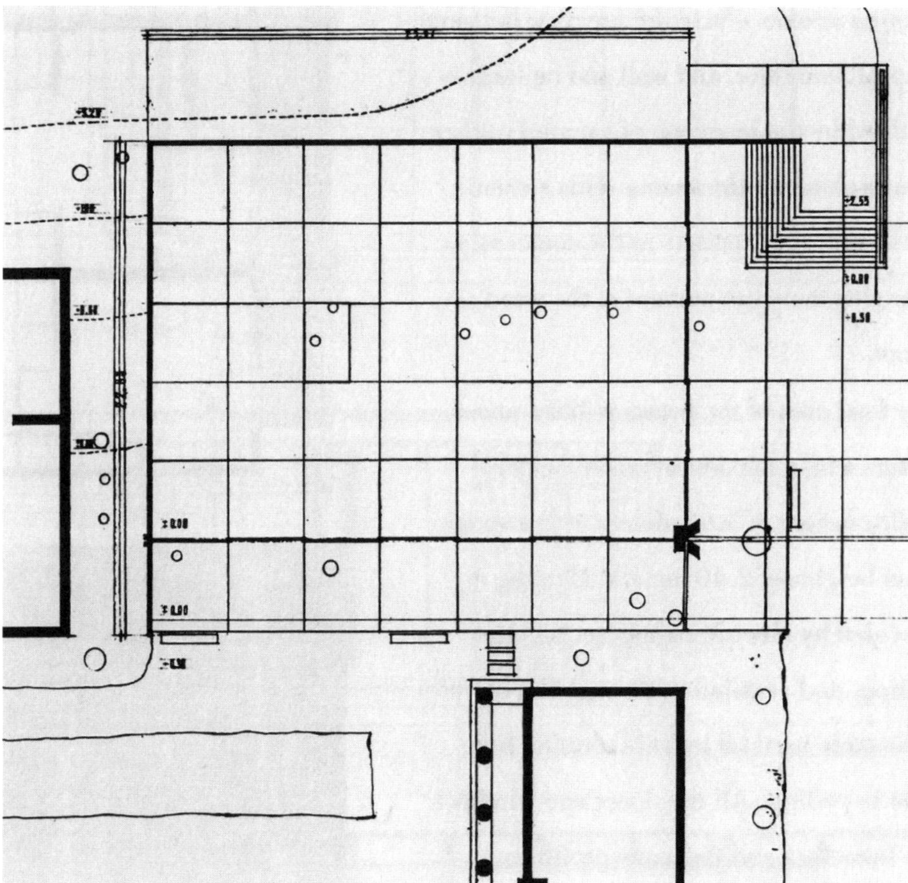

Sverre Fehn, Nordic Pavilion, plan, Venice, 1962.

# Nature and Artifice in the Architecture of Sverre Fehn

David Leatherbarrow

*And he thought of the melancholic and susceptible poet who had once seen the towers and turrets of his dreams rise out of these waves; repeated the rhythms born of his awe, his mingled emotions of joy and suffering.*

Thomas Mann

*For me, there is no culture north of the Alps.*

Carlo Scarpa, quoted by Sverre Fehn

This study aims to add a short chapter to the history of images of nature. Two premises will be supposed: first, that the natural world can be known at least in part through images; and second, that representations of this kind are perforce historical and not only successive, but also cumulative, though incompletely so. There are, of course, different kinds of images—some mathematical, others musical, and still others verbal, visual, or spatial—the design and construction of which requires tools of various kinds.—[1] Further, these types of images often combine. Buildings, my focus, have spatial, visual, and verbal dimensions. *Topographical stories* is a term one can use to describe representations of the natural world that result from constructing cities (or parts of them), buildings, and landscapes.—[2]

My focus is architecture from the postwar period—when the Norwegian architect Sverre Fehn was at

1 The relationships between images and tools as different kinds of artifacts are typically studied in the history of technology and philosophical anthropology. I have in mind the writings of figures such as André Leroi-Gourhan, Arnold Gehlen, and Gilbert Simondon. While interesting in their own right and certainly connected to problems of architectural thought and practice, these relationships are beyond the scope of this paper.

2 I attempt this in *Topographical Stories: Studies in Landscape and Architecture* (Philadelphia: University of Pennsylvania Press, 2004).

work—and on a single building, his Nordic Pavilion, which was built for the Venice Biennale between 1958 and 1962. Although entirely successful as an exhibition pavilion when it was built, and still today, I shall use it to explain how works of architecture can help us see again, and indeed more fully, a world we thought we knew, the world of nature.

While Sverre Fehn's writings are few—mostly autobiographical reflections, responses to interview questions, and allegorical tales—what survives offers clues about how a modern architect understood the relationships between architecture and nature. One of these hints is Fehn's acceptance of the somewhat paradoxical idea that nature is both the context and subject matter of architectural design and construction; the notion that landscapes not only condition design but also result from it, that each site is at once a constraint and construct. In this conception, a work's beginnings and endings anticipate and recall one another, which is how history can be cumulative. The location of Fehn's Archbishopric Museum in Hamar, for example, led him to describe that project's play of elements, first below then above the earth's surface, as "a dance of dead things,"—[3] coupling upright animation to blanketed stillness, communication to silence. The fact that the earth-crypt was also a treasury would not have been known, of course, until excavations opened and formwork constructed the site. When one recalls the delicacy, refinement, and freshness of the spaces and details that typify his buildings, it is surprising that mortality played such an important role in what he called "the constructive act."—[4] Nevertheless, for Fehn creative work in the world of nature meant accepting it as it had been given, while recognizing its remoteness. One of his allegorical tales illustrates his inventive but consistently melancholic way of thinking. The story's ostensible theme—human scale and size—is less significant than its rendition of architectural origins, for that topic holds the key to Fehn's sense of the relationships

3 Sverre Fehn, "The Dance Round Dead Things," in *Poetry of the Straight Line*, ed. Marja-Ritta Norri and Maija Kärkkäinen (Helsinki: Museum of Finnish Architecture, 1992), 4–5.

4 Sverre Fehn, "The Thought of Construction," in *The Thought of Construction*, Per Olaf Fjeld (New York: Rizzoli, 1983), 45–47.

Sverre Fehn, Nordic Pavilion, Venice, 1962.

Sverre Fehn, Hedmark Museum, interior exhibition and site plan, Hamar, 1967–79.

Sverre Fehn, *How Our Dimensions Were Born*, sketch.

between art and nature. The first few paragraphs of "How Our Dimensions are Born" should be sufficient for our purposes.

> In the beginning the cave and the earth itself were the dimensions of the cave. The floor had its own thickness of earth and the dimension of the walls of the cave also stopped at the beginning of the sea.
>
> In reality there was no defined dimension when your comprehension of the world carried infinity within it. The only ultimate was the killed animal outside the cavemouth,—[5] the only thing that kept you firmly in the universe. And that animal corpse was resurrected on the walls of the cave. An abode was sought in the nature of the animal.
>
> I have no idea how many years went by before *the autonomous* dimension was born in front of the cavemouth . . . the stone, hacked in one rectangular volume. Height, Length, Width. How incomprehensible the work of creation in a limited malleable quantity must have been.
>
> The greatest poetic manifestation in limited form. The first security, the first written sign in the landscape resting secretively in the hewn stone.
>
> The story of you and I again standing on the plain. Time was given a dimension.—[6]

The cave is of course a familiar site of mythical beginnings, even among moderns. Frank Lloyd Wright, for example, narrated cave origins in *The Living City*. "Back in time," he said, "mankind was divided into cave-dwelling agrarians and wandering tribes of hunter-warriors."—[7] The first group sheltered themselves in the "shadow-of-the-wall," while the second enjoyed life under the sun, resting now and then under a bower of trees or a tent. When not collecting the fruits of the earth or tilling the soil, cave dwellers—he also called them "wall-lovers"—found security within the hill's hollow. For the adventurers at home on the open savannah, however, freedom of movement was their safety. Although Wright put a spear in the hand of the adventurer,—[8] Fehn seems to have given a weapon to the man of shadows. Just outside the cave lay the body of a lifeless animal. One

5 Rendering the Norwegian *det drepte dyr* as "the killed animal" accents the act. Perhaps the fact that the animal was dead is more important in this tale, given the attention to death in Fehn's other writings and the phrase "animal corpse" (*dyreliket*) that follows. On these points, I follow the interpretation suggested by Per Olaf Fjeld in a recent conversation.

6 Sverre Fehn, "How our Dimensions are Born," in *Poetry of the Straight Line*, ed. Marja-Ritta Norri and Maija Kärkkäinen (Helsinki: Museum of Finnish Architecture, 1992), 4–5.

7 Frank Lloyd Wright, "The Shadow-of-the-Wall—Primitive Instincts Still Alive," in *The Living City* (New York: Braham House, 1958), 21 ff.

8 It was only in Wright's third version of this tale that the cave dwellers were described as agrarians. Before he modified the text for *The Living City*, which is to say in the versions published in *The Disappearing City* (1932) and *When Democracy Builds* (1944), they were described as "more stolid lover[s] of the wall [who] lurked in such hidden holes and material cavities." Richard Wesley pointed me to these different versions of Wright's story.

might assume it was killed for food, but Fehn didn't say that. In a sketch that accompanied his text, the carcass appears outside the cave on the ground directly under the sun or the moon.—[9] The other planetary body rests on the horizon. The appearance of the carcass on the horizon is like that of the snake in the Garden of Eden—no small surprise. What is the connection between a dead animal and the first act of building? And what might Fehn's story say about the relationship between architecture and nature?

9 It is equally possible that the object outside the cave is the upright stone, to be discussed shortly.

The appearance of the lifeless animal outside the cave indicated a break in the continuity of the natural world; not so much with the land that included the cave and extended to the sea, but with the animate kinds of life the soil had nourished. The distinction between human and animal life was less decisive than that between the living and dead. Something living had met its end, *naturally* one can say—whether the cave dweller had a hand in it or not. Less propitiatory than simply preliminary—Fehn never said the animal was sacrificed—awareness of mortality opened a new "dimension," one that somehow kept you (once you had left the cave) "in the universe."

To repeat the initial steps: before the appearance of the dead animal, there was the earth-world within the cave, circled in on itself, expressing infinity (nature's unending cycles I think); after its appearance, something different became possible (something Fehn elsewhere called *history*).—[10] No tears should dampen the death or the departure from the shadows, mortality was a fact of life and enclosed infinity was not all that great: nonspatial, nonsocial, and ahistorical, therefore, prearchitectural. Insofar as death led to a sense of being "kept in the universe," it was somehow connected to knowledge of the person's participation in the whole and was perhaps its prerequisite.—[11]

10 Two different senses of time are also implied in this before and after: cyclical and periodic, or a time of breaks and of unlimited extension, just as *Chronos* and *Aion* embodied ideas of sequence and duration. The Latin stem, *tempus*, the origins of which are still contested by philologists, had two distinct senses: "to cut" (*from temno*) and "to extend" (*from teino*).

11 Here I use the word "participation" in the sense of playing one's allotted part, which is what the now more technical term "proportion" once signified—hence "dimensionality" for Fehn.

What followed next in Fehn's tale is stunning. The existence of the carcass set the stage for creativity. Fissures or facets of the cave wall were carved or colored in ways that brought the animal back to life. The image, Fehn said, was a resurrection. His use of the term resurrection (*oppstandelse*) suggests that the animal's death was some kind of sacrifice, but he never said that. Had sacrifice preceded resurrection, bringing the animal back to life as an image could be seen as some sort of atonement, especially if the cave dweller felt kinship with the animal and had killed it. The real key is that creative work—image-making—was for Fehn a productive response to the end of life in nature.

As they adhered to the stone and elaborated the "natural" modulations of its surfaces—the way cosmetics vivify the lights, darks, and colors of a face—the images, in imitation of figures from elsewhere, were both native and foreign to the cave, there but not.—[12] Fehn also wrote that "an abode was sought in the nature of the animal." This observation recalls the ways people throughout the world—certainly in Scandinavia—clothed themselves and their rooms with animal skins, and still do today. While dressed surfaces may elaborate Fehn's sense of *abode* (also to *abide*), what he meant by "the nature of the animal" raises another question. I'll turn to that shortly. Nevertheless, imitation was not construction. Despite the iconographic richness of its image-laden walls, the cave was still prearchitectural. Why? Because it still lacked both the constructive dimension and the autonomy that would result.

The next and really decisive step in the story required the use of a tool—something capable of hacking stone out of the earth so that it could be turned upright in front of the cavemouth. The materials with which the first "building" was built were not found in nature, premade for construction, but "torn out of the earth," as Hannah Arendt once wrote when explaining the nature of human work and the origin of works of art.—[13] While her account allows violence and he mentioned "hacking," he also alluded to "birth." What those last two have in common are pain and a cut. And something

12 On this point, the philosopher Maurice Merleau-Ponty's observation is helpful: "the animals painted on the walls of Lascaux are not there in the same way as the fissures and limestone formations. But they are not *elsewhere* . . . held up by the wall's mass they use so adroitly, they spread around the wall without ever breaking from their elusive moorings in it." Maurice Merleau-Ponty, "Eye and Mind," in *Primacy of Perception* (Evanston: Northwestern University Press, 1964), 164.

13 Arendt wrote: "the tree must be destroyed in order to provide wood … [building materials, such as] iron, stone, or marble [must be] torn out of the womb of the hearth.… violence is present in all fabrication, and *homo faber*, the creator of the human artifice, has always been a destroyer of nature." Hannah Arendt, *The Human Condition* (Chicago: University of Chicago, 1958), 139. Fehn's Nordic Pavilion broke ground the same year her text was published. Violence was not, however, a part of Fehn's account; he was mostly concerned with death or the lifelessness of the animal outside the cave.

else characterizes the constructive act: unlike cave labor, work on the horizon under the sun didn't result in any sort of likeness. Fehn wrote that the stone upright was "incomprehensible." What is the thought here? And how could something incomprehensible also be the first "written sign in the landscape?"

Thanks to the constructive act—the use of a tool, making a cut, and assisting in a birth—something hidden in the earth's darkness was brought into visibility. At the very least, this would have been the "bones of the earth," but we've also seen "dead things" could "dance," as in the soil and spaces of the Hamar Museum. A rectangular volume—height, length, and width in stone—now stood upright. Although the sketch shows nothing more than a smudge, his specification of a weighty volume recalls stones in Japanese dry gardens, although they were sometimes thought to imitate mountains. Another figure that comes to mind is the archaic *menhir* or *colossos*. Fehn's sense of underground life may make this connection more relevant.

The anthropologist Jean-Pierre Vernant wrote of the archaic colossos: "what it embodies in permanent form in stone is not the image of the dead man but his life in the beyond, the life that is [as] opposed to that of the living man as the world of night is opposed to the world of light."—[14] Afterlife was also Fehn's concern. But the abode that resulted from construction was not sought in the nature of an animal, nor in a mimetic image. To grasp the expressivity of the stone another type of image must be imagined—an *aniconic* figure, featureless and blank. The upright was visible, but not really intelligible, some kind of sign, yet not a likeness, a figure hacked out of and birthed from the earth but remote from it, the present form of a past life. The first act of construction resulted in a figure that invited and defeated understanding insofar as the stone was both visible and impenetrable, expressive but silent.

14 Jean-Pierre Vernant, "The Representation of the Invisible and the Psychological Category of the Double: The Colossos," in *Myth and Thought Among the Greeks* (London: Routledge, 1983), 306.

This account of architectural origins could be taken to suggest that Fehn was not exactly a friend of nature. At most, his affection would seem to have been elegiac, as if *eros* had been ignited by *thanatos*. Yet, in reply to a question about the encounter between buildings and their locations, he once said, "we must again find a dialogue with the earth."—[15] The question, I think, consists in understanding the character of this *dialogue*. Taking physical nature as a model for buildings was certainly not what he had in mind. When commenting on the "feeling for the landscape" in much of modern architecture, he said he was "sick of the sentimental way of dealing with these matters." The physicalism, literalism, or copyism of anything "natural" that presents itself to the senses was what he abhorred. "On the other hand," he observed, "if you look at my buildings and their surroundings, you can see that I tried to preserve every single tree." Thus the "dialogue" to which he referred involved saying yes and saying no; it was, he said, "a love-hate story."—[16]

15 Sverre Fehn, "Has a Doll Life?" (1984, Fehn in conversation with Per Olaf Fjeld), *Perspecta* 24 (1988).

16 Sverre Fehn, "An Architectural Autobiography," *Poetry of the Straight Line*, ed. Marja-Ritta Norri and Maija Kärkkäinen (Helsinki: Museum of Finnish Architecture, 1992), 48.

The appearance of the trees inside Fehn's Nordic Pavilion is striking in two ways: first, that they are there at all; and second, that some of their upper and lower extensions have been cut off from one view, marginalized. He apparently surprised commissioning authorities with his decision to keep the trees he found on the site. Yet, if they seem familiar today, one must also admit they are rather odd—oddly abbreviated, apparently leaf- and rootless. I'm not referring to what one knows but what one sees (and does not see). The loss represented a gain in Fehn's view because thus framed they were given human dimensions—made bodylike. Framing also gave them human qualities. In a short text called "The Dream of Great Construction," he wrote: "the warmth [of the tree] radiates, the temperature it contains, gives you the privilege of closeness."—[17] Of course the body-tree analogy is a commonplace in architectural thought, but he never mentioned how it has been discussed.

17 Sevrre Fehn, "The Dream of Great Construction," ibid., 34.

A second thought is that "the dimensions of the tree … have functioned as an inspiration for constructions of use to human beings." Fehn's focus on the tree's midsection might seem arbitrary, but for him the tree's existence was defined by a "dramatic confrontation between earth and sky." The trunk, which he also called the tree's "horizon," was where it gathered "all its strength and reached its maximum constructive size"—columnlike. Here, again, is an unmentioned commonplace—column as tree. Even though the high and low framing transformed the trunk into a stump, what thus appeared was something "autonomous," somewhat like the rock hacked out of the earth in his allegorical account of architectural origins. Thus, once the tree's natural connections to sky and the soil were visually cut off from the artificial body-horizon, the *natural* topic that really matters in architecture came into view: an upright—found and framed—became capable of marking a place, of becoming a "poetic manifestation in limited form," a "written sign in the landscape," giving time, the time of human history, "a dimension."—18

18 Sverre Fehn, "How our Dimensions are Born," ibid., 4–5.

What kinds of roof and deck staged this disclosure? In simple terms, but unexpectedly: very thick above and very thin below. The roof consists of two layers of wafer-thin concrete joists—each is one meter deep by six centimeters thick—equally spaced from side to side, spanning north to south below and east to west above. Rainwater is collected at the midspans and shed at the ends by hammock-shaped transparent fiberglass gutters that cap the upper edges of the top layer of joists. Although rather immoderate in its depth, the biplanar grid would be fine as a roof, but the joists—and therefore the rain-catchers—were sliced off in their running length wherever trees had to pass out of sight (before branching, for the stump-making just described). This meant that in several places, severed joist ends were allowed to hang—or seem to—in midair, deferential to the stumps but self-defeating from a load-bearing point of view. What was ostensibly supporting was supported. Stability was preserved through midspan joints

Sverre Fehn, *Nordic Pavilion*, sketch, Venice, circa 1960.

between the two levels. Thanks to the cuts, however, rainwater still found its way onto the pavement.

The deck one sees today suffers from two regrettable alterations: 1) the dark Norwegian slate Fehn had installed has been replaced by white travertine; and 2) a number of the tree lawns have been covered over, presumably because the trees they nourished died after construction or were removed. The topographical significance of the floor's flatness is hard to grasp from photographs, but on the site—i.e., within the Biennale gardens—its contrast with the surrounding terrain, which rises from front to back, is significant. Some sense of this can be gained by imagining the spatial implications of the steps at the front and side: a single step up in the first case and a two-sided pyramidal incline of treads and risers in the second. For Fehn, leveling the land and constructing a platform were tantamount to making a building. In a caption to a sketch from 1980, he wrote, "The platform. That is already a building. Platform for exposition. The one platform has to protect the objects by moving walls."—[19] No less important than flatness was blackness. The topographical meaning of the dark color has been explained by Per Olaf Fjeld: the sense of hovering that would have resulted from a white plane raised above the earth was defeated by the somber earth tone.—[20] The slate's color also absorbed—*stopped*, one can say—the ambient light.—[21]

Firm stability would seem to have been the result, but not exactly, for that general impression was qualified by the tree lawn cutouts, which not only covered the roots (defining the stump's bottom), but also exposed the stone and soil of the substrate—muddy on rainy days and no more stable than the ground beneath the entire city, which still barely keeps itself afloat, thanks to the draining and turbulence of the aquifer.—[22]

White and black, thick and thin, the roof and deck complement one another as the key elements of a space of display. A rather unique form of *in-definition* is the

19 Cited in Per Olaf Fjeld, *Sverre Fehn The Pattern of Thoughts* (New York: Monacelli Press, 2009), 59.

20 Ibid., 54.

21 I owe this italicized term to Emily Brune Randall Fjeld, who graciously shared her insights into this building, as well as a number of comments Fehn made to her about it.

22 No less indicative of the instability of the substrate is the fact that the large pier that supports the great girder on the front side, while wrapping its arms around a preexisting tree at the corner, sunk a little after the building was finished, making the use of the large glass sliding doors impossible—because the beam from which they had been hung also dropped at the pier end. Per Olaf Fjeld reported this chapter of the building's history to me in a recent conversation.

result. Enclosure at the sides is partial: two are walled in rather solidly, two by glass only. The walls augmented the place-making function of the horizontals, mixing the solidity of the deck with the color of the roof—rather cave-like as a result—while the open sides extended what would have been apertures to their extreme limits, in the way that many modern buildings transformed traditional openings into "window walls." This manner of enclosure construction and plan composition made the floor and ceiling, cut-up though they were, the decisive instruments of spatial definition. While no one who has been there has any doubt about the presence of an exceedingly singular space, its boundaries are so porous that the "interior" seems coextensive with its vicinity—not just the gardens, but also the wider horizon of the city. I suppose that is why some observers drop the proper name "Nordic Pavilion" and refer to the building as Fehn's "Venice Pavilion."

Yet, unbroken continuity was neither the aim nor the result of this design. Perhaps we have used the term "continuity" and its synonyms too often and uncritically in descriptions of modern buildings. Since the time of Sigfried Giedion's *Befreites Wohnen* (1929), the unmediated transmission of light, air, and views has been repeatedly presented as a key aspect of modern buildings; the more open the better, approximating non-separation between inside and outside, so-called man-made and natural conditions. But how would such a work be a work? Doesn't victory in this battle mean defeat? The more one looks at the buildings themselves, the more it appears that boundaries were not eliminated in modern architecture—for the sake of continuity, flow, or interpenetration—but constructed in new ways. That is certainly what occurred in this case. Boundary-making should come as no surprise from an architect who had such clear, if lyrical, ideas about the ways human dimensions are born. He explained that animals, not humans, enjoy unbroken topographical continuity; their world is a closely woven fabric with no breaks, gaps, or separations between their bodies, their houses, and the land and air on and in which they live. His thesis is a commonplace in modern science. The pioneering biologist Jakob von Uexküll described the animal's environment, its habitat as a *closed circle*: "when [the animal] comes into relation with something else, [it] can only come upon that which 'affects' [it] and thus starts its being capable. Everything else is *a priori* unable to penetrate the ring around the animal."—[23] The real question, then, concerns the discovery of *discontinuities* within the natural world, breaks or distances that both allow and result from construction. In the case we are considering, land, light, and trees were cut into and off from their "natural" surroundings. Their new situation could be called "unnatural" except for the fact that they still stood within the unbuilt environment Fehn had been given.

23 Jakob von Uexküll and Georg Kriszat, *Streifzüge durch die Umwelten von Tieren und Menschen* (Hamburg: Rowohlt, 1956), 85–86; cited in Giorgio Agamben, *The Open: Man and Animal* (Stanford: Stanford University Press, 2004), 51. Von Uexküll's observation formed the conceptual background for Martin Heidegger's much-discussed thesis that animals are "world-poor."

Fehn constructed a gallery in a grove between the soil and sky, connected to but also detached from them because his roof and deck were perforated and the trees seemed to be abbreviated. The relationships were intricate because the two orders of phenomena—built and unbuilt elements—were not only distinct but dependent. That Fehn used the term "calculation" to describe how nature arranges itself makes his understanding of interconnections between nature and artifice hard to grasp. Here is what he wrote:

> . . . nature itself is pure calculation; nature is everything and nothing . . . the constructions of animals are precise and unchanged, they are the same from day to day, from year to year, because the animal doesn't think of death . . . a bird believes it will live forever . . . nest construction never changes . . . the door of the fox is constantly the same, exactly as big as the fox itself. The constructions of animals are based on calculations, they take a very technical and precise stand to the earth and environment.—[24]

24 Sverre Fehn, "About Rationalism and Spiritual Content," in *Sverre Fehn Works, Projects, Writings, 1949–1996*, by Christian Norberg-Schulz and Gennaro Postiglione (New York: Monacelli Press, 1997), 249.

The difficulty here is that we tend to think that art and architecture result from mathematical thinking, at least in part. Fehn doesn't deny the mathematical aspect of project-making, but makes animals the specialists. What's more, once animals get sizes right, they don't change them.

There is no history of bird nests or of fox holes, no anticipations of better solutions or recollections of inferior ones, no approximations of or divergences from an ideal; instead, there is an unending repetition of designs that meet the requirements of (bare) life.

People partly understand this. "Man's thinking," Fehn observed, "is not steadily [though partly] rational and logical; it includes jokes, lies, and irrational caprices."—25 More positively, the kind of thinking that remakes nature because it is insufficient for human life includes fiction and dream. When this is missing, human life is reduced, not really worth living. "If architecture is made completely rational, people become animals." He referred to modern suburbs when making this prediction. But of course fictions and dreams always only approximate the worlds in which people—as people, not animals—really live. The inevitability of approximation, of partial realizations, and of human finitude is also why existence is historical, why stories are invented to transform natural cycles into periods (of life) that are both successive and cumulative, ages that make sense in the manner of a book's chapters. In fact, the awareness of endings is precisely what inaugurates acts of construction, the architectural form of beginnings. Human history also begins in this way, life in the natural world distancing itself from itself. We have seen this already in Fehn's story about the "autonomous dimension": human freedom arose from the end of animal life. He said the same thing about fiction transcending calculation: "the dome of St. Peter's church was not calculated, it was based on the dream of a space devoted to a world beyond death."—26 Awareness of mortality, fear of death, anxiety about endings … these, Fehn said, give rise to construction. "The greatest story, the greatest poetic construction is the idea of life after death."—27

25 Sverre Fehn, "An Architectural Autobiography," ibid., 245.

26 Sverre Fehn, "About Rationalism and Spiritual Content," ibid., 249.

27 Sverre Fehn, "An Architectural Autobiography," ibid., 245.

Of course there are other stories in architecture. Maybe it is better to say there are shorter chapters within the epic narrative that chronicles the discipline, as it is

Johan Christian Dahl, *Danish Coast by Moonlight*, 1828.

Giovanni Bellini, *St. Jerome Reading in Countryside*, detail, 1480.

now and was before. What about the Nordic Pavilion? What story does it tell?—[28] We have described it as a gallery in a grove between soil and sky; not much story in that. More particularly, Fehn's calculations specified a level deck, protective covering, legible displays, and the preservation of ancient trees; once again, nothing particularly dramatic. But it is also true that Fehn allowed cuts, leaks, layers, perforations, abbreviations, and transparencies that qualified—one could also say compromised—the obvious or typical solutions. Why?

28 Marc Neveu had elaborated the significance of storytelling in this building. See, Marc J. Neveu, "On Stories: Architecture and Identity," *Architectur N* 02 (2008): 2–7.

Although the building is sometimes called Fehn's Venice Pavilion, because of its location in that city and congeniality with the immediate surroundings, the proper name is the Pavilion of Nordic Nations. The governments of three countries sponsored the construction: Finland, Norway, and Sweden. As mentioned earlier, the task was to house works of Scandinavian art. In principle, this meant providing an enclosure and protective roof, as well as adequate lighting. Yet for Fehn, the matter of lighting was not only a problem of correct light levels, expression was equally important. He observed that there is a particular kind of light in Scandinavian countries, *shadowless*. To explain himself he drew a comparison with the light in southern countries, such as Italy. There the slightest break in a surface produces sharply defined shadows, profiles that faithfully record their source. Two distinct kinds of light (and shadow) can be seen in paintings of these two parts of the world; in the landscapes of Johan Christian Dahl and Giovanni Bellini, for example. Fehn had made this realization early on in his career. During his trip to Morocco he observed: "In Africa, shadows are strong and provide the landscape with sharp contours. In the north, nothing is discerned so clearly, the sun does not make such shadows, the world is hazier and more obscure, almost without shadows."—[29] Fehn's problem in Venice was the creation of northern light in a southern climate. In its absence, the works of art to be put on show would have been out of place. This meant

29 Sverre Fehn, "An Architectural Autobiography," 247.

that while the pavilion was "naturally" sited in Venice, its other location was the one he constructed there. Conditions taken to be "natural" had to be constructed. It wasn't only construction methods, materials also played a part in constructing the building's "natural" site.

Added to the mix that made up the in-situ concrete of the roof joists was the particularly white limestone typical of Venetian construction.—[30] The result, of course, was that the typical gray-white of concrete was made whiter—and not only the white of the concrete, also of the light. It is mostly architects who look from the art on show to the ceiling, but when they do they see a web of fins that seems to vibrate with a soft white luminosity, not so much the light of clouds (often dark on their undersides or streaky), more like the light diffused through fog or mist on a cold morning. Many Scandinavian paintings glow with this kind of light. Yet, thus "increased," the pavilion's light was also decreased. The two-layer or biplanar grid of roof joists has been called *brise soleil*, invoking Le Corbusier's term, albeit rotated ninety degrees from the typical vertical plane. The best translation of the French name is "sunbreaker," a term entirely apposite in this case, because the light had to be broken by the double layer of planes to avoid the projection of sharp profiles, to allow, instead, the "shadowless" interior that was right for Scandinavian artifacts. The key point is that the light, like the level terrain, was an artifact. Perhaps it is better to call such a construction an image; better still, a page in the story the building was designed to tell. A story of what? Of displacement, of northern environments and artifacts at home in the south, of Scandinavian light in Venetian gardens. For this to make sense, the building had to make one believe that environmental and cultural conditions that were so distinct were also compatible. Carlo Scarpa told Fehn there was, for him, no culture north of the Alps. Fehn obviously thought otherwise, but was not correspondingly provincial. The fiction of compatibility, of the mutuality of cultures, so hard—maybe impossible—to

30 Marc Neveu made this observation in the article cited above.

believe in the years after the war, is what he wanted his building to say and show.

More largely, the building's *artificial nature* argued that once ways of living are dislocated, cut out of or off from their native sites, they can become representations of that way of living. And images—unlike animals and trees—are things that last, things that can free themselves into the type of time that persists, not through repetition but accumulation. Stories, according to the philosopher Paul Ricoeur, transmute natural into human time. Fehn's story, or the final chapter of this story of art and nature in Venice, is a tale about an afterlife—not his, but the dimension of nature his building brings before our eyes.

Bruno Taut, *Oberstenfeld and Beilstein*, pencil drawing, 1904.

# Bruno Taut
# Landscape as Aesthetic Substrate

Manfred Speidel

## Landscape Portraits

From the beginning of his professional activity in large cities, Bruno Taut (1880–1938), who was born in Königsberg, visited rural areas for relaxation on his days off. This was quite normal for city dwellers; however, the experience of landscapes was crucial for Taut's artistic development.

In 1903, he worked in the architectural office of Bruno Möhring in Berlin, who sustained a large office with the design of industrial buildings and elevated train stations. The staff spent their weekends at the Gothic Chorin Abbey in the moraine landscape of the Uckermark, where a lake and vast forests were perfect for long walks and the Wollgast family's six daughters waited on guests in the abbey's tavern. Taut later married one of them, Hedwig, in 1906.

Taut enjoyed the socializing and was inspired to produce countless sketches and systematic nature studies in pencil and pastels. Beyond a representation of nature scenes, he believed that he was able to communicate spiritually in painting, and perhaps more importantly to find the way to new building forms through the study of nature, for which he also sought to internalize nature and landscape depictions of the Japanese art of printing, as he later wrote.—[1]

1 Bruno Taut, "Zu meiner bevorstehenden Reise nach Japan," in Bruno Taut, *Ich liebe die japanische Kultur*, ed. Manfred Speidel (Berlin: Gebr. Mann, 2003), 45–48; Manfred Speidel, "Farbe und Licht. Zum malerischen Werk von Bruno Taut," *Daidalos* 15, no. 45, (September 1992): 117–35; Manfred Speidel, ed., *Bruno Taut. Natur und Fantasie* (Berlin: Gebr. Mann, 1995).

When Taut moved to Stuttgart in 1904 and received a job for four years with the architect Theodor Fischer, the firm's young employees went on weekend excursions to the Hohenlohe hilly landscape north of the city, to Oberstenfeld and Beilstein, picturesquely situated villages in the vineyards of the beautiful Keuper Mountains. Taut painted landscapes even more atmospherically and compared his visits with those to Chorin. He wrote to his fiancée Hedwig in Chorin: "From Oberstenfeld to Beilstein—a constant back and forth between huts, as between Berlin and Chorin." Until his marriage, Oberstenfeld was Taut's "Stuttgarter Chorin."

In 1904, Taut wrote a short essay in two variations: "Natur und Kunst" (Nature and Art).—[2] He believed that the old masters were closer to nature than we are today. "We have to learn to sense nature again like [the old masters] could ... There [in the forest], we find the space that we can never reproduce but that drives us to create an image of its glory in our buildings." To that point Taut quoted from John Ruskin's *The Stones of Venice*: "We cannot all have our gardens now, nor our pleasant fields to meditate in at eventide. Then the function of our architecture is, as far as may be, to replace these; to tell us about nature; to possess us with memories of her quietness; to be solemn and full of tenderness, like her, and rich in portraitures of her; full of delicate imagery of the flowers we can no more gather, and of the living creatures now far away from us in their own solitude."—[3] Taut summarizes in the second essay: "Everywhere, where the halls and vaults of the ancient builders infuse us with a certain calm and reverence, they trigger in us sensations that are awakened at the sight of space formations of free nature."—[4]

Taut recommended to his younger brother Max that he should study nature and painting: "Look, look, do not brood, which is always the highest philosophy. The world is our work of art." In another letter we read, "With my

2 Bruno Taut, "Natur und Kunst," and "Natur und Baukunst," 1904, in Bruno Taut, *Ex Oriente Lux. Die Wirklichkeit einer Idee*, ed. Manfred Speidel (Berlin: Gebr. Mann, 2007), 50–55. All Translations by the author.

3 Ibid., 51. The original text of John Ruskin, *Stones of Venice*, Vol. 1, Chapter XXX, The Vestibule, 353.

4 Ibid., 53.

painterly studies … I only want to nurture my sense of color to nature! It is necessary to keep views open to all sides, otherwise your work never becomes a welling spring, but a sluggish, seeping, little brook that ultimately dries out."—[5]

5 BTA-01-2 Letters to Max Taut from August 21, 1903 and August 26, 1903; and BTA-01-03 from July 20, 1904. Baukunst Archiv, Akademie der Künste, Berlin.

## "Rural Landscape" in the Interior
## The Church in Unterriexingen

Taut's first architectural commission in 1905 was the restoration of the church in the village Unterriexingen near Stuttgart. The congregation commissioned a new spatial planning of the altar and pulpit. Taut complemented it with an extensive colorful frame, which though no longer preserved is reproduced in sketches and illustrations.

Taut rendered Ruskin's "talk" about nature into naturalistic depictions: he painted grapes and ears of corn on the railings of the pews, flowers on a part of the gallery, the flat ceiling was covered with white butterfly silhouettes, and stars between the ribs of the Gothic choir vault turned it into a firmament. He covered the entire space with colors: the pews were resplendent in lush (Schweinfurt) green, the ceiling of the nave glowed red-brown, the walls were pale blue, the Gothic choir vault nocturnal dark blue, the base behind the altar Pompeian red, the galleries with old Apostle images were framed in white.

The color tone was meant to turn the church interior into a symbolic, rural landscape, which Taut believed corresponded to the farmers' wishes. The parish priest evaluated the first color sketch similarly: "The little church, simple, modest, colorful, a space in which my farmers will not seem strange, homelike for them."—[6] If one compares the different sketches and illustrations, Taut seems to have also factored in the color effect of the change of light and shadow during the execution: the gray-blue of the walls in the shade becomes a shining light blue in the light, and the Pompeian red of the lower choir wall becomes orange in the sun.

6 BTA-01-10 Letter of Priest Gastpar to Bruno Taut 13.01.1906. Baukunst Archiv, Akademie der Künste, Berlin.

The existing architectural space, hardly changed in its substance, became a work of art that indeed reproduced "nature," but as a whole—in the colors—wanted to recount its "glory" rather than its details, as Taut made it the program in 1904.

In his inaugural speech in autumn 1913 in Leipzig as the architect of the German garden city movement, Taut of course declared himself committed to "social ideas" in the design of housing developments, but waved aside functional concerns—such as the direction of the houses and streets or the consideration of contour lines—as incidental. Rather, he called for a new garden city a whole, as something organically grown, a work of art to be created with which residents are able to identify.—[7] That year, he built the garden suburb Falkenberg near Berlin, and with a rich color palette set the rows of houses in the hilly landscape like colorful flower beds.

7 Bruno Taut, "Kleinhausbau und Landaufschließung vom Standpunkt des Architekten," quoted in Speidel, *Bruno Taut. Natur und Fantasie*, 116–17.

## Colorful Interior Landscape

After the First World War—during which Taut was able to avoid entry into the military through different alternative services—he worked in Bergisch Gladbach near Cologne in a furnace factory from 1917–18; he moved to Dahlewitz in 1919. The village—now part of the municipality Mahlow, in the Teltow administrative district, six kilometers south of Berlin's city limits—had been developed after 1900 on a modest scale for Berlin's middle class. The new, small housing development area was called "the colony." It was located in a pleasant, flat landscape of meadows and fields, surrounded by woods.—[8] The rural surroundings promised quiet for concentrated work. Taut moved with his companion Erica Wittich and her children in a house in the colony in Dahlewitz, which was built in 1910,—[9] and had it painted inside and outside—according to his draft from 1905—in bold colors. In one room, the floor was painted in narrow stripes and the walls in large areas. The

8 A keen interest in the purchase of land began with a development plan from 1904. The so-called colony emerged near the train station. Land and homeowners came mostly from Berlin; building first took place on the farmland, the northern side of the main street. Vera Seidel, contribution to Taut House Chronicle based the municipality acts. October 22, 2010. (unpublished)

9 Today Wiesenstrasse 4. The house was purchased on June 18, 1919 and registered under the name Erica Wittich on July 3, 1919.

living room had a floor in diagonally structured sections of white, blue, yellow, and black, with walls in narrow stripes of blue, red yellow, green, gray, and brown under a black ceiling.—[10] One could interpret the striped walls as an abstracted landscape.

10 In his book, Taut depicted the rooms in black-gray-white with color designations. See: Bruno Taut, *Die neue Wohnung—Die Frau als Schöpferin* (Leipzig: Klinkhardt und Biermann, 1924), 46.

For the couple's bedroom under the roof, he selected two colors, which in the changing of daylight would symbolize the lovers' mood changes. In his magazine supplement *Frühlicht* (*Dawn's Light*), founded in 1920, Taut wrote a hymn to the slanting walls and ceiling of the attic room—alternately painted ultramarine blue and royal red—naming it "Kosmische Farbenliebe" (Cosmic Love of Color). "Chrome yellow, orange, and black as an accompaniment to vertical surfaces. Play of the blue and red: in the reflection of the sunlight, both glow absolutely equally, in the simple bright daylight, red becomes light, almost pink, blue accompanies in the uttermost depth, and when twilight comes, the blue becomes always lighter with the increasing darkness, appearing almost white, but purple always deeper and almost black. The exchange of stepping forward and stepping back. The lamp, however, the human light, makes both equally calm and mild. The cosmic game of the double star, blue and red, ends."—[11]

11 "Stadtbaukunst Alter und Neuer Zeit 1," *Beilage Frühlicht,* Heft 14 (Juli): 221.

"It is not the construction of the building that decides the color distribution, but the light as it is reflected and absorbed by the walls or gives shadows."—[12]

12 Bruno Taut, "Beobachtungen über Farbwirkung aus meiner Praxis," Bauwelt 10, 38 (1919): 12.

The transformations of the colors under changing light were far more important to Taut than the architectural framework or his ability to aesthetically enjoy the nature/landscape from the house; the interior landscape was more important than the "natural" outside.

## Colored Glass in the Sunlight
## Vibrant Landscapes

With the Glass Pavilion at the Werkbund exhibition in Cologne in 1914, Taut created an architectural work of art, sparkling in the colored light of the interior, whose sole task was "to be beautiful." The glass "Tempietto" seemed like a fruit that had grown out of the ground. It had a net latticed cupola of colored background glass prisms above, and in the lower part—embedded in the high plinth—a cascading waterfall enclosed by two glass staircases.

From top to bottom, the unevenly colored, rhombic cupola had symbolic colors of the sky—from bright daylight to dark night: "In the cupola space where the light was always scattered by reflective glasses in sunshine and in rainy weather, there was no gloomy mood. A uniformly distributed light, whose colors began deep blue below, always passed upwards from moss green to yellow gold, and at the top of the space in a brilliant pale yellow."—[13] In contrast, the ornamental space of the lower floor was a natural landscape abstracted into an art form. From a circular pond, a six-tiered cascading waterfall spilled over yellowish shining glass plates, and the flowing water formed wave images between the colored glass blocks. Red ornamental walls surrounded the space.

13 Ibid., 12–13. Taut gave this color sequence before in 1920, in the architectural stage drama *Der Weltbaumeister* (World Master Builder) for the transformation of the evening sky. See: Bruno Taut, *Der Weltbaumeister* (Hagen: Folkwang, 1920). Reprint, ed. Manfred Speidel (Berlin: Gebr. Mann, 1999).

Three years later, in 1917, Taut drew a towering crystalline glass tower, in whose interior a "landscape" steeped in light from the sun was intended to glow over the middle of a large and rationally planned, circular garden city of 500,000 inhabitants. In the vast interior of this crystal "City Crown," the "lonely" visitor was to be surprised and overwhelmed by the splendor it presented. "All of the great sensations will awaken when the full sunlight pours over the high room and breaks into countless fine reflections—when the evening sun suffuses the upper ceiling vault and deepens the rich colors of the stained-glass windows with its red glow ..." The plastic design of the space should appear as a "free form world, which also leads the soul of the artist beyond everything thus far in the waves, clouds, mountains, all elements and creatures ... in the full harmony of a rich structure."—[14] As in the space in Unterriexingen, the artist internalized the natural landscape and was able to create a landscape of light and color.

14 Bruno Taut, *Die Stadtkrone* (Jena: Eugen Diederichs, 1919), 68.

## Country Style and the Difficult Path

After completion of the book *Die Stadtkrone* (*The City Crown*) in the fall of 1917, Taut turned his attention from the crowned, densely populated garden city towards the natural landscapes of the Alps, which he thought to decorate with glass crystal structures to create an *Alpine Architektur* (*Alpine Architecture*) from the mountain ranges.—15 Using this title, he drew thirty illustrated plates in 1918. In the first four frames, he "published" those probably most important to him, the crystalline glass tower of the "City Crown," as a visionary crystal temple in a fictional, remote mountain scenery and called it "Temple of Silence." It was meant to be hard to find and accessible only with great difficulty. As that which is most sacred, art should not mix with the daily life of the city for easy enjoyment. One should make a pilgrimage to a pure work of art. With a difficult climb in a region with even higher mountains, Miaio tai tze—a Chinese mountain temple, which Taut had depicted in the book *Die Stadtkrone* —may have served as a model for the location of the temple in the mountains.—16 In these mountains, the design of the Glass Pavilion's small cascading waterfall from 1914 becomes a mountain torrent's multilevel waterfall in a steep canyon, which is overbuilt with colored, bridge-like, glass structures into a great "land art."—17

The pilgrimage route begins on a mountain lake that has to be crossed as the first obstacle, to be able to go into the narrow mountain valley. A decorative tower stands on the lakeside as a sign. "From the terrace at the tower, steep flight of steps as ascent to the crystal building – Difficult ascent".—18

15 *Alpine Architektur* (*Alpine Architecture*) is the title of a large-format book with thirty illustrated plates, twenty-two black-and-white and eight multicolored panels in five sections. The originals are pen and ink drawings and watercolors, which Taut painted in 1918 on cardboard. Originally intended as a portfolio, it was released in February 1920 as a book in the Folkwang Verlag, Hagen, with the date 1919. Matthias Schirren, ed., Bruno Taut, *Alpine Architektur, Eine Utopie* (München, Berlin, London, New York: Prestel, 2004).

16 Taut, *Die Stadtkrone,* 43.

17 Taut, *Alpine Architektur*, part 1, "Kristallhaus," plates 1 to 4.

18 Ibid., plate 1 and 2.

## The Rocky Path to the Tea House

Taut must have had the image of the arduous approach to the remote temple of art in mind, when he similarly

Villa Katsura, “Shokintei” (garden pavilion), Tokyo, circa 1645 and “Shinshoin” (new palace), circa 1658.
Bruno Taut, “Glashaus” (glass house), Cologne, 1914 and Pathway to the “Kristallhaus” (crystal house).

interpreted one of the most beautiful landscape scenes of Japanese garden art. In the park of the seventeenth-century Katsura Imperial Villa in Kyoto, which he was able to see in detail in 1934 and analyzed with twenty-eight sketches,—19 the path to the teahouse Shokintei—the place of silence and artistic meditation—is designed as a path through the highly praised landscape Amanohashidate, a "sky bridge" on the Sea of Japan. As Taut observed, after the idyll of a brook and a small waterfall, the mood of the scene changes once the view opens onto a stony "coast scene," beyond which one sees the rural pavilion covered with reeds. "There were rough stones, there was something like a stony wilderness of the sea, and a small promontory of round beach stones with a stone lantern on top spoke of loneliness. Further along, the nature of the path, with its large stones, became even rougher and more forbidding up to the bridge that led over to the tea house and consisted of a large, four-sided, long stone."—20 In Taut's analytic sketches, this section challenges the visitor to make a decision: "Think about it!" And in quite the same sense as the path to the "crystal house in the mountains," he continues: "Hard is the path, and hard is the bridge to the destination." After the effort to pass the stony landscape, to be ready to experience the great work of art in the tea house, Taut finds a gentle path beyond the tea house under trees on the Hill of Flowers: "Soft and free is the path and we walk happily through nature."—21

19 Bruno Taut, *Gedanken nach dem Besuch in Katsura*, Mai 1934 (Tokyo: Faksimile Druck Iwanami Verlag, 1981).

20 Bruno Taut, *Das japanische Haus und sein Leben*, ed. Manfred Speidel (Berlin: Gebr. Mann, 1997 [originally published 1935/1936]), 274–75.

21 Taut, *Gedanken nach dem Besuch in Katsura*, plates 6 and 9.

## Radiating Earth's Crust
## Alpine Architecture

The sequence of images in *Alpine Architektur*, which Taut drew in 1918, is a collection of ideas of giant glass structures and crystal forms, which were intended to be built on the mountains of the Alps, to extend to a global utopia of a brilliant crowning of all of the earth's high summits, and ultimately be transferred to the world of stars—incorporating nebulae as great "world architectures" and uniting the earth and the cosmos into a comprehensive, artistic landscape.—[22]

22 The idea of the earth-adorning mountain structures originated with Paul Scheerbart (1863–1915), the poet of the fantastic. There may have also been a point of reference in Friedrich Nietzsche's *Zarathustra*.

Taut believed war would then be avoided when artists issued people oversized tasks, such as the adorning the earth—thus placing art on the natural landscapes, instead of devastating these landscapes through war. The architecturization of mountains should follow the motto: AEDIFICARE NECCESSE EST. VIVERE NON EST NECESSE. (Building is necessary. Life is not necessary.) By implication, this also means that Taut did not intend a renaturalization of the landscape. Today, one may be chilled by such an obsessive idea.

## Building on the Earth's Crust

Nietzsche's formulation from 1880, "to raise the Alps from their approaches and motifs of beauty to perfection,"—[23] may have stood behind the call to adorn the earth. In his novel *The Sea Serpent*, Paul Scheerbart went even further: from the Earth's crust out, one could harmonize the unbalanced forces within the Earth by beautifying the surface. Ultimately, wars—as an effect of opposing forces within the Earth—would thus cease to exist. For Taut, the crystallization of the mountains may have additionally meant a recovery of perfect forms—an ideal condition, so to speak, before geological erosion began to ruin their purity.

23 Hubertus Adam, "Die Alpen zur Vollkommenheit zu erheben. Bruno Tauts 'Alpine Architektur' – eine Vision aus dem Geist Friedrich Nietzsches," in: *Symposium BRUNO TAUT*, 1995, ed. Landeshauptstadt Magdeburg (Magdeburg, 1995), 131–45.

In Japan, Taut found a form of natural perfection in the figure of Mount Fuji, the highest mountain of the islands and an extinct volcano. He gave the majestic figure the title *Fuji Tenno*, Fuji Emperor, and wrote in his diary on September 2, 1933. "Yesterday evening Fuji very clearly, the only fixed line—one thinks: art form!—in the landscape. First sun above it with silver clouds, and at the bottom silver bands, then the sun went to the right of it, where its asymmetry, below and later evening clouds arranged decoratively around it. (Watercolor) landscape, nature—pure aesthetics."—[24]

August 15th: "Yesterday evening, Fuji brilliant. A natural wonder—but it looks like 'well done.' Task 'mountain' also from the standpoint of Alpine architecture perfectly solved. Nature-form—the secret of Japan."—[25]

One is also tempted to see in the idea of building on the earth's crust a parallel to the concepts of Chinese Feng Shui—achieving a channeling and harmonizing of forces, through additions to the earth's surface which are caused by the topography, mountains, and streams.

In *Alpine Architektur*, the most magnificent contribution to earth's adornment should indeed be made in Asia. In the colored, silver-flecked page 25—"Earth, Asian Side"—the gigantic glass developments from the Himalayas to the island chains of the Pacific Ocean, in comparison with Europe, "Asia [would be] the brightness in the darkness of the colored night" with crystal trimmings in ruby red, golden yellow, and emerald green, which would decorate the earth for the universe much more than the cultivated European Alps.

24 Manfred Speidel, ed., *Bruno Taut in Japan. The Diary*. First Volume 1933. (Berlin Gebr. Mann, 2013), 104.

25 Ibid., 102.

## Retreat from the Big City
## Residences for Loners in the Community

In a detailed critique of *Die Stadtkrone* in 1919, Leberecht Migge—garden architect and staunch supporter of individual horticulture for self-sufficiency—advised Taut that instead of building an "astral" glass tower over the "dictatorial accumulation of people" of a city of 300,000 inhabitants, it would be more important to begin with the intensive horticulture in glasshouses, in a real "socialism" of "communities, with everything high and noble that blossoms from this living with and for each other." It is necessary "to increase crop soil for a richer and safe nourishment" as a condition for "good people," who will then also be prone to "important things." The order has to be: "from hotbed windows to glass palace" and not vice versa, as Taut conceived.—26

26 Leberecht Migge, Review: "Die Stadtkrone," in *Die Tat*, 1919, 461–64.

I suspect Migge's criticism moved Taut to turn his concept of *Die Stadtkrone* and *Alpine Architektur* upside down, and to conceive a further utopia in 1919: Die *Auflösung der Städte* (*The Dissolution of Cities*).—27

27 Bruno Taut, *Die Auflösung der Städte: oder die Erde, eine gute Wohnung, oder auch: Der Weg zur Alpinen Architektur* (Hagen: Folkwang-Verlag, 1920).

In thirty drawings, Taut now designed structures for mixed cohabitation and production communities, which are regularly arranged like points on circular segments, lie scattered far apart, and complement each other in the exchange of their products. The joint action of farming or crafts is spatially combined in "collective buildings," but the living takes place in individual houses on long, narrow, spaciously laid out plots of land.

The open spaces between them were intended to be mixed, with individual buildings as foldable and transformable huts for the "loners." Whether in the community or individually, it is ensured that the lives of the families take place in suitably distanced coexistence. Taut urges: "Each person everywhere must have the earth's surface that he needs from nature."—28 "The distanced feeling requires distance in space and form and color."—29

28 Ibid., plate 4.

29 Ibid., plate 8.

The built-up, wide natural landscape on earth makes it "a good dwelling," according to the book's subtitle, and gives everyone the basis of existence and guarantees individuality with distance to the others in communal organizations. Nevertheless, there have to be culturally and spiritually bound community facilities, but already Migge pointed out that "in East Asia and antiquity the temples were located originally apart from their human accumulation of cities."—30 Taut concentrated huge futuristic complexes—such as the People's House as arena and fun park, the scholars' home with observatories at the sea shore, the energy production from sun as light transforming phallic towers and mirror rosettes, the sanctuaries of glowing, the Great Star Temple or a church of cumulated halls by the work of generations—far from

30 Migge, *Die Stadtkrone*, 463.

each other and from the production groups of the living areas.—[31] Surrounded by dense forests or on the open sea, "such buildings are in complete solitude, distance from person to person and distance in things of the whole. What belongs to everyone is equally far and equally close to everyone."—[32] Distance became Taut's ideal of living, like the art experience as a cult.

31 Taut, *Dissolution of Cities*, plates 12 to 19 and 24, 25.

32 Ibid., plate 15.

## Horseshoe Base
## Community Symbol with a Guarantee of Distance

For us Bruno Taut is not the loner, but the architect of the "social housing." He gave the cooperative major housing developments in Berlin their architectural form. The most famous is the Hufeisensiedlung (Horseshoe Estate) Britz (1925–31), whose large center—the circa sixty-meter-wide, three-story horseshoe crescent—gave the settlement its name, and the organizing GEHAG (the cooperative homes savings and construction corporation) its easily recognizable icon. In its execution as a symmetrical layout with a single-story, courtyard access was set back a bit from the main road, in order to retain a public forecourt in front of the shops located there and to serve as a freely accessible center for the entire settlement. The strict symmetry and the low additions flanking the access may recall feudal residence architecture. Yet instead of an expected Cour d'Honneur, or as a socialist symbol a "central meeting place for workers," one is faced with an architecturally conceived nature scene. In the design by Leberecht Migge, the pond in the end moraine of the glacial period had a lancet shape and was so large that only two-thirds of greenarena was useable—namely as a lawn for recreation. Nevertheless, the symbolism of the large community was strong, and in autumn Labor Day celebrations were put on there by the union.—[33]

However, Taut structured the large shape so that the privacy of the residents could be preserved. The

33 Ludovica Scarpa, *Martin Wagner und Berlin* (Braunschweig: Vieweg, 1986), 38.

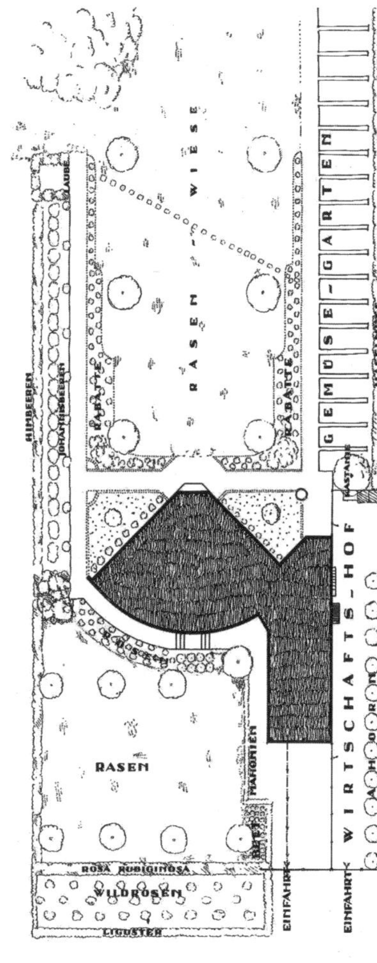


Bruno Taut's house in Berlin–Dahlewitz, 1926.

apartments are oriented to the center of the pond, but with more than sixty meters in diameter, the form is pulled far apart, and one can hardly notice the neighbors on the opposite side. The apartments are arranged in groups of six, two neighboring in three floors one above the other, but the deep loggias also give the feeling of distance to the closest neighbors. To the center, towards the public park, small gardens lie in three steps in front of the apartments and shield them from passers-by with hedges. This seemed necessary because the gardens along the path that follows the shape of a horseshoe were planted with cherry trees, and Britz was a popular destination for Berliners from the city center during cherry blossom season. The garden plan was intended—in contrast to the architectural gesture of the community—to give individuals the opportunity to be able to live in the community while maintaining the feeling of individual freedom.

## Retreat and Landscape View

In 1925, Taut bought a large plot with open views to fields and forest across from the house he had purchased in 1919 in Dahlewitz (today Wiesenstrasse 13) to build his own house.—34

34 Taut, *Ein Wohnhaus.*

The new house received the fragmentary form of a cube rounded to a "slice of pie," which lies diagonally on the twenty-seven- by eighty-meter-long plot about fifteen meters away from the road, and forms a front garden closed by a single-story side wing to the street. The right-angled corner, and thus its major axis, is like the bow of a boat facing west with the view of the fifty-five-meter-deep garden, to the open countryside, to meadow and forest; the circle segment of the rear side to the east closes itself off with few window openings to the street. Taut justified the strange form and the position on the plot in the fourth edition of his book *Die neue Wohnung: Die Frau als Schöpferin* (*The New Dwelling: Woman as Creator*):

“To avoid the uncomfortable juxtaposition of the houses and looking into the windows of the neighbors, they are placed in an angle.”—[35] This means that the two sides, lying diagonally at forty-five-degree angles to the plot boundaries, with the living and sleeping rooms turning demonstratively away from the neighboring buildings. At the time, Taut’s house was the last in the row. As a continuation, he drew two more exactly aligned, identical houses in a site plan.

35 Taut, *Die neue Wohnung*, 120.

The garden is arranged like an architectural cottage garden. From the house edge, 1.5-meter straight paths parallel to the property boundaries lead into the depths of the garden. On the southern side, there was a three-meter-wide strip up to the fence for berry bushes, on the north side a five-meter-wide, perhaps forty-meter-long vegetable garden for “self-supply.” The center formed a sixteen-meter-wide and twenty-seven-meter-deep lawn, lined with narrowing flowerbeds, which led with a slight slope into the open landscape. The wedge-shaped house, which protrudes into the garden, offers a view from the living area—as well as from the terrace upstairs—of the “neutral” lawn, framed by fruit trees, onto meadows and fields to the edge of the woods, and gives the residents the feeling of solitude in an endless expanse. The framing of the view through the trees makes the area an aesthetic object.

The quadrant quarter-circle positioned across the corner, obtains a complex meaning in conjunction with the “objective” garden layout that Leberecht Migge designed for Taut.—[36] Taut emphasized twice in his commentary the importance of the garden’s neutrality. “The garden … is thus not a ‘spatial design,’ it is nothing more than the harmless emphasis of what exists”;—[37] that is, the continuation of the former agricultural land as a lawn at the house. The planting is by no means “artistically” important, because it is only a transition of the landscape to the house, which with the meadow, the bushes, and finally the woods in the background implies everything.”—[38]

36 David H. Haney, *When Modern was Green: Life and Work of Landscape Architect Leberecht Migge* (Abingdon, Oxon: Routledge, 2010).

37 Taut, *Ein Wohnhaus*, 101.

38 Ibid., 105.

Taut explained the choice of colors for his own home with the effect of the central garden area. From the outside: "… the green lawn in contrast to the snow-white home. Fruit trees and a herbaceous border give the green surfaces a firm hold to the house and in turn allow them to fade away into the open landscape."—[39] From the interior: "Through its two large windows and the door in the middle, the living room displays the uncontrived landscape, framed by the border of the woods behind the meadows … for this reason, the three walls with windows and exterior doors are sand gray, while the three remaining walls … are wine red with darker door frames of the same spectrum, namely because the glowing evening sun should be captured warmly, but not garishly. The entire ceiling, on the other hand, has only a somewhat attainable glowing red in the limewater color, so that from the corridor below the red of the ceiling appears as a complementary color to green meadow, without competing with the natural green, because … the garish tones were only used on indirectly illuminated surfaces."—[40] Bright tones, as Taut lectures on, should be applied only where the daylight lies in rays of light or in the shade, and the space obtains a colorful atmosphere, without imposing itself.

39 Ibid., 105.

40 Ibid., 38–39.

Without a more detailed justification, the small, south-facing rooms are painted in colors that are "cooler but not cold": "Ultramarine blue ceiling, three interior walls softer and lighter blue, the end wall with the main window chrome yellow. It is accentuated by the direction of the hall in the garden."—[41] If that were to be regarded as a principle, then the study upstairs would have to have had similar colors. But the surface directly illuminated by the window is chrome yellow, and the shadowed south wall bright red, the inside corner ultramarine blue, while the ceiling remains white.—[42]

41 Ibid., 40.

42 Ibid., 87 (color photo as frontispiece).

That may be enough to show how Taut wants to base the inner color cosmos on the "temperature" of the sunlight on one hand, and the garden colors on the other; however, no classification yields this, rather it is determined by Taut's feelings. The direct, penetrating light of the sun was necessary for the glowing effect of the stained glass in the early works, thus its indirect light is used in the painted interior spaces.

Taut speaks nowhere about the heating effect of the sun, which would indeed require an alignment of the main rooms to the south. The idea of a diagonally positioned floor plan originally came from Hans Soeder, who drafted the plan of a house—"completely in accord with the sun!" with the major axis towards the south—in 1922 for the painter Ewald Dülberg and passed on to Taut.—[43] The similarity with the plan of Taut's own house is amazing, as is Taut's disregarding of the south direction for the living spaces.

43 In a letter to Taut from August 12, 1922 with sketch. Manfred Speidel, Karl Kegler, and Peter Ritterbach, eds., *Wege zu einer neuen Baukunst. Bruno Taut FRÜHLICHT* (Berlin: Gebr. Mann, 2000), 30.

## Garden without Art

Much to his astonishment, Taut again found the mirroring of the colors of the garden in the colors of the room in Japan when he visited the Imperial Villa in Kyoto Shugakuin in 1933. The small garden castle, "takes up the reflex of the garden solely by the color of the walls, which here amazingly have a red plaster, as I have otherwise never seen … The red of the wall plaster is explained here by the garden area in front of the room, whose red maple trees are taken up by the warm gray red walls gently and without contrast in the fall … The color spectrum of the old buildings seems very simple at first; but it is always exactly tuned to the color of the wood and of the garden or the countryside—for example, as a light, delicate yellow in the Park of Shugakuin on the hill, where far from this small pleasure house, the view extends into the openness."—[44]

44 Manfred Speidel, ed., *Bruno Taut. NIPPON mit europäischen Augen gesehen* (Berlin: Gebr. Mann Verlag, 2009 [1934]), 23.

For Taut, the garden at the house in Dahlewitz must have been a kind of general model. In 1933 in Japan, when he visited the Katsura Imperial Villa near Kyoto, he not only admired the art of the landscape garden that, with its pond and island designs, richly complement the simple buildings and their modest interiors in the exterior, but he was also amazed that the large garden area in front of the two residential wings: "… the residential garden of the high residents [was] nothing but grass with trees, almost like a cottage garden, also simple and 'artless,' like no other public garden. The object: the tranquility of the garden view is necessary and useful for working, living, and everyday activities; garden art, however, is disturbing even in the smallest idyll."—[45] Taut is probably the only one who saw a deeper meaning for living in this "non-garden." Nevertheless, in Katsura other reasons may have been important. The lawn was likely used for (light) sports; but it lies so deep that it floods after major rainfalls, when the Katsura River—which is connected to the garden pond—overflows. This happens "only" every few decades, but this is why the buildings are elevated.

45 Bruno Taut, "Das architektonische Weltwunder Japans," in Taut, *Ich liebe die japanische Kultur*, 98.

## Dahlewitz in Japan

In 1932, Taut went to Moscow for ten months. The house in Dahlewitz was rented and the family moved back into the old house across the street, today Wiesenstrasse 4. When Bruno Taut returned from Moscow in February 1933 and planned a world tour, he did not live in Dahlewitz, but in Eichkamp with the family of his office partner, Franz Hoffmann. On March 1, 1933, a day after the Reichstag fire, Bruno fled Berlin with Erica and escaped from the Nazis. Via Stuttgart, Switzerland, Paris, and Marseille, then by boat to Odessa, by train via Moscow to Vladivostok, they arrived in Kyoto, Japan on May 3, 1933. Taut's planned destination was America, but he wasn't able to continue traveling. He and Erica became "emigrants" in Japan, and had no fixed abode for over a year.—[46]

46 Taut described his stay in Japan in great detail in a diary, which he sent in copies to the family in Berlin and Dahlewitz, and which was preserved. Manfred Speidel, ed., *Bruno Taut in Japan. Das Tagebuch*, Band 1, 1933 (Berlin: Gebr, Mann, 2013); Band 2, 1934 was published in 2015, Band 3, 1935–36 in 2016.

Only in August 1934, did Taut get a permanent job and a permanent home. He was to design furniture and objects for everyday life for the Applied Arts Institute of Gumma Prefecture in Takasaki, approximately one hundred kilometers northwest of Tokyo. It was by chance that he could move into a new and uninhabited, small house eight kilometers from Takasaki, at the Shorinzan Zen temple. It was a very mundane, normal two-room wooden house of about forty-five square meters, with a small kitchen and bathroom. But it lay on the brow of a hill with a view of a vast plain with river and villages framed by mountains, and offered an image of fertility and abundance, as Taut could not have more beautifully cited as an example in *Die Auflösung der Städte*. "With the mountains, the land is like a pearl," Taut writes, and certainly because the diary was also addressed to the family in Dahlewitz, he compares his modest home with the old homeland: "Here—as once Dahlewitz by Berlin, only more grandiose, more clear" (August 3, 1935). On October 1, 1934, after many work-filled days, he writes: "Thus our life alternates between calm, visits, trips to the city in the dear little house, also between moisture, mist, rain, and clarity with a distant view of the beautiful mountains. Modern 'romantic' … It is also thus a kind of Dahlewitz—in Japan. And we do not like thinking about the day we have to leave."

Taut's retreats in beautiful landscapes were essential for his creativity. On the occasion of the extensive exhibition of his designed objects in November 15, 1935 in Tokyo, he wrote in his diary: "First, a strange feeling about what I have brought into the world here (and in Dahlewitz) in the greatest silence, thus to see revealed to everybody's gaze." On the quiet Sundays and nights in Dahlewitz, he also indeed brought the "living" form of his housing developments to completion. On December 11, 1935, Taut even wrote: "By the way, in Tokyo I often misspeak and say 'Dahlewitz' instead of 'Shorinzan.'" However, the hot and humid climate in summer and the dry cold in winter afflicted his health to such an extent that he wished to leave.

In October 1936, after three and a half years, the Tauts left Japan and were able to emigrate to Turkey, where Taut became dean of the architecture faculty at the Academy of Fine Arts in Istanbul and head of the construction office for schools and universities of the Ministry of Education. It was a fantastically good arrangement—being able to combine "architectural education" with architectural design and construction work.

Again, Taut lived outside the city on a sunny, steep slope on the European side of the Bosphorus in a rented house, and could build his own house next to it (figures 25 and 26). On June 5, 1938, he wrote to his friend, the architect Carl Krayl: "A new Dahlewitz is rising here, completely different, on the deep blue Bosphorus, on fifteen-meter high concrete pillars, a 'dovecote of the soon 900-year-old Noah.'"—[47] The stilted house had no garden, but it overlooked the treetops like a tower. The privileged location, the panoramic windows of the main room, and the overlying octagonal workspace enabled a great view over a mosque across the Bosphorus, and the city with the hills crowned with mosques in the distance. The "observation tower," which granted distance, was the completion of Taut's dream of being able to live creatively with nature as a recluse.

47 Baukunst Archiv der Akademie der Künste, Berlin.

Taut was not able to move into the nearly finished house, because he died on December 24, 1938, at the age of fifty-eight.

Taut's understanding of landscape and nature was complex, but always referred to architecture, to his manner of designing a human living environment. Architecture had to be a work of art, though not in the sense of a "Gesamtkunstwerk" (complete work of art), but of one whose landscape and whose medium was the nature of light. Light realizes itself architecturally in the colors of walls and ceilings, and in the translucent colored glass; landscape in the pleasant views of the form-addicted architect who completed its design graphically, or preserved a completed form—like the Japanese Fuji-san—in words as well as images. Landscape and designed nature also served Taut in gaining distance to other people, in preserving an undisturbed life of his own, and only thereby being capable of common action. Yet, the great architectural work of art should be secluded in nature, and the visitor only able to fully experience it as a "lonely wanderer" through a difficult approach.

Taut composed these concepts of colorful spaces—which began in 1904 with Ruskin's call to let the dwindling nature emerge again as a reminder in building structures—that were first enriched with images of plants, then later geometrically abstracted, but on the walls and in the glass domes the refractions of light into color relationships were allowed to become reality. In utopian image sequences, Taut did not hesitate to form the natural landscapes of the earth with glowing structures on a large scale, in order—as he said—to make the earth compete with and link to the starry sky.

The prerequisite for this endless major project of humanity was meant to be state-free settler communities scattered around the earth, which guaranteed the ability to earn a living and made the earth into "a good dwelling." Although Taut did not conceive any more utopias after 1920, they formed the hidden foundations of his residential projects, of the housing developments, and of his own dwellings.

Bruno Taut by his house at the Bosporus, Istanbul.

Ludwig Mies van der Rohe, Tugendhat House, Brno, 1929–30, view outside the living area through the conservatory.
Photograph taken by Fritz Tugendhat in the 1930s.

# Mies's Organic Order

Albert Kirchengast

Little thought has been devoted to the gardens of the architect Ludwig Mies van der Rohe. This is completely justified, since it is not really a matter of gardens but of landscape.—[1] However, it is almost impossible to understand why there has not been a discussion of "living in a landscape" with regard to his country houses long before now. Perhaps it has not so much been mosquitoes and flooding that have steered the attention of the experts in other directions as a feeling of literally being "held in nature," an existential aesthetic experience with which a dweller had to cope in the architectural space of Mies.

1 For further information on the bibliography and sources, see Albert Kirchengast, "Das unvollständige Haus. Mies van der Rohe und die Landschaft der Moderne" [The Imperfect House: Mies van der Rohe and the Landscape of Modernity], dissertation, Zurich, 2017.

When it comes to modern architecture, people still think in terms such as "flowing spaces" or "open plans," believing that in this way they are also getting to the bottom of Mies's work. But what is a "free-flowing ground plan" supposed to mean? Certainly, with Mies, "indoors and outdoors are no longer easily defined,"—[2] as Philip Johnson has put it. But then again, what makes the difference? This certainly fits in well with the established image of an apparent obsession with making the greatest possible reduction in technical detail, a trend-setting "abstraction," preparing the ground for mass production—which obviously does not do service to his buildings. Such interpretations miss the point, not least because they are devoid of a deeper understanding of the substance of Mies van der Rohe's work.

2 Philip C. Johnson, *Mies van der Rohe* (Boston and New York: The Museum of Modern Art, 1947), 30.

As long ago as the early 1930s, some architectural critics already described his houses as capturing an atmosphere of "profane sacredness" (*sakrale Profanität*) and triggered a debate about their role in a society that was in need of social reform.—[3] Consequently, a discussion of the intellectual challenge that these kind of houses represented for a *single person* turned out to be merely a large diversion in the internationalization of architecture. The opposing parts of this rather philosophical distinction—involved with the development of a modern, Miesian house—remain virulent today: purpose versus spirit. Nature plays an important part in this.

3 Justus Bier's article followed a discussion of the house by Walter Riezler and triggered the famous debate "Kann man im Haus Tugendhat wohnen?" [Is it possible to live in the Villa Tugendhat?], *Die Form* 10 (1931), 392–4. For the concept of sacred profanity see also Paul Tillich, "Kult und Form," *Die Form* 23/24 (1930), 578–83.

## Ideals

Only recently, in a small publication recounting a lecture given at the Illinois Institute of Technology, where Mies headed and expanded the department of architecture during the years 1938–58, Jacques Herzog wrote—not without some asperity—"Mies's understanding of and interest in nature is just decorative. Nature interests him as the decorative, optical, and plastic opposite of his architecture. The architecture does not adapt to nature and nature remains as it was. It is not transformed and exploited like a vegetable garden, nor is it used to support the architecture and the people."—[4]

Over fifty years before, Mies condensed his own attitude in a rare and enigmatic statement, claiming "Nature should also live its own life."—[5] This only was a response to a visually explicit opposition in his sketches. To "live one's own life" clearly meant different things for architecture and nature according to him. By no means the consequence of a simple formalism intended to distance the technical appeal of his architecture from the *Leistungsform* (performance form) of Hugo Häring—with whom he shared his Berlin office—or from the "technical formalism" of the Bauhaus—an institution he headed

4 Jacques Herzog and Pierre de Meuron, *Treacherous Transparencies: Thoughts and Observations, Triggered by a Visit to Farnsworth House* (New York: Actar, 2016), 55.

5 Christian Norberg-Schulz, "Ein Gespräch mit Mies van der Rohe" [A Conversation with Mies van der Rohe] (1958), in Fritz Neumeyer, *Mies van der Rohe. Das kunstlose Wort. Gedanken zur Baukunst* [The Artless Word: Mies van der Rohe on the Building Art] (Berlin: Siedler, 1986), 404–6, at 405.

before emigrating to the US—his earliest perspective sketches are already characterized by an opposition of the strict straight lines of architecture and the gentle contours of landscapes. Though the sketches were quickly drawn in order to develop and try out an idea, showing evidence of the linking of "outdoors" and "indoors" being an essential element of his architecture, a separation of the architectural space from the world outside is nevertheless established in them. These paper-landscapes are endowed with visual "depth," becoming a compositional complement to the house, in which the outward-looking gaze loses its way and ranges over parts of the spacious interior. Wolf Tegethoff has spoken of an "aesthetic border,"—[6] whereby the exterior is easily accessible—but only by crossing a threshold. They evoke the idea of a stage, transforming an architect's drawing into the scenery of an unwritten and enigmatic play. The calm and protective envelope of the building again stands in opposition to the dynamic, seemingly autonomous appearance of nature, which offers the occupant its aesthetically stimulating drama with giant trees crowding in on the sketchpad, as if these houses were surrounded by ancient forest. The only thing that "flows" here is the view into the distance.

6 Wolf Tegethoff, "On the Development of the Conception of Space in the Works of Mies van der Rohe," in *Daidalos* 13 (1984), 114–23, at 118 and 122.

With the avant-garde projects of the first half of the 1920s, glass became a major part of Mies's architectural repertoire. In 1914, in his influential little volume *Glasarchitektur*, Paul Scheerbart even dreamed of "illuminating the mountains"—[7] with Alpine glass hotels, admitting "In introducing glass architecture, it is best to begin with the garden,"—[8] and spoke of houses as garden pavilions with iron ribs. In 1933, in a text entitled "Was wäre Beton, was Stahl ohne Spiegelglas?" [What Would Concrete, What Would Steel be without Mirror Glass?], Mies firmly asserts that "only here, in a realm of greater freedom, unfettered by narrow purposes, can the architectural value of this technical resource be fully proven … Only now can we divide the space freely, open it up and tie it to the landscape. Only now can we once again see what is wall and

7 Paul Scheerbart, *Glasarchitektur* [Glass Architecture] (Berlin: Der Sturm, 1914), 32.

8 Ibid., 11.

aperture, what is floor and ceiling."—[9] The use of large-format glass panels stretching from ceiling to floor, from wall to wall, in different tones, chastely but clearly mounted in metal frames, is brought together here with the *idea* for a new architecture. Its "glass walls" would only disguise the unmistakable boundary between house and landscape at first glance, while at the same time fulfilling the task of visual opening and spatial closing–glass is a medium of both transparency and reflection. Mies understands it as a dividing element that creates visual relationships, while the basically similar but opaque wall panels rhythmize the adjoining space of the house. A key building material of the period, not only for him, the glass membrane becomes the crystallization point of the close relationship between the landscape and the living area in his houses. But Mies's buildings also allow retreat and intimacy, not only supported by opaque walls—mistakably arranged like an avant-garde-painting—or slender conservatories acting as visual "filters," but also groves of ancient trees that cast shadows and appease the hostile mood of a shimmering hot summers' day, sculptures that point to axes of reference, spanning imaginary boundaries, and so on. And yet again the landscape "out there" develops a strange power to draw you in.

9 Ludwig Mies van der Rohe, "Was wäre Beton, was Stahl ohne Spiegelglas" (1933), in Neumeyer, *Mies van der Rohe*, 378.

The idea of "tying a building to the landscape" put forward in his aforementioned statement refers specifically to the idea of nature experienced as the *other* part of the house. In doing so Mies only follows a major shift in the relationship between man and nature that characterizes a "modernization" on the level of the history of ideas, as Gerd Blum has thoroughly explored in terms of a revolution of the "visual."—[10] After the decay of Vitruvianism and an all-embracing harmonic order, it is down to aesthetic subjectivity, to each single dweller, to "re-embed"—[11] a house (and oneself) in its "surroundings." The aesthetic—i.e. sensuous *and* intellectual—experience of nature is at the core of this process with the cultural landscape as its material backcloth that appears picturesquely undulating.

10 Cf. Gerd Blum, *Fenestra prospectiva* (Berlin and Boston: De Gruyter, 2015).

11 I am borrowing this term from the sociologist Anthony Giddens. Cf. idem, *The Consequences of Modernity* (John Wiley & Sons, 1990).

Only on the intriguing posters produced for clients and exhibitions, with their geometric lines drawn with ruler and pencil, is the restrained vocabulary of Mies's drawings extended by the addition of glued-in "implants," resembling pieces of furniture, sometimes with vividly grained (luxurious) wood veneers or representations of works of art, whose real proportions and size are lost in such collages. The views over wide-open spaces Mies adds here as if they were real landscapes—instead of mere ideas—are none the less important for a pictorial impression. Where a settlement is to be seen at all in these prospects, it is cropped or melts into the landscape. Created from cut out photographs, these backgrounds originate from the same type of scenery as on Mies's blueprints, where people seem to take second place behind them. More than representing a certain building site, they are meant somehow to resemble how a dweller might experience them. His drawings thus make clear a spatial model that owes more to an intellectual concept than to actual conditions. The underlying typology is subdivided into foreground (living space), middle ground (a surrounding garden), and an unavailable distance (landscape).

Despite this designing strategy Mies was perfectly aware of the *genius loci*. What already existed at a certain place prior to his own architectural considerations—which is to say "natural" conditions such as trees, topography, view, etc.—turn out to be most relevant to him. In his plans for the Gericke House, he even modifies the requested spatial program in order to reconcile a real site with his ideal. In the project description required for the small private competition run by Herbert Gericke (1932), the Director of the German Academy in Rome, he emphasizes the importance of the location of the house and the specific configuration of the landscape by the Wannsee in Berlin. The main view from the fully glazed living area is deliberately guided toward the scenery opposite, so that the contours of the lakeside landscape are piled up one behind the other, forming the backdrop of an expansive, open landscape of water and forest, “this living area does not lie exactly at the center of the previous axis, but has been moved further forward to the southeast because, in the author’s opinion, the view from here over both the lower garden and the lake is much more interesting.”—[12] In order to learn to understand the natural atmosphere on the spot and consider how to proceed with the design, he went to the Grosse Seestrasse at different times of day, and different weather conditions. Ultimately, it was all about the “most beautiful view over the Wannsee,” as he concludes in his account to Gericke, constantly seeking ways to build a house that corresponds to the picturesque scenery.

12 Published in Wolf Tegethoff, *Mies van der Rohe. Die Villen und Landhausprojekte* [Mies van der Rohe: The Villas and Country Houses] (Essen: Richard Bacht, 1981), 115f.

Mies van der Rohe’s repertoire subsequently matured, with a couple of projects in the 1930s, which were unbuilt. While his 1924 sketch of the Brick Country House, which became famous for its radical lines, could be discussed as a model for linking a house with “infinity”—[13] beyond the confines of a sheet of drawing paper, he transformed the sublime distance, prevalent in all of his houses, into more suitable concepts for the urban environment. Such houses might only partially open up to their surroundings, their walls framing a mountain or a river—as Mies demonstrated in the Hubbe House Project (1934–35) on the Elbe Island near Magdeburg, whereas the adjacent houses on less favorable sections of the same plot remain completely surrounded by walls. The residential building for Margarete Hubbe appeared less imposing, showing the public a simple pierced façade on the street side and only displaying its spatial qualities on the river side. The view toward the River Elbe is defined by brick walls, with another glass-box set alone in between, though without reaching out into the river landscape itself. Here, too, Mies relies on the natural qualities of the place, orchestrating it without “owning” it. Self-confident and respectful, the building keeps its distance from the tranquil happenings by the water, for which Mies now draws the symbol of a heeling boat with billowing sails in all the three surviving

13 The free-flowing lines of the walls in the ground plan go right to the edge of the sheet.

perspectives of this project. As we observe these imaginary scenes like a movie through the skillful sketches of an architect, we might share the eyes of a prospective dweller and contemplate the distance that opens up.

In the small, "dark" courtyard of the famous Barcelona Pavilion (1929), which was reconstructed in the 1980s, however, it remains possible to retain the distant landscape, the changing moods of nature and its vivid fabric, as well as the sky and its reflection in stone and water, within the enclosed building. A horizon is now symbolized by the precise copings of the embracing walls, with the sky and the crowns of tall trees above them. Standing there, Georg Kolbe's more-than-life-size statue *Der Morgen* [Morning] clarifies the role of the sculptures belonging to such houses. They have internalized the auratic relationship of distance and nearness, which, of course, could not always be present in the sometimes hectic, sometimes distracted daily life of an occupant. In one of the most recent comprehensive works in the tradition of German aesthetics of nature, Martin Seel described the meaning of such an experience, mediated by a house, with its "dynamische Eigenmächtigkeit" (dynamic autonomy), "sinnliche Wahrnehmbarkeit" (sensuous vitality), and "lebensweltliche Anwesenheit" (meaningful presence).—[14] Clearly, a house of this kind not only suits the physical comfort of its inhabitants, but is truly attuned to nature, while its architectural structure gives expression to its impressionistic setting.—[15]

14 Martin Seel, *Eine Ästhetik der Natur* [The Aesthetics of Nature] (Frankfurt am Main: Suhrkamp, 1996), 20f.

15 For the role of construction and Mies's comments on "epoch," "chaos," "technology," etc., cf. my dissertation, "Raumkunst und Technik," 289–326 (Chapter 7).

## Theory

Mies was never able to erect any of these country houses from the 1930s true to his primary sketches. Today they may serve as evidence of his thoughts on landscape. The landscape toward which this kind of *contemplative living* was oriented, is not in any way "decorative" but is connected with the unavailability that lies at the core of the aesthetic

The profundity of Tugendhat House: views through the rear parts of the living area.
Photographs taken by Fritz Tugendhat in the 1930s.

A distant Špilberk hill in the historic center of Brno staged by Tugendhat House.
Photograph taken by Fritz Tugendhat in the 1930s.

experience of nature. It is an experience no older than modernity itself, in an epoch best characterized by the "awakening" of a sensitivity to the aesthetics of nature and likewise by the loss of that "order" in architecture and society and a subsequent "chaos," which was to preoccupy Mies throughout his life. The very fact that the countryside is, for a dweller in such houses, no longer a place for agriculture has already been widely discussed in modern landscape theory. Only rarely are such theoretical concepts matched with the development of architecture or even translated into the environment we live in. So what is the intellectual, even spiritual aspect of unavailability promised by the "distance" of Mies's country houses?

Robert Levit has stated that Mies "marries" the abstract architectural space to a quite different, picturesque landscape, which lies *beyond* the modern house and retains the old form of an English landscape garden.—[16] This leads him logically to the crucial issue: "if we assume the project for architecture was not simply one of updating its techniques, but of lending to architecture an epistemological role in revealing the underlying circumstances of contemporary life, it is strange that landscape should not have been subject to similar scrutiny."—[17] Mies must have given equally little consideration to the privileged landscape of a historical style in the history of gardens, as he turned his attention to modern technology for its own sake. He saw modern technology as merely a tool. Only in this way could a *work* ("Werk") of architecture remain an expression of more deeply rooted, immaterial qualities.

As this interaction between the modern concept of nature and the history of architecture helps to show, Mies goes through a period of development. The houses and landscaped gardens of Lenné and Schinkel are not the only significant elements in this. To begin with, the garden also occupies a prominent place in Mies's spatial concept. He considers it in the same way as the garden reformers of the first decades of the new century; gardens become a natural part of an architect's design project. When Mies,

16 Robert Levit, "Afterword: The Persistence of the Picturesque," in Charles Waldheim, *Hilberseimer/Mies van der Rohe. Lafayette Park Detroit* (Munich, Berlin, London, and New York: Prestel, 2004), 135–41, at 136.

17 Ibid., 138.

who had not yet even reached twenty years of age, left his home city of Aachen for Berlin, where he worked first as a draughtsman and then for Bruno Paul, a leading furniture designer, he soon came into contact with the philosopher Alois Riehl and his wife Sofie, and built his first house for them in 1908. It stands in the suburban surroundings of the archetypal modern city, which the architectural historian Julius Posener identified as the nexus of "country-house culture."—[18] Under the influence of the reformers of that time, who included Hermann Muthesius and also Mies's later teacher and employer, Peter Behrens, the garden became the key feature of these houses, arranged geometrically as an Albertian "outdoor room" with terraces, steps, pergolas, and clearly structured flowerbeds. The Riehl's garden, which was established in cooperation with the important plant cultivator Karl Foerster in Neubabelsberg, also looks like this. However, the typical distant landscape, which accompanies Mies's work like a basso continuo, starts at the Griebnitzsee with its ranges of wooded hills beyond the loggia of the house. Correspondingly, the hall of Riehl House, a place of philosophical discussion, hints at the great living room of his future room typology as a place of aesthetic reflection.

18 Cf. Julius Posener, *Berlin auf dem Wege zu einer neuen Architektur* [Berlin on the Way to a New Architecture] (Munich: Prestel, 1979).

It was then that Mies learned to understand the garden as an architectural task and went on to produce designs—which still survive today—for flowerbeds right up against the walls of his Krefeld Villas (1927–30). Christiane Kruse examined his activity in this area, and in conversation with Mies's collaborator Sergius Ruegenberg in the 1990s she discovered that the majority of the documents from the early years of the office were already destroyed in the 1920s.—[19] Mies van der Rohe's "gardening activity"—including the records remaining at the Mies-van-der-Rohe Archive at MoMA in New York—can no longer be perfectly reconstructed. It seems that he happily handed over this task to experts in the closely related discipline. The Riehl House can also be taken as a paradigm for this. The favorite rose beds of a single color that were drawn on his

19 Christiane Kruse, "Garten, Natur und Landschaftsprospekt. Zur ästhetischen Inszenierung des Aussenraums in den Landhausanlagen Mies van der Rohes," dissertation, Berlin, 1994, 5.

own plans, which, together with the plans of the house, Muthesius published in the second edition of his book *Landhaus und Garten* [Country House and Garden], were not laid out; Foerster's herbaceous plantings were accepted instead. For Mies himself, the garden is a matter of that extra "stratum," which in later development became simple terraces and platforms. In his successive projects he designed strictly geometrical paved terraces around the house, which act as an abstract link, separated by a simple straight line from the immediately adjacent natural topography, which begins around the house and vanishes somewhere in the distance. In the case of the Lemke House (1932–33), which was actually built in a modified version, the house and terrace stand on a subtle "plinth," a mound of earth that does not immediately attract the visitor's attention. Mies had the site banked up and levelled in places by a few centimeters with some of the soil from the excavation. The house is a part of the landscape, and yet not quite; it stands out, only to link up with it as major part of the visual experience.—[20]

20 This is probably the basis of the difficulty modern architects sometimes have with cultural landscapes, in which they would like to position their houses but consider it simply as what lies in opposition, needing no maintenance or design.

In his *Geschichte des Horizonts* [History of the Horizon], Albrecht Koschorke comments that the recent phenomenon of the landscape horizon, which began to replace the gold background of paintings as far back as the Renaissance, corresponds to the freedom experienced by the modern individual. It takes over the function of an opposite pole in relation to the secularized "world of immanence." "Only in a profane form and within the a priori spatial organization of the profane can the sacred still be rendered visible."—[21] In fact, a special perceptivity ("Organ") was needed for this high regard for nature. In 1963 Joachim Ritter contributed an influential essay to German landscape theory in which he talks of a modern adaptation of the ancient Greek concept of *theoria*—philosophical contemplation. Looked at in this way, the historic cultural landscape, which has been relieved of the burden of action but, of course, bears traces of human life and was even formed by human activity, stands in opposition to the pressure of expansive,

21 Albrecht Koschorke, *Die Geschichte des Horizonts. Grenze und Grenzüberschreitung in literarischen Landschaftsbildern* [The History of the Horizon: Borders and Crossing Borders in Literary Images of Landscape] (Frankfurt am Main: Suhrkamp, 1990), 61.

modern civilization.—[22] The idea of "relief from the burden of action" as a genuine value of "organic" nature dates from the history of the aesthetic experience itself, which developed in parallel with the landscape garden. Here the critical date for Ritter is Kant's *Critique of Judgment* of 1790. As designing a "nature unadorned" in the English Landscape Garden became the province of landscape architects, Friedrich Schiller—following Kant—epitomized its experience as one of "naturalness" in his treatise *Über naive und sentimentalische Dichtung* [On Naive and Sentimental Poetry].—[23] Only when man had begun to master nature through technology and understand it rationally did the capacity for aesthetically distanced appreciation develop. Ritter's treatise, which bears the apposite title *Landschaft—Zur Funktion des Ästhetischen in der modernen Gesellschaft* [Landscape—On the Function of the Aesthetic in Modern Society] helps not only to interpret the relationship of Mies's houses to the landscape but also to sum up the profound changes in the history of the relationship to nature, defining what he describes as the phenomenon of *Entzweiung* ("dissociation"). The modern human is, so to speak, incomplete if his technical-rational access to the world is not completed by an aesthetic-moral aspect—[24]—a state that seems to be reflected in the spatiality of Mies's modern country house.

The fact that this theoretical view of landscape, which refers back to the eighteenth century and links up with the postwar debate, meant more than just a broad arc of philosophical thought, is borne out by Georg Simmel's contemporary *Philosophie der Landschaft* [Philosophy of Landscape] of 1913. Simmel's work was part of Mies's reading at the time, which alternated between philosophical essays and writings on social and technological criticism, as can be seen from Fritz Neumeyer's research into Mies's library and the publication of parts of his written legacy.—[25] Mies himself spoke of the year 1926—so before the projects of the 1930s—as a "peculiar year," concerning what he had found to be his own

22 Joachim Ritter, "Landschaft" [Landscape] (1963), in idem, *Metaphysik und Politik. Studien zu Aristoteles und Hegel* [Metaphysics and Politics: Studies of Aristotle and Hegel] (Frankfurt am Main: Suhrkamp, 2003), 407–41, passim.

23 Friedrich Schiller, *Über naive und sentimentalische Dichtung* [On Naive and Sentimental Poetry] (Stuttgart: Reclam, 2002 [1795]), 33.

24 Cf. Cornelia Klinger, *Flucht, Trost, Revolte. Die Moderne und ihre ästhetischen Gegenwelten* [Flight, Consolation, Revolt: The Modern and Its Aesthetic Alternative World] (Munich: Hanser, 1995).

25 Neumeyer, *Mies van der Rohe*, Appendix, Manifestos, Texts, and Lectures, 295–406.

standpoint. In 1927 he was avidly reading and selecting extracts from Friedrich Dessauer's book *Philosophie der Technik* [Philosophy of Technology] and Leopold Ziegler's *Zwischen Mensch und Wirtschaft* [Between Man and Business]. In the latter, he occasionally found criticism of the organizational form of the modern economy, which is said to fragment the individual. Ziegler subsequently put forward the suggestion of an organic way of doing business.—[26] Simmel's visionary writing not only recognizes the landscape as an artistically "envisoned" section of nature, but accords it the meaning of an experienced "whole" (Ganzheit) that achieves ontological potential where the modern city-dweller finds himself reduced to a fragment in a reifying mass culture. To understand this condition, Mies is aware of the term *coincidentia oppositorum*, which he probably adopted from his mentor Romano Guardini, to describe the essential "bridging" between ratio and instinct, individual and society that is alluded to here—the chasm between the wholeness of nature experienced through landscape and manifestations of cultural alienation. The modern individual can transcend these antitheses only through the aesthetic experience.

26 Leopold Ziegler, *Zwischen Mensch und Wirtschaft* [Between Man and Business] (Darmstadt: Königshausen & Neumann, 1927), 52f.

In 1938, on the occasion of his inaugural lecture at the IIT, Mies spoke of an "organic order"—[27] to be achieved through the means of architecture, a dwelling that gives equal recognition to a given landscape and the tools of modern technology. Richard Ingersoll is therefore right when he hints at the secret "program" of this architecture behind the oft-repeated misunderstanding of the apparent disconnectedness of the picturesque "green space" and the cubic "house space." He suggests that, "while one usually thinks of Mies as a master of inert steel-and-glass boxes, it could just as well be said that his true mission was to create grand vistas using natural elements of water and plants."—[28] Although Mies designed houses for a privileged social class, he spoke, with unusual pathos, of a "higher unity" that was to be communicated by the view through the glass walls of his houses, a "deeper meaning"

27 Mies van der Rohe, "Inaugural Address" (November 20, 1938), in Neumeyer, *Mies van der Rohe*, 381.

28 Richard Ingersoll, "Mies van der Rohe and the Conservation of the American Landscape," in Christophe Girot and Albert Kirchengast (eds.), *Mies als Gärtner* [Mies as Gardener] (Zürich: gta, 2011), 11–22, at 11.

of nature, and a "greater whole,"—[29] that could be experienced by everyone. A house now becomes a medium, a lens of a high degree of constructive refinement through which to engage in a dialogue with "nature," that, at the same time, transcends its technical foundations.

29 Christian Norberg-Schulz, Ein Gespräch mit Mies van der Rohe [A Conversation with Mies van der Rohe] (1958), in Neumeyer, *Mies van der Rohe*, 404–6, at 405.

## A House

The Villa Tugendhat in Brno can be seen not only as the high point of the houses built by Mies in Europe but also as the most ingenious realization of the "country house model" of the 1930s. The very topography of the steep slope below Černopolni Street (then known as Schwarzfeldgasse) in the Černá Pole residential district of Brno prompted Mies to design a house on three levels. At the request of Grete und Fritz Tugendhat, he included separate private rooms and bedrooms, which he was fortunately able to place on the upper, street-level floor, above the large, central living space.

"And when I contemplate the leaves and flowers that shine out like diamonds against appropriate backgrounds, when I let these rooms and everything in them affect me as a whole, I have a distinct feeling that this is beauty, this is truth."—[30] That is how the owner expressed himself in his letter to the editor of *Die Form*, the journal of the Deutsche Werkbund. It is his reaction to the debate about whether it was actually possible to live in the Villa Tugendhat. As an amateur photographer, Fritz Tugendhat caught the transient moments of the aesthetic effects of nature that he experienced every day—the play of light and shadow, reflection and vividness in the conservatory, and family get-togethers under the great weeping willow in front of the house, which unfortunately fell victim to a storm in the 1980s. He captured the image of a lively house that he had made his own—"large and austere—but in a way that releases rather than oppresses,"—[31] as his wife Grete described it.

30 "Die Bewohner des Hauses Tugendhat äussern sich" [The Occupants of the Villa Tugendhat Speak], *Die Form* 11 (1931), 437–9, at 438.

31 Ibid., 437.

At the foot of a shared old villa garden, directly connected by garden paths, lies the house of Grete Tugendhat's parents—erected when the style of Viennese Historicism was still in vogue. When Mies arrived in Brno to view the site, after a positive meeting in Berlin with the wealthy Jewish intellectual Tugendhats, he was impressed by the view over the city center and Špilberk hill. The new house for the young couple and their children was to be built right next to the garden pavilion, at the highest point of the villa garden in an expanding area of the aspiring industrial city, known historically as the "Belvedere." The aforementioned weeping willow, directly referred to visually on the ground plan with a semicircular wooden screen, played an instrumental role in Mies's sketches, as did the familiar spatial scaling with flowerbeds. However, once again, Mies left the detailed formulation of the connection to the winding garden paths and the final layout and planting of the beds to a professional. Markéta Roderová-Müllerová (a.k.a. Grete Roder-Müller) seems to have acted just as Mies would have wished. She was taking over the design of sparse additions to the older landscape-garden from him and in a 1969 conversation about their collaboration, she mentions the "emphasized emptiness"—[32] that he wanted—small "clearings" with lawns surrounded by trees and shrubs that would draw the eye to the view of the Špilberk, which could be enjoyed from the glass-walled living room as well as from the private rooms on the upper floor. By and large, moving the living areas to the middle level of the house—withdrawing it from the city into the garden—helps to create the impression conveyed by the house that one is living in a large clearing. Hidden in the "plinth level" below are the extensive machine rooms of the "Wohnmaschine" (machine for living). They constitute the complementary side of the special *Wohngefühl* ("feeling of living"), include an "air conditioning plant" that was a luxury at the time, and a unique mechanism for lowering two monumental plate-glass windows.

32 Recording of a conversation of April 1, 1969, cited in German translation in Kruse, *Garten, Natur und Landschaftsprospekt*, 191–3.

It was Romano Guardini, whose writings greatly influenced Mies van der Rohe, who considered the Italian villa landscape as a role model for future living. The intellectual reflection on the spatial structure of a cultural landscape had its origins in the late Renaissance, when *prima natura* was first thought of as the opposing pole to a villa.—[33] This must have been a major inspiration for Mies's concept of "organic order" that he never explained publically after his speech at IIT. Also Guardini drew guidance for the present from it. As a thought experiment, he challenged the readers of his 1927 *Briefe vom Comer See* [Letters from Lake Como] to "take a sailing boat"—[34]—thus challenging Mies to do the same. What he describes is a simile expressed in terms of the mechanics of sailing. The wind, a force of nature, poetically propels a wooden boat by means of the swollen sails: "When this kind of boat sailed with the wind behind it, my heart sang, as probably happens when perfection of form has caused something to become light and bright from the inside."—[35] Only the design of a man-made object in aesthetic interplay with natural forces makes the wind "visible." The opposition of intuition and understanding—the basis of the perception of *Entzweiung*—has been stirred and overcome in the spectator through the "contemplation" of the *Lebendige-Konkretheit* ("living concreteness")—as Guardini describes the aesthetic experience, coining his own term. His response to what Mies was searching for came from the fundamental personal experience of a specific place to which he was traveling in a thoughtful mood and sending letters back about it. What was revealed to him in the centuries-old landscape around Lake Como, which is still threatened by technological invasion, had to do with conveying opposites based on two completely different but related ways in which modern man approaches nature. Only the experience of the presence of the "living concrete," the experience of the inherent insufficiency to get to grips with it, therefore saving it from its "reification," would promise *beauty*. Human dwelling in this landscape that nevertheless includes modern technology would only

33 Cf. John Dixon Hunt, *Greater Perfections: The Practice of Garden Theory* (London: Thames & Hudson, 2000), 32–75.

34 Romano Guardini, *Briefe vom Comer See* [Letters from Lake Como] (Mainz: Grünewald, 1927), 17f.

35 Ibid.

Family gathering in the shadow of the weeping willow next to Tugendhat House.
Photograph taken by Fritz Tugendhat in the 1930s.

be successful if the house is "held" (gehalten) in it, as Joachim Ritter has put it.

Mies devoted a large part of his Notebook to *Letters from Lake Como* and commented, paraphrasing his experience of reading it: "The struggle against the new does not inevitably have to mean holding on to the old, and we like to believe that deep down it is a struggle against the rational. We want to save the supra-rational. To question whether it is possible in this way."—[36] Also for him, the "villa landscape" seems to have become an answer to his quest. Echoing the idealistic aesthetics of nature, reformulated as a critical social theory, what is described here is a spatial "apologia for distance," "the ability to step back and look on."—[37]

It was in his critique of Villa Tugendhat that Walter Riezler introduced the term profane sacredness to the debate. In a later lecture "Zur Theologie der bildenden Kunst und Architektur" [On the Theology of Art and Architecture] 1961, Paul Tillich—who originally coined the term—stated that he had found "categories of spiritual creation"—[38] in functionalist art and architecture that allowed the quality of sacredness to be experienced in everyday life; a state of "intimacy with nature" that paradoxically included a "promise of distance," helping towards a modern reality that encourages the immediate power to make use of things. In the modern age, this experience has found its place—alongside art—in the aesthetic manifestations of nature, deeply convincing us with a "free play"—[39] of the organic and affecting our idea of our own capacity for free decision and feeling—the very notion of the modern individual. It would be in the modern landscape, in the shelter of a house—nonetheless a place of natural dynamics—that this kind of aesthetic experience finds its place. *Theoria* exactly translates into Latin as contemplation: the present centered on a distant incident, a *templum*.

36 Ludwig Mies van der Rohe, "Notebook" (1929–28), cited in Neumeyer, *Mies van der Rohe*, 330.

37 Martin Seel, *Adornos Philosophie der Kontemplation* [Adorno's Philosophy of Contemplation] (Frankfurt am Main: Suhrkamp, 2004), 18. Cf. also Richard Padovan, "Machines à méditer" [Machines to Meditate In], in Kevin P. Harrington, *Mies van der Rohe: Architect as Educator* (Chicago: University of Chicago Press, 1986), 17–26.

38 Paul Tillich, "Zur Theologie der bildenden Kunst und der Architektur" [On the Theology of Art and Architecture] (1961), in idem, *Selected Texts* (Berlin and New York: De Gruyter, 2008), 407–18, at 407.

39 Immanuel Kant, *Kritik der Urteilskraft* [Critique of Judgment] (Frankfurt am Main: Suhrkamp, 1974 [1790]), 132.

Ludwig Hilberseimer, planner, and Alfred Caldwell, delineator, aerial perspective, *The City in the Landscape*, pen and ink with graphite, 1942.

# Ludwig Hilberseimer's Ecological Urbanism

Charles Waldheim

*There are, in fact, no cities anymore.*
*It goes on like a forest.*—1

A German architect and art critic immersed in the *Neue Sachlichkeit* (New Objectivity), Ludwig Hilberseimer first came to prominence for his unbuilt urban projects from the nineteen-twenties, most notoriously known for totalizing rationally planned schemes—such as Hochhausstadt (Highrise City, 1924) and Groszstadtarchitektur (Metropolis or Big City Architecture, 1927). Referring to this earlier work as "more a necropolis than a metropolis,"—2 he quickly abandoned those schemes in favor of projects that explored decentralization and landscape as remedies for the ills of the industrial city. This was evident as early as 1927 in a sketch titled *The Metropolis as a Garden-City"*—3 Hilberseimer's work over the course of the nineteen-thirties was clearly influenced by European precedents for the garden city and favored the use of landscape and mixed-height housing in a low-density pattern. Particularly formative in this regard were his early projects for *Mischbebauung* (mixed-height housing, circa 1930) and for the University of Berlin (1935), the principles of which would inform the balance of his career.—4 His preference for landscape and mixed-height housing in a low-density pattern would continue to appear in his work in the United States (US).

1 Ludwig Mies van der Rohe, Transcript of an interview with John Peter, 1955, Library of Congress, 14–15.

2 Richard Pommer, "'More a Necropolis than a Metropolis,' Ludwig Hilberseimer's Highrise City and Modern City Planning," in *In the Shadow of Mies: Ludwig Hilberseimer. Architect, Educator, and Urban Planner*, ed. Richard Pommer, David Spaeth, and Kevin Harrington (Chicago: Art Institute of Chicago, 1988), 16–53.

3 See David Spaeth, "Ludwig Hilberseimer's Settlement Unit: Origins and Applications," in Pommer, *In the Shadow of Mies*, 54–68.

4 Ibid.

While Hilberseimer's early work was immersed in German planning circles of the day and notions of *Stadtlandschaft*, it was also influenced by the then evident reality that mature industrial production would tend toward the decentralization of traditional urban form.—[5] He was a committed socialist, having been radicalized by the social conditions of the nineteen-twenties and thirties. In Germany, he espoused a public socialist position informed by traditional Marxist social critique. Hilberseimer's planning projects from that time are imbued with his sense of "fairness."—[6] His interest in social equity informed planning projects that embodied equitable conditions for all, most notably through equitable access to healthful housing. By correlating social equity to arable land and access to sunlight, he proposed an ecological urbanism informed by social, environmental, and cultural determinates.—[7]

By the time he immigrated to Chicago in 1938, Hilberseimer's planning projects had explored the spatial and urban implications of these issues. While he maintained his social commitments throughout his Chicago years, he eschewed a public position on socialism in the US, most often relying upon his colleagues and students to take more critical public positions.—[8] By the mid-nineteen-forties, Hilberseimer's notion of the Settlement Unit took clearer form as the basic building block of urban structure and social order. The Settlement Unit was rendered as a self-contained, repeatable structure in which residential settlement was embodied in mixed-height housing with equal access to networks of pedestrian greenways and surface streets for the automobile. Hilberseimer's drawings at this time anticipate the development of an interstate highway system, articulating precise relationships between transportation networks, Settlement Units, and the regional landscape. His interest in an organic urban expression for the North American continent was further fueled by civil defense imperatives toward decentralization in the years following the Second World War. In the wake

5 Ludwig Hilberseimer, *The New Regional Pattern: Industries and Gardens, Workshops and Farms* (Chicago: Paul Theobald & Co., 1949), 171, 174. See also Detlef Mertins, "Mies, Organic Architecture, and the Art of City Building," in *Mies in America* (New York: Harry Abrams, 2001), 591–641; and Detlef Mertins, "Collaboration in Order," in *Case Lafayette Park Detroit*, ed. Charles Waldheim (Munich: Prestel/Harvard GSD), 11–17.

6 Phyllis Lambert, *In the Shadow of Mies*, symposium, Art Institute of Chicago, September 1988, 14–17.

7 Hilberseimer's commitment to equity informed planning projects that embodied equal conditions for all, most notably through equitable access to healthful housing. For Hilberseimer, this suggested the necessity for equitable distribution of land as well as access to sunlight throughout the year. By correlating social equity to arable land and access to sunlight, Hilberseimer proposed a proto-ecological urbanism.

8 Lambert, *In the Shadow of Mies*, symposium.

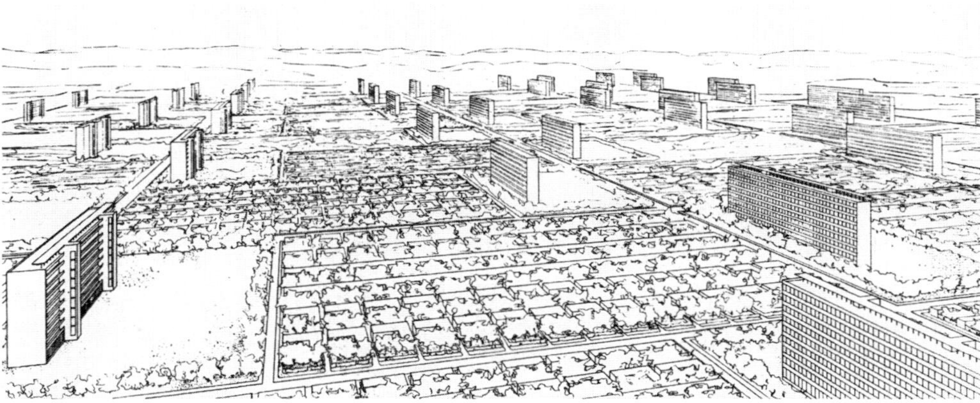

Ludwig Hilberseimer, aerial view of mixed-height housing (*Mischbebauung*), 1930.

Ludwig Hilberseimer, planner, with Alfred Caldwell delineator, aerial perspective, Settlement Unit with commercial area, circa 1942.

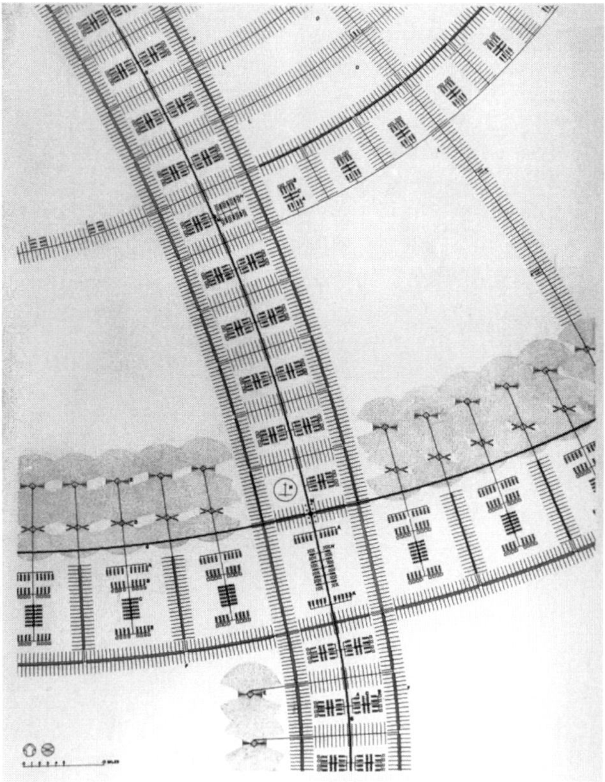

Ludwig Hilberseimer, New Regional Pattern, Final Planning System, circa 1945.

of Hiroshima, he adapted his proposals to anticipate the construction of the interstate highway system as a civil defense infrastructure and an extension of Fordist production logics. Hilberseimer was conversant with Wright's Broadacre City, as well as the progressive Tennessee Valley Authority project of regional electrification and landscape improvements. In this context, Hilberseimer developed his "New City" planning proposal for the urbanization of a low-density North American settlement pattern based on a contemporary understanding of regional infrastructure and environment.

## Regional Patterns

Between 1944 and 1955, Hilberseimer authored three major English-language books on his theories and planning methods. While the three books overlap and share fundamental material with each other, they each advance Hilberseimer's arguments in consequential and distinct ways. The first of these, *The New City: Principles of Planning* (1944) introduced his commitment to an Augustinian sense of order, as an organic relation of equal and unequal parts, each in their own relation to the whole. In this regard, Hilberseimer and Mies shared an interest in architecture and planning as embodiments of culture, rather than mechanisms of reform. Mies contributed the introduction to *The New City* and described Hilberseimer's city planning as a work of order:

> Reason is the first principle of all human work. Consciously or unconsciously Hilberseimer follows this principle and makes it the basis for his work … City planning is, in essence, a work of order.—[9]

9 Ludwig Mies van der Rohe, "Introduction," in Ludwig Hilberseimer, *The New City: Principles of Planning* (Chicago: Paul Theobald, 1944), xv.

*The New City* incorporates much of the analytical and methodological underpinnings for *The New Regional Pattern: Industries and Gardens, Workshops and Farms* (1949). Hilberseimer's planning proposals in his following book were organized around the distribution of transportation and communication networks across an essentially horizontal field of landscape. Within this extensive horizontal territory, housing, farms, light industry, commercial buildings, and civic spaces formed variously scaled networks across a field of decentralized distribution. *The New Regional Pattern's* organizational structure did not defer to the abstraction of the grid, but was informed by the natural environment: topography, hydrology, vegetation, wind patterns, and the like. It conflated infrastructural systems with built landscapes and found environmental conditions to produce a radically reconceived settlement pattern for the North American continent.

Hilberseimer's proposals for an organic American urbanism centered on a radical reconceptualization of the agrarian in relationship to the urban. Central to such a concept of "structural change" for the American city was the role of the region as understood through an ecological lens. Hilberseimer's *The New Regional Pattern* was conceived in response to the English garden city movement and the work of Ebenezer Howard. In contrast to the persistent radial centrality of Howard's diagrams with a dense interior core and sparse exterior hinterlands, Hilberseimer's mature work in the US moved quickly to explore notions of decentralization, abandoning concepts of center and periphery almost entirely. At this time, his projects began to deploy a horizontal field of agrarian industrial decentralization that invoked the French and Soviet desurbanist traditions, in which the sites of industrial labor were diffused into the agricultural territory. *The New Regional Pattern* also referenced Frank Lloyd Wright's Broadacre City project and Petr Kropotkin's conflation of the fields and factories.—[10] In so doing, it proposed the commingling of the agrarian and the urban as the fundaments of an ecological approach to urban order.

10 The subtitle to Hilberseimer's *The New Regional Pattern: Industries and Gardens, Workshops and Farms* makes explicit reference to Petr Kropotkin's 1898 disurbanist manifesto, *Fields, Factories, and Workshops.*

Many twentieth-century urban planning projects explicitly aspired to construct an agrarian urbanism. These agrarian aspirations were often an attempt to reconcile the seemingly contradictory impulses of the industrial metropolis with the social and cultural conditions of agrarian settlement. In many of these projects, agrarianism came to stand as an alternative to the dense metropolitan form of industrial arrangement that grew from the great migrations from farm villages to industrial cities in the nineteenth- and early twentieth-century cities of Western Europe and North America. In the first instance, the agrarian aspirations of many modernist urban planning proposals lay in the relatively decentralized model of industrial order favored by Henry Ford and other industrialists as early as the nineteen-tens and twenties.—11

11 Henry Ford with Samuel Crowther, *My Life and Work* (New York: Doubleday, Page, and Co., 1922).

While the long-standing tradition of regionally informed planning practice from Patrick Geddes through Ian McHarg certainly points to this potential, Hilberseimer's *The New Regional Pattern* diverges from that lineage in affording priority to a complex cultural conflation of civil engineering and ecological artifact. His organic conception of urban order rendered basic distinctions between city and countryside irrelevant, in favor of a non-hierarchical horizontal field shaped by the contextual referents of industrial economy and regional ecology. In this regard, Hilberseimer's work goes well beyond the canonical works of progressive regional planning. In lieu of traditional conceptions of central city and peripheral hinterlands, *The New Regional Pattern* abandons the historical opposition between city (read culture) and landscape (read nature), in favor of a mature Fordist order of industrial economy distributed across the North American continent. In this regard, the pattern's scale (the continent) and contextual referents (industrial economy and regional ecology) exceed the scale and contexts associated with the tradition of landscape planning. While

Hilberseimer shared much by way of social critique and political commitment with aspects of that tradition, his work moved well beyond its reliance upon that tradition's uncritical inheritance of the transcendentalist and organicist traditions.

In response to the social conditions of the Depression era, Hilberseimer's ecological agrarianism came to be seen as a form of continuity between formerly rural populations based on subsistence farming and the relatively vulnerable industrial workforce of the modern metropolis. By mixing industry with agriculture, he imagined a rotational labor system in which workers alternated between factory jobs and collective farms. Most often these new territorial spatial orders were understood as vast regional landscapes. In this regard, Hilberseimer appropriated aspects of the anarchic strain of US agrarianism evidenced in Wright's Broadacre City, while distancing himself from the intellectual tradition that Wright embodied. In this regard, his concepts offer a clear contrast to—and implicit critique of—much of the inheritance of American landscape architecture and planning, and its reliance upon a metaphysics of nature outside of and beyond human agency. In contrast to the American landscape tradition from Downing and Olmsted through Wright and beyond, Hilberseimer's conception of landscape dispensed with notions of nature outside of human construction, in favor of an explicit social agenda to insulate populations from the worst impacts of advanced Fordist decentralization. He conceives of a modern American landscape without notions of center or place, in which industrial economy and regional ecology provide context and meaning. Ironically, Hilberseimer's intellectual commitments represent a clear contrast to the transcendentalist tendencies of Alfred Caldwell—the collaborator who realized his most important drawings and the landscape planting of his only built work. Trained as an architect, Caldwell had apprenticed with the Danish-American, Midwestern landscape architect Jens Jensen, who had himself collaborated with

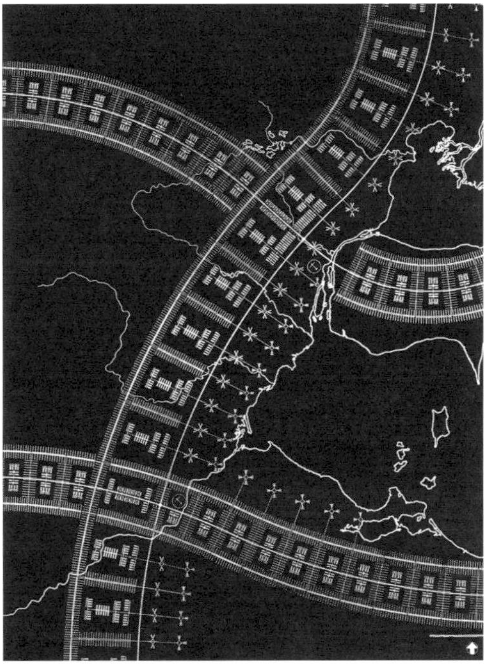

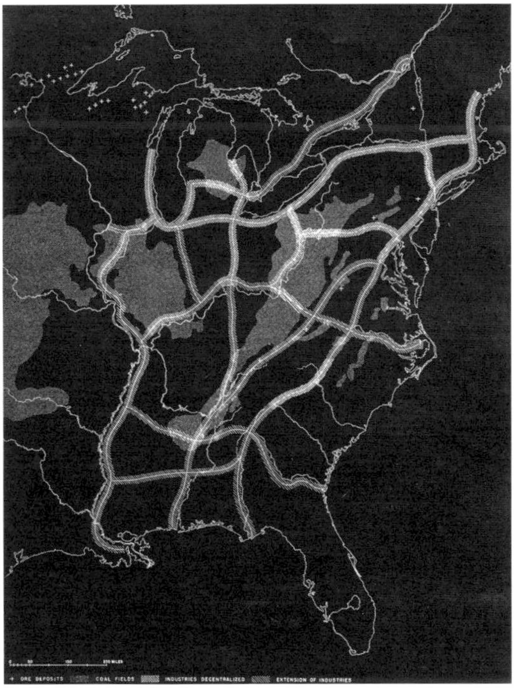


Ludwig Hilberseimer, Urban Planning System (variation) and planning diagram, from *The New Regional Pattern*.

Gratiot Redevelopment (Lafayette Park), Detroit, site razed, aerial photograph and site model, 1955.

Frank Lloyd Wright. From Jensen and Wright, Caldwell inherited a commitment to Prairie style landscape design, as well as a devout antiurban bias associated with US transcendentalist and naturalist traditions. In this regard, Hilberseimer and Caldwell approached their collaboration from distinctly contrasting intellectual traditions.—12

12 For more on the intellectual contrasts between Hilberseimer and Caldwell, see Caroline Constant, "Hilberseimer and Caldwell: Merging Ideologies in the Lafayette Park Landscape," in Waldheim, *Case Lafayette Park Detroit*, 95–111.

## Structural Change

In *The New Regional Pattern*, Hilberseimer proposed the restructuring of Detroit as necessitated by contemporary industrial economy. He argued that in Detroit "[t]he structure of the city is wrong … Only a structural change of the city could bring about the necessary order."—13 Just six years after publishing this impassioned argument for structural change, he was commissioned to plan the urban "renewal" of one of the city's deteriorating downtown neighborhoods. At the beginning of a half-century of urban exodus from the city of Detroit, Hilberseimer's plan applied the theoretical principles he had developed in the first half of the century. It fundamentally reconceived the urban pattern for this portion of the "motor city," and provided the urban diagram orchestrating the contributions of a uniquely talented interdisciplinary design team assembled for the project. Hilberseimer and his collaborators produced a continuously viable and still vibrant community of publicly subsidized housing in the midst of Detroit's ongoing deterioration.

13 Hilberseimer, *The New Regional Pattern*, 174.

As conceived by Chicago developer Herbert Greenwald in association with Samuel Katzin, the Lafayette Park project was developed as a mixed-income and ethnically diverse development. Greenwald enlisted the services of architect Ludwig Mies van der Rohe for the design of the project, with whom he had previously worked on the development of the 860–880 Lake Shore Drive Apartments in Chicago. Mies invited Hilberseimer to plan the site, and Alfred Caldwell to execute the landscape design.

Hilberseimer's plans for the site proposed landscape as its primary material element, and the commission offered both sufficient acreage and budget for what could have otherwise been an uninspired urban void. Central to this was Greenwald's finance and marketing scheme, which positioned landscape as the central amenity in the form of a seventeen-acre park bisecting the site and providing a much sought-after social and environmental amenity in the midst of Detroit. Hilberseimer's plan for Lafayette Park removed the vestiges of the obsolete nineteenth-century street grid, in favor of a verdant landscape interspersed with mixed-height housing. The landscape planting formed the primary framework for the development of the site at the scale of both planning and the individual residences—an architectural ensemble of townhouses, courthouses, and apartment slabs.

Hilberseimer found in Herbert Greenwald a developer client equally committed to making "structural change" in the city. While the overwhelming majority of federally funded urban renewal projects tended toward single race, single class concentrations, Greenwald argued for a diverse future, through a mix of class and tenancy. Both imagined a new spatial structure, built upon landscape, would enable such a radical social transformation. In this regard, both imagined the project would become a national model. At Lafayette Park, Hilberseimer's plan produced one of the most successful and enduring examples of publicly subsidized social housing, through a radical reconsideration of both spatial and social structure for the American city.

## Modern Myths

In spite of their progressive social and ecological aspirations, and the success of his single built project, Hilberseimer's planning projects were largely ignored and later discredited as evidence of the "failures of modernist

Presentation of Gratiot Redevelopment (Lafayette Park), Detroit, 1955.

planning." By the late nineteen-sixties, Hilberseimer's longtime collaborator Mies van der Rohe lamented the relative lack of recognition for Hilberseimer's work, in the context of increasing attention to energy conservation, solar orientation, and environmental topics. "Maybe the importance of his work will finally come out. The present concern about energy conservation, solar orientation … etc. were long-time [*sic*] common issues in Hilbs's work."—14

14 Ludwig Mies van der Rohe as quoted by George Danforth, "Hilberseimer Remembered," in Lambert, *In the Shadow of Mies*, symposium, 13.

Hilberseimer's projects for an ecologically informed organic urbanism in the US have been read by many as respectively prefiguring or collaborating with the postwar project of suburbanization. This was to mistake effect for cause in the causal relations between industrial economy, spatial fix, and urban project. In this misreading, postmodern critics of modernist planning attacked Hilberseimer's proposals for a landscape-based urban pattern as ultimately antiurban, often labeling any landscape-based urban proposal as insufficiently committed to the reconstruction of the nineteenth-century structure of street wall and block structure. Among these critics, George Baird has been one of the most eloquent and effective. Baird's seminal *The Space of Appearance* (2003) includes a chapter on this subject entitled "Organicist Yearnings and their Consequences." While not mentioning Hilberseimer directly, Baird argues that the organicist strain of urban through exhibits a "mistrust of any extant form of the public realm."—15 Baird claims this organicist tradition to be ultimately antiurban, a bias that he argues can be traced in many respects to the longstanding lineage of regional progressive planning from the Scottish planner Patrick Geddes to Geddes's influence on Lewis Mumford, and perhaps as late as Ian McHarg's 1969 *Design with Nature.*

15 George Baird, "Organicist Yearnings and Their Consequences," in *The Space of Appearance* (Cambridge: MIT Press, 2003), 193–238.

The most enduring narrative critique of Hilberseimer's plans would come from Charles Jencks. In an article immodestly titled "The Problem of Mies," published in May 1966 in the *Architectural Associate Journal*, Jencks—who was then a graduate student—begins what would be a two-decade attack on Mies and Hilberseimer. He uses Hilberseimer's Lafayette Park as an exemplary case where "the purity of form leads to an inarticulate architecture, or one extraneous element, a bathroom vent, leads to monumental bathos."—[16] A decade later in a series of issues of *Architectural Design*, Jencks would launch a headlong assault on the perceived failures of modern architecture and urbanism, with Hilberseimer the surrogate for attacks against Mies. Infamously, Jencks ultimately declared the "death of modern architecture," on April 22, 1972 with the televised demolition of the Pruitt-Igoe public housing project in St. Louis.—[17] The most common claim in Jencks's line of attack was the notion that Hilberseimer had fallen "out of fashion." In his 1977 essay on the work of Rem Koolhaas, Jencks's collaborator George Baird referred to Hilberseimer as the "least fashionable modern architect."—[18] By the early nineteen-eighties, Joseph Rykwert concluded that Hilberseimer's success was astonishing, given the obvious lack of merit in the work. Further, Rykwert argued that his plans were worse than anything that modernist planning had wrought.—[19] By this time, his planning projects had been relegated to a subject of ridicule on both sides of the Atlantic. This was largely accomplished by ignoring the merits of Hilberseimer's ecological planning and returning to his *Groszstadtarchitektur* of the nineteen-twenties. In 1989—in the context of a review of the Art Institute of Chicago's Hilberseimer symposium, *In the Shadow of Mies*—Peter Blundell Jones reiterated the by then commonly held position that he was hopelessly out of fashion.—[20]

16 Charles Jencks, "The Problem of Mies," *Architectural Association Journal* (May 1966): 301–04.

17 Charles Jencks, *The Language of Post-Modern Architecture* (New York: Rizzoli, 1977). The televised event on April 22, 1972 was actually the second in a series of demolitions that began in March and ended in June of that year. For a historically informed rebuttal of Jencks, see Katharine G. Bristol, "The Pruitt-Igoe Myth," *Journal of Architectural Education* 44, no. 3 (May 1991): 163–71.

18 George Baird, "Les Extremes Qui se Touchant?" *Architectural Design*, 47 no. 5 (1977): 326–27.

19 Joseph Rykwert, "A Balance-Sheet of the City," *Diogenes* 31, no. 121 (1983).

20 Peter Blundell Jones, "City Father," book review of David Spaeth and Kevin Harrington, *In the Shadow of Mies: Ludwig Hilberseimer: architect, educator and urban planner*, *Architect's Journal* 190, no. 7 (August 1989): 75.

In stark contrast to the critical reception of Ludwig Hilberseimer's work by proponents of postmodernism, for contemporary readings of ecological urbanism his work offers a number of significant insights. The first of these is the notion of program or plan as a social agenda, as evidenced in quite distinct political points of view. Hilberseimer's project was conceived as a critical response, at least in part, to the social pathologies, economic injustices, and unhealthful conditions of the traditional industrial city. He advocated for limits on the physical scale of industry, agriculture, and housing, arguing in favor of meaningful proximate relationships between work, family, food, and civic life. The project proposed remedies to the social inequities and ill health of pure capitalist development, especially in the form of limits on private ownership, accumulation, and speculation.

His mature planning proposals embody a decentralized urban order as the organic condition of North American settlement patterns. They located an organic urbanism in the conditions of modern industrial economy itself as the basis for a truly ecological urbanism. This work stretches the traditional bounds of the landscape medium understood as a decorative art or environmental science. No small part of that relevance is landscape's promise to work across scales, rendering meaningful relationships between the larger regional environment and local social conditions. This potential is evident in Hilberseimer's use of variously scaled courts, yards, and gardens to relate domestic life to the larger public parklands that connect them. In his Settlement Unit, kitchen gardens give way to small-scale cooperative farms and their markets, in the formation of a public landscape primarily formed by agricultural uses at a variety of scales. The cumulative effect of these strategies for contemporary interest in an ecological urbanism is to inflect the local conditions of individual dwelling and the broader civic realm of public infrastructure, toward a more mature and robustly realized set of relationships with their ecological contexts.

## Plural Ecologies

Ecology has emerged as one of the most important epistemological frameworks of our age.—[21] This assertion coincides with the understanding that ecology has transcended its origins as a natural science to encompass a

21 This claim has been made most recently by Christopher Hight. See Hight, "Designing Ecologies," in *Projective Ecologies*, ed. Chris Reed and Nina-Marie Lister (Harvard GSD/Actar, 2014), 84–105.

range of meanings across the natural and social sciences, history and the humanities, design, and the arts. It has developed from a proto-disciplinary branch of biology in the nineteenth century, into a modern science in the twentieth century, and increasingly toward a multidisciplinary intellectual framework in the first decades of the twenty-first century. This disciplinary promiscuity is not without its challenges—intellectually and practically. The slippage of ecology from natural science to cultural lens remains a source of confusion within and across the design disciplines. We might also postulate that the effects of urbanization are effectively planetary in scope.—[22] If so, what are the implications for thinking about the relation between ecology and urbanization?

22 Henri Lefebvre, *The Urban Revolution*, trans. Robert Bononno (Minneapolis: University of Minnesota Press, 2003).

The theoretical frameworks, analytical tools, and projective practices of the urban arts have been developed on a presumed distinction between the urban and the ecological. For much of their history, the urban and the ecological have been conceived and constructed to occlude each other. The origins of urbanism in architectural culture and a preoccupation with the architectonic form of the city have contributed to this condition. Equally, the classical definition of ecology as the description of species in relation to their environments, absent human agency, is equally problematic. Taken together, the cumulative effect of describing ecology as outside the city and the urban as external to ecology continues to have a profound impact on thinking across the urban arts.

Contemporary readings of ecology offer at least three distinct potentials for the design disciplines.—[23] These begin with the enduring understanding of ecology as offering a models to predict and account for the natural world. Contemporary accounts of ecology in design invoke a point of tangency between the production of scientific models through testing and falsification and the symmetrical activity of design through making and matching. While the historical split between the habits of mind and methods in the sciences and design persists, contemporary

23 See for example, Chris Reed and Nina-Marie Lister, “Introduction,” and “Parallel Genealogies,” in Reed, *Projective Ecologies*, 14, 22.

readings propose a plausible relation between ecology as a model of the world and the agency of design in the shaping of that world. In addition to its status as model, ecology has come to be an equally effective metaphor for a range of intellectual and disciplinary pursuits. Ecology has been found relevant as an epistemological framework operating at the level of a metaphor in the social or human sciences, the humanities, history, philosophy, and the arts. References to this potential are evident in the work of Gregory Bateson, Giorgio Agamben, and Félix Guattari, to name but a few. These authors illustrate the fecundity of ecological thinking across a range of fields.

The metaphorical understanding of ecology has been particularly significant for its subsequent absorption into the discourse and practices of the design disciplines. Among the challenges of this translation is the differential reading of ecology across the disparate disciplinary and professional concerns of architecture, landscape architecture, and urban planning. While landscape architecture and urban planning have historically tended to view ecology as a kind of applied natural science, architecture and design culture have received ecology as a metaphor imported from the social sciences, humanities, and philosophy. More recently, a third reading of ecology as a medium of thought, representation, and projection has been proposed to reconcile this opposition. The prospect of "projective" ecologies has recently been articulated as one theme under the more general theoretical project of an "ecological urbanism."

The emergent discourse of "ecological urbanism" has been proposed to more precisely describe the aspirations of an urban practice informed by environmental issues and imbued with the sensibilities associated with landscape. This most recent adjectival modifier of urbanism reveals the ongoing need to requalify urban design as it attempts to describe the environmental, economic, and social conditions of the contemporary city. In his introduction to the Ecological Urbanism conference, Mohsen Mostafavi described the topic as both a critique and a continuation of other terms of the discourse of landscape urbanism.—24 Ecological urbanism proposes multiplying the available lines of thought on the contemporary city to include environmental and ecological concepts, while expanding traditional disciplinary and professional frameworks for describing those urban conditions. Mostafavi suggested that ecological urbanism "implied the projective potential of the design disciplines to render alternative future scenarios."—25

24 Mohsen Mostafavi, "Introduction," Ecological Urbanism Conference, Harvard University Graduate School of Design, April 3, 2009.

25 Ibid.

One productive way to pursue projective potentials of an ecological urbanism would be to construct useful histories of the relationship between ecology and urbanism specific to the design disciplines. Among the models of twentieth-century modernist planners, none offer a more critical alternative vision of the city in relation to ecology than Hilberseimer, who provides a unique case study in the critical and social potentials of an ecologically informed planning project for the contemporary city. His radical planning concepts presented their audiences with a profound reconceptualization of the city, by proposing radical decentralization and dissolution of the urban figure into the landscape. This rendered the classical distinction between city and countryside irrelevant, in favor of a conflated condition of suburbanized regionalism. From the perspective of contemporary interest in an ecological urbanism, his projects show compelling alternatives to the canonical history of urban landscape, from progressive garden city models to the tradition of urban parks as exceptions to the industrial city. Through this work, he reconceptualized the fundamental distinctions between city and countryside, village, and farmland; urbanism and landscape are dissolved in favor of a third term, an ecological urbanism for the mature North American industrial economy. In so doing, he offers a useful historical case study for contemporary interests in the social, environmental, and cultural potentials for ecologically informed urban practice.

# Álvaro Siza: Nature and Architecture as a Living Body

Dedicated to the memory of Bernardo Secchi.

Pierre-Alain Croset

*Nothing has changed as far as the essence of Architecture is concerned. No tree felled to build—or stone wrested from the mountain—will be restored. No yellowed photograph restores past beauty. All that remains is to attempt—to continue—the construction of Beauty. Natural or constructed, we transform everything with excessive haste, excessive ambition or indifference. The freedom attained, unlimitedly necessary, can also destroy.*—1

1 Álvaro Siza, *Scritti di architettura*, ed. Antonio Angelillo (Milan: Skira Editore, 1997), 70.

More than any other contemporary architect, Álvaro Siza embodies the ideal of an architect who listens prior to speaking, who observes prior to designing, who interprets places, programs, and desires of inhabitants prior to building. He operates far away from the modernist paradigm of the breakthrough, the leap forward; rather than a cult of the New, he cultivates the art of *transformation* and critical dialogue with the context. Nature, for Siza, is not a static concept, not Other-than-Architecture; nature is mutable and dynamic, and like architecture it is a *living body*. What is decisive for architecture is the relation between nature and construction—a *relation* that is the "permanent source of any project," which Siza perceives "as an obsession."—2

2 Álvaro Siza, *Immaginare l'evidenza*, ed. Guido Giangregorio (Bari: Laterza, 1998), 5.

Depending on the context, he intervenes in two opposing ways. The first might be illustrated in an exemplary way by the project for the access to the Casino of Salzburg (1986), where the new construction—a tower-elevator shaft that

Sketch for the Pavilion of Anyang, South Korea, 2005–2006.

Sketch for the Casino of Salzburg, 1986.

makes the connection between the historic center and the hill visible—forms a clear contrast with the natural profile of the rock. This contrast seems necessary to gauge and thus enhance the specific topographical condition. The second way, aptly illustrated by the small multifunctional Pavilion of Anyang (South Korea, 2005–2006), has to do with intervention in the open landscape: in this case, the impulse to obtain a form springs from the inside, from the specific needs of the architectural organism, though the building does not withdraw into itself, but branches out to create a meaningful relationship with the natural context. Actually, Siza often mixes these two modes of intervention, because his design action is based on the conviction that places are *the work of time*, in keeping with the stimulating hypothesis of interpretation made by Francesco Dal Co: "Natural stratifications reveal that work with the same clarity with which cities offer, to those who know how to see it … the extraordinary wealth of their constituent sedimentation, making constructed environments like coral reefs, offered to view by the waves of the sea and of time."—3

3 Francesco Dal Co, "Prefazione. Álvaro Siza e l'arte della mescolanza," in *Álvaro Siza. Tutte le opere*, by Kenneth Frampton (Milan: Electa, 1999), 10.

To understand Álvaro Siza's extraordinary landscape sensibility, we can walk down the approximately two kilometers of Atlantic coast connecting the port of Matosinhos to the chapel of Boa Nova—a promenade Siza himself recently redesigned (2002–07)—with his first two important works at its two extremities: to the north, the Boa Nova Tea House and Restaurant (1958–63), and to the south the Tidal Swimming Pools of Leça de Palmeira (1961–66).

Almost fifty years separate the first project from the recent reorganization of Avenida da Liberdade—a very long time span that underlines Siza's profound relationship with a place he began to love with a passion during his childhood in Matosinhos. Siza recalls the first drawing lessons in the studio of Isolino Vaz, in the summer of 1949: "At the end of the second week, Isolino Vaz took us to the Leça beach. There was no talk of drawing. We played football and ran against the wind until we were almost out of breath. Lying on the sand, we stared with amazement at the constant, rhythmical passes of a tireless teacher, until the sky and the sea were stained with purple."—[4]

When Siza began to work, this place was almost empty: a pure presence of rocks, sand and sea, a place of extraordinary beauty that "instilled fear in the fledgling architect."—[5] We know that the choice of the precise position of the Boa Nova Tea House amidst the rocks was made by Fernando Távora,—[6] and that later—while Távora was out of the studio—Siza, on his own, developed the project that won the competition held for its construction. In a handsome photograph conserved in the Távora archives,—[7] we see a group of architects and administrators making a visit to the Boa Nova site: behind Távora, a very young Siza bends slightly forward, observing the scene with a worried look.

Since the very first press coverage,—[8] critics have unanimously praised the exceptional qualities of this first

4 Siza, *Scritti di architettura*, 20.

5 Siza, *Immaginare l'evidenza*, 11.

6 Giovanni Leoni, "Costruzione, esperienza, linguaggi. L'architettura di Álvaro Siza," in id., *Álvaro Siza*, (Rome: La Biblioteca di Repubblica—L'Espresso, 2010), 34.

7 Fundação Instituto Arquitecto José Marques da Silva, University of Porto, Document FIMS_FT_Foto4052, published in *Fernando Távora Modernidade Permanente*, ed. José António Bandeirinha (Matosinhos: Associação Casa da Arquitectura, 2012), 196.

8 N. Portas and V. Rosa, "Álvaro Siza Vieira, Casa de Chá da Boa Nova," *Arquitectura* 88 (1965).

Boa Nova Tea House and Restaurant, 1958–63.

Tidal Swimming Pools of Leça de Palmeira, 1961–66.

work by Siza. The path of approach is already memorable. At the foot of the mass of rocks topped by the building, a white wall borders the parking area and accompanies visitors to the access staircase. Like an ascent to a tiny acropolis, the path zigzags its way up, constantly varying the viewpoints on the landscape. At the bottom of the first ramp, the volume of the nine stone steps conceals the sea from view: the horizon reappears only when you are halfway up. From this first podium, you turn right to approach the building on a second flight of steps, followed by another change of direction to reach the entrance. The promenade continues inside, and it is only at this point that you realize the entrance is located on the upper level, meaning that you have to descend along the natural slope of the rocks to reach the tea room on the left, and the restaurant dining room on the right. From inside, the discovery of the seascape is astonishing: the foreground rocks frame the distant view, and the sound of the waves makes a forceful contribution to the atmosphere of the place.

In the form and the materials, everything contributes to create a vivid sense of the architecture's belonging to the place: the exposed concrete walls have a color that makes them seem to have grown out of the ground, while the large, slightly sloped roofs echo the natural gradient of the site. The experience of the architecture-nature relationship is conveyed by the correlation of just three elements: the

Tidal Swimming Pools of Leça de Palmeira, 1961–66.

jagged profile of the rocks, the horizon line, and the artificial profile of the roofs.

The project for the Leça Swimming Pools makes this essential nature-architecture relationship even more radical, completely eliminating the lively profile of the roofing. Siza focuses on the presence of a precise *limit* in this place, when he narrates the origin of the design: "A wall, the support of the urban zone, contains the beach, the rocks and the ocean, with all that force the Atlantic possesses. Nature is almost entirely undisturbed, thanks to the existence of a zone of protection, for military purposes, that prevents construction throughout that area."—[9] The place, "a site where the rocks close off a small lake," had already been chosen by Fernando Távora's brother,—[10] the engineer Bernardo Ferrão, who due to the great impact of the project on the landscape decided to call in an architect, and therefore contacted Siza. Whereas the engineer had already begun to design a swimming pool enclosed by four walls, Siza decided to "optimize the conditions created by nature, which had already started the design of a swimming pool here. What was needed was to take advantage of those same rocks, completing the enclosure of the water only with those walls that were strictly necessary. This generated a very close link between what is natural and what is constructed."—[11]

9 Siza, *Immaginare l'evidenza*, 11.

10 For a complete reconstruction of the design and building process, see Christian Gänshirt, *Álvaro Siza, Swimming pool on the beach at Leça de Palmeira* (Lisbon: Editorial Blau, 2004).

11 Siza, *Immaginare l'evidenza*, 13.

Thus Siza completes the work of nature—the age-old labor of erosion of the rocks caused by the tides and the waves—using the specific tools of architecture: big horizontal lines and flat surfaces, vertical walls in exposed concrete, with a color resembling that of the rocks, and horizontal surfaces of water. With respect to the Boa Nova Restaurant, Siza himself clarifies the need for a purification of the architectural language: "I considered that this solution [for the Boa Nova Restaurant and Tea House] was too direct a translation of the accidents of the landscape. The profile of the restaurant is almost a direct parallel to the profile of the rocks. After I finished, I found it much too dependent on the existing landscape."—12

12 Álvaro Siza, "Interview," in *GA Document Extra*, 11 (Tokyo: A.D.A. Edita Tokyo Ltd. Co., 1998), 20.

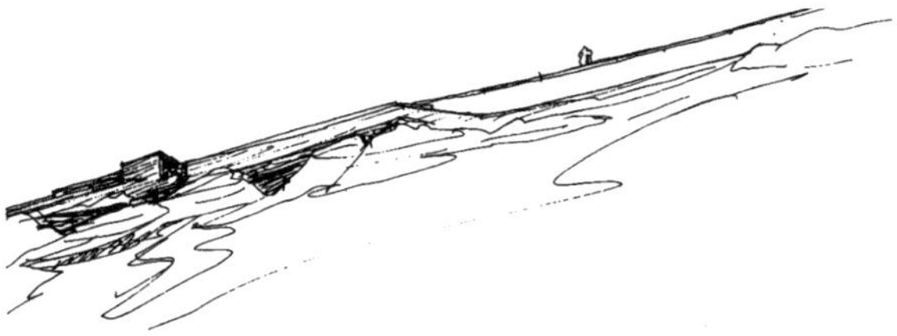

A very beautiful sketch provides an apt illustration of this necessary essentiality: in a view from the sea, it shows the horizontal line of the embankment wall of the street as the background, while in the foreground the profile of the rocks establishes a dialogue with other horizontal lines that reveal the presence of the new walls containing the pools of water. This sketch helps us to understand that the line of the street should be interpreted as an artificial horizon, and that the project has been conceived by Siza as a work of delicate completion of the natural site bordered by these two existing horizon lines: the line of the ocean and the line of the wall.

Siza would have liked the essential character of this place contained between these two horizons to be maintained over time, conserving the character of the whole zone as a *non-constructed border*. This was the drift of the coordination plan he had already developed in 1974, but which was unfortunately never approved, thus causing the subdivision of the place by speculators. Today, the view of the wall from the beach is no longer that of the artificial horizon so eloquently represented in Siza's sketch, but of a simple line above which brutal residential hulks stand out. Nevertheless, one of the primary qualities of Siza's intervention remains—that of having concealed from view the dressing rooms and service spaces, absorbed by the parallel volumes built in front of the existing wall. The result is a system of masonry screens that organizes the route as a gradual discovery of the landscape through a sequence of thresholds between the public space of the promenade and the internal space of the pool facility.—[13]

## 2. Topography: Nature and City

Regarding the Boa Nova Restaurant, Siza has acknowledged the evident influence of Alvar Aalto, citing in particular, "Maison Carré, with its undulated wooden roofs and white stucco."—[14] The profound affinity between Siza and Aalto, nevertheless, goes well beyond mere stylistic aspects, and has to do first of all with their shared, exceptional *topographical sensibility*. Speaking of Aalto, Siza has pointed to deep affinities in the ways of designing "what strikes him most,"—[15] using knowledge of places and works of architecture as the "seed of the transformation."—[16] This aptitude for transfiguring references, shared by Siza and Aalto, becomes explicit in the following passage: "I mean to say that by taming the models experienced (the model is universal), [Aalto] transforms them, deforms and hybridizes them, setting them down inside different realities, and making surprising, enlightening use of them; foreign objects that rest on the ground and immediately put down roots."—[17] To "put down roots" is clearly what Siza's first works of architecture do; so strong is the sense one gets of rooting to the place when one visits the Boa Nova Restaurant and the Leça de Palmeira swimming facility. However, it is not only in the case of "natural" sites that Siza pursues this sense of rootedness. He also intervenes with the same spirit in urban sites, for which he again evokes the question of

13 Christian Gänshirt has described the quality of this experience of the path in precise terms: "From the coastal road, little can be seen of the swimming pool-grey concrete … A few meters below is a landscape of rocks and sand. The view from above encompasses the Atlantic Ocean, two swimming pools, stairs, and concrete walls … Along the retaining wall, a ramp sinks down into the earth … The dressing rooms: suddenly it is cool and dark … From the dressing rooms, the path leads into a long courtyard enclosed by weathered concrete walls … A tall gateway, twice as high as the building, points the way. The space widens; you step down, and a view of the sea, the horizon, opens up to the right … Street and cars have disappeared; you have become part of a scene viewed from above only shortly before. No paths are visible in this miniature landscape of rock formations and sand plateaux, but small, geometric constructions point the way through the craggy terrain … Steps lead downward, a small landing turns toward the horizon, then three more steps. The water in the white basin sparkles almost as green as the sea." Gänshirt, *Álvaro Siza*, 5–9.

14 Siza, *Immaginare l'evidenza*, 22.

15 Siza, *Scritti di architettura*, 102.

16 Ibid.

17 Ibid.

roots: “In one way or another, all cities are my city. The charm of every city—always different—irresistibly obliges us to adopt it, or to be adopted by it … The essence of every city springs from a very ancient, almost inexplicable alchemy, beyond Geography and recorded History, and the weight of its own materials … The weight of the roots arises again, therefore, in the same way, wherever we find ourselves working; the present possibility of being called upon to make great voyages stimulates us through the eyes and the mind … The alternative is that of a universal receptivity capable of reawakening the roots of every city, prolonging them in trunks, branches, leaves, flowers, fruits, in any place.”—[18] In this very significant text, Siza aptly describes the condition of the architect as sensitive *interpreter* of cities, of their local and specific characteristics. To understand the “roots” of a city means making the new architecture able to extend these roots into “branches, leaves, flowers, fruits,” so the architecture can be perceived as an *almost natural* offshoot of the urban site.

18 Álvaro Siza, in *Casabella,* 630–631 (January–February 1996), 108.

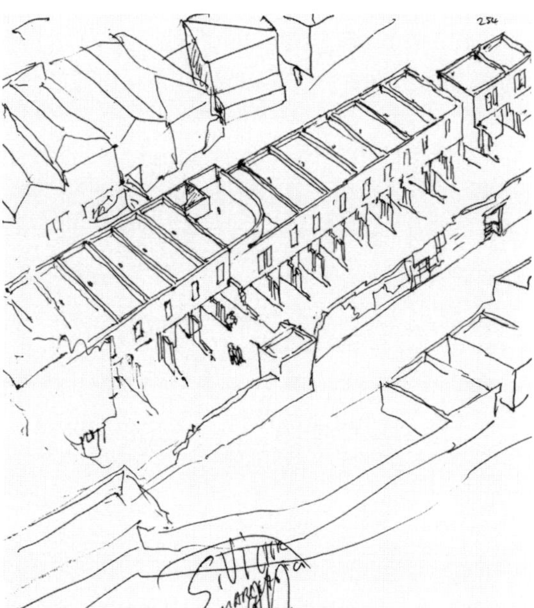

Sketch for the SAAL of São Victor in Porto, 1974–77.

This is precisely Siza's procedure in the project for the SAAL of São Victor in Porto (1974–77). The new architecture, though in forceful contrast with the stylistic characteristics of the vernacular architecture of the center of Porto, is delicately set down on the terrain, absorbing even its smallest irregularities, and above all every physical presence of urban memory: "I have spoken of the moments of patient gathering and grouping of fragments of the city, of traces of the deepest collective heritage, scattered, truncated and yet contained in even the smallest stone. And it will never be possible to bury all the little stones."—[19] So for Siza, it appears decisive to act on the crest between conserving and destroying, to think of architecture as dialogue with the context, interpreted as a "seed of the transformation." As we saw previously regarding Aalto, nature can therefore be interpreted as a metaphor for everything that comes prior to the project's action of modification. Paying attention to the smallest traces—just as he was sensitive to the rocks of Leça de Palmeira—in the São Victor project, Siza decides to conserve the ruins of the old divider walls inside the block. This choice is not just the result of an empirical, non-dogmatic operation that is open, close to the concerns of the inhabitants. Above all, it is also a *poetic* choice: the choice of resorting to a language that is neither abstract nor imitative, but characterized by deft *crossing between the new and the existing*, a language that clearly displays to the observer the fact that the place had previously undergone a process of modification. Unfortunately Siza's "poetics of the hybrid" met with the violent opposition of the municipal services of Porto, leading to the demolition of the ruins of the historic walls, and depriving the works of architecture of their context: all that remains of the original idea are some very intriguing sketches.

19 Siza, *Scritti di architettura*, 167.

The Malagueira area in Évora, after over thirty years of construction, can instead be seen as the successful outcome of a design strategy based on sensitivity, on empathy with places and even their smallest traces, be they "natural"

Malagueira Quarter in Évora, 1977–97.

presences or products of the urbanization process. In the midst of a thousand difficulties, the territory patiently designed by Siza is slowly taking form, revealing a wealth of strata. Recalling the start of the project, Siza does not simply speak of the multiple existing features: the unauthorized settlements of Santa Marta and Nostra Senhora da Glória, an Arabian bath, a cork tree, a cistern, a reservoir, the Quinta da Malagueirinha with its orange groves, a school and two old mills, as well as many other relics of the original agricultural character of the site, and the new seven-story residential buildings. Instead, he also considers the movements of people, who have left signs on the ground of the most convenient paths: "These very clear trails also help us to explain behaviors and topography, and indicate the possibilities of transformations and relations. It immediately seemed clear that the link between the two unauthorized zones was one of the fundamental issues that had to be taken into consideration by the project."—[20] Hence, there is nothing nostalgic, nothing contemplative in Siza's attitude. Nothing could be further from a stance inspired by Ruskin, since here no appeal is made to some romantic "aesthetic of ruins." Siza's position is based on an authentic *critical realism*, on the observation of the life of local populations.

20 Siza, *Immaginare l'evidenza*, 102–03.

It is interesting to talk about Évora as a slow, laborious process, not a traditional "work."—[21] Siza transforms a piece of the periphery—marked by a rural past and urbanized at first through processes that mixed unauthorized construction and planning—into a new city form. A new, low-density city based on the principle of temporal stratification, as in any true city. To talk about the long time span of this process of construction of the territory, Siza uses an apt metaphor: what the architect imagines, "manifests itself and is placed on the undulating ground like a white and heavy sheet, revealing thousands of things no one paid any attention to: emerging rocks, trees, walls and paths, washing troughs and cisterns, furrows created by water, ruined constructions, animal skeletons. Simple ideas are disrupted by all this, by the wrinkles and undulated surfaces. Humble things and houses take on the dimension of a living presence, interrupting the new foundations."—[22]

21 For a complete reconstruction of the design and building process, see Enrico Molteni, *Álvaro Siza. Barrio de la Malagueira*, Évora (Barcelona: Edicions UPC, 1997).

22 Siza, *Scritti di architettura*, 178.

To make use of the "thousand things no one paid any attention to," Siza works not only on the architecture of the buildings, but also and above all on the urban connections and the design of open spaces, created with the landscape architect João Gomes da Silva (1987–91). Starting with in-depth study of local farming techniques and traditions, with a particular focus on irrigation systems (the subject of Gomes da Silva's degree thesis), the main interventions are defined that should evoke the deeply *rural* character of the landscape. As in the Leça swimming pools, Siza again applies an essential language of walls, stairs, and ramps: large horizontal lines in the territory, like the big dam bordering the central pond, that bring out all the topographic irregularities by means of contrast.—[23]

23 L. Biondi, "Progetto per gli spazi pubblici di Malagueira," *Casabella* 597–598 (January–February 1993): 105–07.

This new landscape designed by Siza seems original and singular: neither Arcadian nor modern. It proposes a different way of making a hybrid between different traditions, of conserving traces of the historic rural landscape without avoiding the need to construct a new urban identity.

## 3. The Inaccessible Garden of Eden

The new School of Architecture of Porto (1986–96) offers an outstanding illustration of Siza's great ability to exploit the relationship between architecture and topography. Wilfried Wang sees a pedagogical value in Siza's architecture that stimulates students to discover the importance of the relationship between architecture and nature, and between architecture and the constructed environment: "The Porto 'Acropolis' situates the educational process in a privileged and raised surrounding from which the students and teachers might draw their references in an analogous manner. This in turn prepares them for a process of transformation of the built context, a process that is infused with a responsibility as one views the other side of the river through and across the drawing studios."—24

24 Wilfried Wang, "A Forum for the Architecture," *Casabella* 547 (June 1988): 10.

School of Architecture of Porto, 1986–96.

This reference to an acropolis should not be taken literally, since the site—though in a position overlooking the Douro River—is actually more like a sequence of terraces, harking back to the agricultural use of the slope. Wang associates the figure of the open courtyard with the "picturesque" compositions of Alvar Aalto, influenced by the particular interpretation of the Acropolis of Athens provided by Auguste Choisy. Choisy's text (*Histoire de l'Architecture*, 1899) is famous for having influenced many modern architects—including Le Corbusier, Aalto, Kahn, and Stirling—as well as artists like Richard Serra and

Robert Smithson who have investigated the relationship between the work of art and the experience of the path. Choisy's reading of the Acropolis appears in the chapter entitled "The Picturesque in Greek Art: Asymmetrical Compositions, Ponderation of Masses," in which we read: "The Greeks cannot imagine a building independently of the site and the surrounding buildings. The idea of leveling the surroundings is absolutely foreign to them: barely adjusting it, they accept the terrain as nature made it, and their only concern is to put the architecture into harmony with the landscape; the Greek temples have value as much for the choice of their location as for the art with which they were built."—25

25 Auguste Choisy, *Histoire de l'Architecture*, Tome Premier (Ivry: Éditions SERG, 1976), 325.

Like the Greeks in Choisy's suggestive interpretation, Siza makes minimal interventions, adjusting the existing topography to make it more regular, and arranges the

Galician Center for Contemporary Art in Santiago de Compostela, 1988–93.

buildings in such a way as to create a sequence of open spaces that can be gradually discovered as one penetrates the site. The quality of the experience of the path manifests itself if one stays outside or if one enters the buildings. In both cases, it is possible to verify, with steps, the precision with which Siza arranges ramps, staircases, and passages in relation to the existing and new terraces. From the outside, arriving from the lower end of the site to the west, the path begins with an initial courtyard of nearly domestic size, enhanced by two large trees, prior to the ascent onto the central terrace: the view suddenly widens, thanks to a dilated perspective caused by the divergence between the two sides of the plaza, and one can enjoy the panorama of the river, glimpsed through the openings placed between the small towers of the Ateliers, along with the fine view of the dense mass of trees of the Quinta da Póvoa that concludes the background perspective. The beautiful stone support walls are exploited by Siza to construct a system of ramps and steps that offer access to the Quinta da Póvoa from the corner that hosts the Carlos Ramos Pavilion (1985–86), which contains the first-year ateliers. Venturing into the old garden, one discovers the refined architecture of this small pavilion: an original interpretation of the age-old theme of the courtyard house, bent and shaped to create a meaningful tension with the existing natural and architectural features of the garden.

Serralves Foundation in Porto, 1991–99.

While the presence of the small, precious garden of Quinta da Póvoa was undoubtedly a catalyst for Siza's creative imagination in the design of the Porto School of Architecture, in two other major public works of the same period—the Galician Center for Contemporary Art in Santiago de Compostela (1988–93) and the Serralves Foundation in Porto (1991–99)—other gardens have a profound impact on his design choices. In Santiago, he decides to put the new museum on the edge of the lot, along the street, and to organize it as a compact stone volume to make optimal use of a historic site marked by the forceful monumental presence of the old monastery of Santo Domingo de Bonaval. This choice was also driven by the need to reconstruct the abandoned garden to the rear: Siza explains how the "slow perfecting of the form" was obtained "through the simultaneous work on the garden, which turned out to be a perfect machine for the utilization of nature."—[26] This *utilization* is revealed in the experience of walking through the place, starting at the small triangular plaza created between the new museum and the old monastery, and then zigzagging through a sequence of terraces that very delicately mix old walls and new intervention, conserving the traces and features

26 Siza, *Immaginare l'evidenza*, 63.

unearthed during construction, including an ancient spring and the granite canals of the original irrigation system. Marc Dubois comments on this precious, discreet project by talking about Siza as a *topographer*, who "exploits level shifts to gradually make the walls emerge from the ground, in a solution already applied in his first work, the Boa Nova Restaurant, and in the Leça da Palmeira swimming pools. By building geometric, linear walls, the forms and contours of the terrain are emphasized."—[27]

Thus in the garden at Santiago, Siza prolongs the experience of the *architectural promenade* we find in every

27 M. Dubois, "Álvaro Siza Vieira," in *Dentro la città*, by A. Siza (Milan: Motta Architettura, 1996), 14–15.

museum—as demonstrated by well-known specimens by Le Corbusier, Wright, Mies, or Kahn—but he does so without producing any effect of excessive "museumization": the Bonaval garden is effectively restored to the use of the townspeople and takes on a civic role that transcends its original monastic function. In the Serralves Foundation, on the other hand, the garden from the nineteen-thirties—[28] was already part of the museum itinerary prior to Siza's intervention, in which he therefore attempts to limit the impact of the new contemporary art museum on the site. Though larger than the existing villa that was previously the foundation's headquarters, Siza's museum appears as a harmonious, silent work of architecture, serenely placed in the garden revitalized by a few, precise interventions carried out by the landscape designer João Gomes da Silva, who had already worked with Siza on the design of the park in Évora. The access sequence to the museum is a good illustration of Siza's assertion that, "in the crossing between inside and outside a mediation, a transition always becomes necessary":—[29] a lateral, not central route that crosses smaller and smaller open spaces, leading to the covered lobby that evokes the vestibule of the house from the nineteen-thirties. The first space encountered underlines the intense, privileged relationship with the large garden: those who walk along the solid wall of the access portico are instinctively prompted to turn the gaze and to discover a beautiful lawn, closed at the sides by the white volumes of the small entrance pavilion and the auditorium, which frame the view of the vegetation of the historic garden. It is a threshold space, a place of waiting, from which one decides whether to proceed towards the museum, or to change course in the direction of the garden. A low, stone wall provides a vestige of an earlier enclosure to decisively indicate the role of this space as a threshold. Rather than bordering the new space, this wall makes it possible to perceive the mass of trees of the historic garden as nature *enclosed by the wall*: a clear limit, with a value that is more symbolic than practical, since the Serralves

28 The author of this beautiful garden was the French landscape architect Jacques Gréber.

29 Siza, *Immaginare l'evidenza*, 33.

site is a single complex that combines museum, park, and historic villa.

Siza emphasizes this act of *enclosing* a fragment of nature in many of his projects. This is the case, for example, of another major public work from the same years: the school in Setúbal (1986–92), where the central space, organized like a cloister, encloses two ancient cork oaks. Regarding this splendid space, Kenneth Frampton has spoken of a "solemn gesture" with which Siza isolates the tree to "establish a connection between tree and loggia that reminds us of the way the Erechtheion protects the sacred olive tree planted by Athena on the Acropolis."—30 Hence for Siza, enclosing a fragment of nature, constructing an enclosure, has a symbolic meaning that can sometimes be associated with the memory of an ancient ritual of a sacred character. This is confirmed by a singular sketch he made during the project for the transformation of the J. Paul Getty Museum at Malibu, Santa Monica (with Peter Testa, 1993). Invited to submit proposals to modify the access and the use of the existing villa—a modern reconstruction (1970) of the Villa of the Papyri of Herculaneum—Siza delivers a fine album of sketches, again displaying his obsession with the creation of spaces of transition and mediation between architecture and nature. He titles the most singular sketch "door to inaccessible Garden of Eden." Though it addresses one of the concrete strategies proposed to resolve the relationship between the villa and the park, the sketch takes on particular symbolic value: a double white wall with a square opening at the center, beyond which one can see dense vegetation. Once again, it is the wall that transforms a fragment of nature into a "Garden of Eden": but why is it "inaccessible"? In the foreground, a nude woman—perhaps Eve herself—is shown with amputated legs, curiously enough, like certain ancient Greek or Roman statues; she lingers outside the garden, while beyond the door the trees look like masks, with eyes, noses, and smiling mouths. Apart from the enigmatic, almost

30 Frampton, *Álvaro Siza*, 42.

dream-like atmosphere of the drawing, there can be no doubt regarding the overall meaning of the project, which Siza sums up in the resolve, “to enhance accessibility within the site itself and to build on the present atmosphere of discretion and deference with respect to the landscape … My design proposal crosses conventional boundaries between architecture and landscape by fusing and juxtaposing human movement, intellectual activity, artifacts, topography, plant materials, sunlight, water, and enclosures.”—31

31 Álvaro Siza and Peter Testa, *J. Paul Getty Museum Villa Malibu* (Oporto: Fundaçao Serralves / Edicoes Asa, 2005).

Sketch for the J. Paul Getty Museum at Malibu, 1993.

## 4. Architecture as an Animated Body

Nature appears in two different ways in Siza’s sketches. The first has to do with the traditional relationship between architecture and landscape—expressed for example when the building frames a particular view, or exploits the value of trees or any other “natural” material. The second involves the figures that are often seen in the drawings, not just as inhabitants of the spaces represented, but also at times as living beings freely sketched in the margins of plans, façades or technical drawings: above all women and angels, but also animals, especially horses and cats. These "organic" figures do not contribute directly to the development of the architectural form, as could have happened in the work of Le Corbusier, who mixed—first in his paintings and later in his architecture—abstract forms and forms derived from the study of the objects found in nature (which, not coincidentally, he called *objets à réaction poétique*). Siza, on the other hand, draws "for pleasure, necessity and habit,"—[32] and his interest in the concept of the *organic* in architecture is connected to the conception of Frank Lloyd Wright, regarding "the relationship among all the elements of the construction, so that the whole and the parts mutually generate and influence each other. Syncretism and not formal prerequisites."—[33]

32 Álvaro Siza, *Stadtskizzen / City Sketches / Desenhos urbanos*, ed. Brigitte Fleck (Basel-Berlin-Boston: Birkhäuser 1994), 15.

33 Siza, *Scritti di architettura*, 96.

The animal is not of interest for its form, but for its functioning and its behavior as an *animated body*. In Siza's imaginary, rather than the individual building it is the very act of designing that comes alive, taking on a "life of its own," which Siza himself describes using words as precise as those of a zoologist: "[The project] transforms into a moody, restlessly pacing animal, with a wary gaze. If its transfigurations are not understood, if its desires are fulfilled beyond the essential, it changes into a monster. It becomes ridiculous … If excessively restrained, it cannot breathe and it dies. The project, for the architect, is like the character for the novelist: it constantly gets beyond him. It is necessary not to lose it. The drawing keeps up the chase."—[34] This striking metaphor does a good job of clarifying Siza's method: the analogy with animals "is not figurative, but intimate," as Eduardo Souto de Moura has correctly observed.—[35]

34 Ibid., 51.

35 Eduardo Souto de Moura, "Vocaçao Animal," in Leoni, *Álvaro Siza*, 118.

Nevertheless, in certain situations during the development of the project, specific images of animals come spontaneously to the surface, drawn by an *inner* necessity of the project, not by an a priori intention of form. Siza often explains this process by using the example of the Mário Bahia house at Gondomar (1993), which is located on a terraced lot along the Douro that made a traditional solution for the garage and the entrance impossible. This led to the idea of a platform extended towards the river, supported by a tall pillar used to contain an elevator: "This tower develops by degrees, and the elevator extends like a neck. The patio-house, conveniently placed on the only possible terrace, stretches its legs down to the river, stairs like toes, steps like breaths, windows like eyes."—[36] In one of the first sketches, in the margin Siza writes "*oiseau maladroit*" (clumsy bird), making explicit reference to the animal as the project's guide. This is not a question of form, because it would be hard to glimpse the figure of a bird in the decidedly unconventional shapes of the house. Siza tells us that "this rather crazy idea of a volume suspended in the void, with bridge and elevator" had made the image of the building "something very complicated": so the image of the bird was useful "to tame the growth of the design, which was almost out of control. The animal alights delicately on the ground, with lightness."—[37]

36 Siza, *Scritti di architettura*, 192.

37 Álvaro Siza, interview with the author, September 12, 2014.

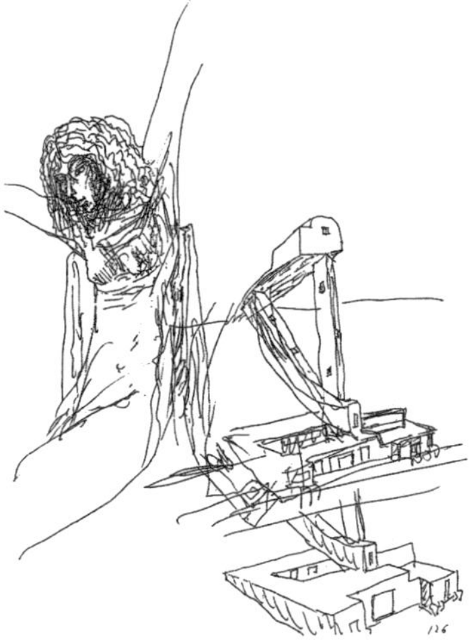

Sketch for the Mário Bahia house at Gondomar, 1993.

Sketches for the corner building of Berlin-Kreuzberg, 1980–84.

The bird image had appeared previously, during the design of the corner building of Berlin-Kreuzberg (Bonjour Tristesse, 1980–84). Though the curved form of the building was an explicit tribute to the Berlin expressionism of Scharoun and Mendelsohn, it is not this form that evokes a bird, but once again a particular *movement of the body* that seems to bring the architecture to life. Observing the triangular terrace that emerges from the curved corner in the sketches, the pillar that supports it seems to rise off the ground: this strange movement suggests that of a large bird, which flees with its wings spread, pushing off the ground with one leg only. Siza explains that the Berlin authorities did not want the triangular terrace to be built, claiming that it would be impossible to make the foundation of the pillar due to the presence of underground conduits: "So I replied that I had no need of this pillar, that I could leave it suspended from the terrace. It is true that when this image emerged, I thought: 'That looks like the leg of an animal!' In any case,

Iberê Camargo Foundation in Porto Alegre, 1998–2008.

I hadn't drawn it to make it seem, a priori, like the leg of an animal, because my real aim was to somewhat cut the smoothness of the curve. I discovered it afterwards!"—38

With precise words, Siza describes what the analysis of the many sketches reveals: the surfacing of animated figures "is a consequence, not a premise" because "it is not a voluntary action."—39 This extremely free way of working, open to the almost unconscious surfacing of figures, reminds us of the mental process described in an exact, penetrating way by Alvar Aalto in the famous article titled "The Trout and the Stream" published in the magazine *Domus* in 1947: "I then move on to a method of working that is very much like abstract art. I simply draw by instinct, not architectural syntheses, but what are sometimes like childlike compositions, and in this way, on an abstract basis, the main idea gradually takes shape, a kind of universal substance that helps me to bring the numerous contradictory components into harmony."—40

38 Ibid.

39 Ibid.

40 Alvar Aalto, "The Trout and the Stream" (1947), in *Alvar Aalto in His Own Words*, by Göran Schildt (Helsinki: Otava Publishing Company, 1997), 108.

Siza has acknowledged many affinities with these words from Aalto, also in the antidogmatic way of looking at the relationship between design practice and theoretical thinking: "A few lines that suffice to make me be astonished if by chance I hear someone saying (and I have heard it): Aalto, architect, Finnish, did not theorize, did not talk about method; instead he did, and in a brilliant manner."—[41]

Among more recent works, the Iberê Camargo Foundation in Porto Alegre (1998–2008) demonstrates Siza's sculptural virtuosity: an apparently extravagant, excessive building that resembles no other previous work of architecture.—[42] Faced with the three broken ramps that emerge from the curved volume of the museum, at first the observer thinks of enormous arms, or fingers, or the tentacles of an octopus. Yet the zoological image is misleading, because Siza, as in earlier works, develops the form above all on the basis of functional and contextual necessities. In fact, he explains that the very small size of the site—an old quarry squeezed between the street and a hill—hampered the original intention of creating a continuous museum itinerary with long ramps, as in Wright's Guggenheim: "So the idea arose of advancing towards the river, of making the ramps emerge from the compact volume. It was inevitable. It is true that in the final result the ramps look like arms, but this reference to the body did not happen as a premise, but as the result of the difficulties of the design."—[43] The *sculptural* dimension of these ramps, aided by the high quality of the construction in exposed white concrete, can also be seen as a tribute to the modern Brazilian tradition: we are immediately reminded of the walkways freely inserted by Lina Bo Bardi between the powerful volumes of the SESC Pompéia in São Paulo (1976–82). Nevertheless, once again it is the experience of the *path* that reveals the building's deeper nature as an authentic *animated body*. Approaching the museum, the visitor discovers that the building continuously changes shape, and above all notices

41 Siza, *Scritti di architettura*, 102–03.

42 R. Segre, "Bodily Metaphors," in *Fundação Iberê Camargo, Álvaro Siza*, ed. F. Kiefer (São Paulo: Cosac Naify, 2008).

43 Álvaro Siza, interview with the author, September 12, 2014.

the modification of the relationships between the main volume and the ramps. Reaching the base of the building, visitors find themselves in a singular space: an external lobby, symbolically enclosed by the suspended ramps that welcome, yet also create an *estranged* relationship with the context, due to their slope that deforms and skews the frame through which the landscape is observed. Also in the interior route, the relationship with the landscape is not direct, but filtered by the few, irregular openings that accentuate the effect of disorientation. Rather than a visual relationship, it is a *tactile* rapport with the landscape that is proposed by the unusual interplay of internal and external ramps: while the inner ramps overlook the central void of the museum, contributing to create a strong sensation of introversion and of openness of the exhibition space, the outer ramps encourage visitors to temporarily *exit* this space; though paradoxically, the act of leaving coincides with that of penetrating into a closed space, a dim tube that makes the path enigmatic. With one's own body, then, one lives the singular experience of walking suspended in the void, embodying this idea of "advancing towards the river," which Siza saw as "inevitable" due to the attraction exerted by the large expanse of water.

In this extraordinary work, Siza interprets the relationship between nature and construction in profoundly renewed terms, having always viewed it as "decisive in architecture" and as a "permanent source of any project,"—[44] as discussed at the start of this essay. While in the first works, this relationship leaned towards a sort of erasure of the form, now the forcefully sculptural expression of the architecture stands out in avowed contrast to the vegetation and the geographical context. This is not, however, a formalist choice, because the strong tension Siza is able to create between artifact and nature is recognizable as unique and specific: it bears witness, as in the early works, to a profound sense of rooting to the place.

44 Siza, *Immaginare l'evidenza*, 5.

Sketch for the Iberê Camargo Foundation in Porto Alegre, 1998–2008.

# Postscript: Turf Wars

Caroline Constant

I am grateful to Maria Arquero, Albert Kirchengast, Nancy Levinson, and Karen M'Closkey who provided critical feedback on early drafts of this paper.

Recent speculation concerning the relative agency of architecture and landscape architecture, including landscape urbanism and ecological urbanism, can be viewed as responses to the contemporary understanding of the physical environment as a complex and ever-changing phenomenon, for which new tools of analysis and creative thought are needed if we are to address the changing circumstances of life on this planet. Disciplinary boundaries are inherently fluid and malleable; indeed such malleability provides a stimulus for productive cross-fertilization. Yet the prevalent propensity to "blur" the boundaries between architecture and landscape architecture has also contributed to a professional milieu, in which theorists and practitioners of the two disciplines are operating under different, albeit related, assumptions about concepts that are key to their respective undertakings. As a result, architects tend to use ideas that originate within landscape discourse—such as issues of temporality associated with a focus on process over product—in a limited analogical sense, rather than for their deeper cultural and environmental implications. Probing two examples of this phenomenon, these preliminary notes are directed to speculating about possible means of augmenting disciplinary efficacy at a time when issues of inter- and transdisciplinary exchange have become increasingly relevant.

In many ways, the results of the Parisian Parc de la Villette Competition of 1982 served as a wake-up call for architects and landscape architects alike. The first- and second-place entries—by Bernard Tschumi and OMA/Rem Koolhaas respectively—were not only designed by teams led by architects, they also signaled an approach to landscape design that eschewed mimicry of natural appearances in favor of design tactics that were both open-ended and decidedly urban. Not only had landscape returned to the cultural prominence that it supposedly lacked since the late nineteenth century, but landscape design was also seemingly re-ensconced within the disciplinary milieu of architecture.—[1] Yet the ensuing appropriation of landscape terms and concepts by architects has obscured significant differences in disciplinary approaches, thereby limiting the efficacy of interdisciplinary exchange at a time when the value of such efforts is increasingly being recognized.

1 For a critique of the supposed decline of landscape as a significant aspect of Western culture in the late nineteenth and early twentieth centuries, see Caroline Constant, *The Modern Architectural Landscape* (Minneapolis: University of Minnesota Press, 2012). There I argue that landscape was crucial not only to the social and political aspirations associated with the so-called Modern Movement in architecture, but also to the ability of twentieth-century architects and landscape architects to engage new, more democratic and collective forms of social organization.

Although numerous projects could be cited in support of this claim, two contrasting examples will suffice for this abbreviated discussion: the Thomson Optronics Factory in the satellite new town of Saint-Quentin-en-Yvelines, France (1988–91) by the Renzo Piano Building Workshop (RPBW) with landscape architects Michel Desvigne and Christine Dalnoky, and the winning competition proposal for Downsview Park in Toronto, Canada (1999) by the team of Bruce Mau Design, OMA/Rem Koolhaas, Oleson Worland Architects, and Inside/Outside (Petra Blaise). Whereas the scheme for Downsview Park exemplifies the propensity for architects and designers to use landscape analogies in a manner that is more literal than figurative, blurring disciplinary boundaries, the architectural and landscape solutions at the Thomson factory invoked analogous temporal processes and analogous sources of geometric logic in a manner that benefited from the distinct contributions of each discipline. Moreover, these two projects engage issues of temporality in diverse ways, provoking necessarily open questions of how best to address the substantive challenges associated with interdisciplinary work.

Inspired in part by the results of the Parc de la Villette competition, the Downsview Park competition brief called for a structured transformation of the site that would remain open to change, engage the complexity of ecological thinking, and challenge disciplinary scopes and boundaries. Although the interdisciplinary team of Bruce Mau, OMA, Oleson Worland Architects and Inside/Outside prevailed with their competition proposal "Tree City," the collaborators abandoned the approach that underlay OMA's Parc de la Villette competition proposal, in which the site was imagined as a locus of social and political engagement, in favor of analogically modeling certain landscape principles: "Manufacture Nature"; "Grow the Park." Whereas the first principle is a tautology, owing to our understanding of nature as a cultural construct, the second—which reflects the temporal duration of the project—invokes landscape processes independent of landscape form. The team's winning proposal is more graphic than tactical; failing to take the complexity of ecological and hydrological systems into account, it left landscape appearance open to natural processes, just as it left potential commercial activities open to economic circumstances. In emphasizing the scheme's performative aspects, its stress on temporal versus finite solutions, the collaborators neglected to engage what Anita Berrizbeitia describes as "landscape's capacity for precision of form notwithstanding flexibility of program—for the precisely open rather than the vaguely loose."—[2] As a result, "Tree City" offers little to challenge the traditional notion of the urban park as a counterpoint to the contemporary metropolis.

2 Anita Berrizbeitia, "Scales of Undecidability," in *CASE: Downsview Park Toronto*, ed. Julia Czerniak (Cambridge, MA: Prestel and Harvard Graduate School of Design, 2001), 124.

In contrast to the weak appropriation of landscape concepts at Downsview Park, the design for the Thomson Optronics Factory reflects a symbiotic relationship of architecture and landscape, a condition that emerged in part from the circumstances of the commission. Here, the site was also to remain open to change and engage the complexity of ecological systems, while the architecture was itself required to accommodate temporal flux,

Bruce Mau Design, OMA/Rem Koolhaas, Oleson Worland Architects, and Inside/Outside, Downsview Park competition entry, Toronto, Canada, 1999, design tactics.

Downsview Park competition entry, site diagram.

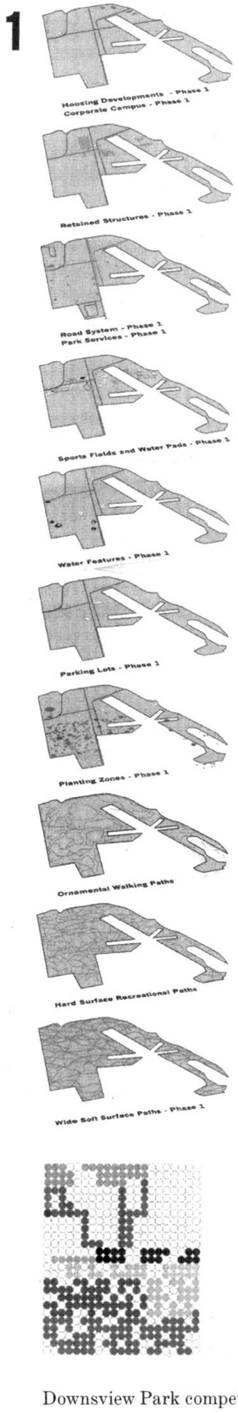


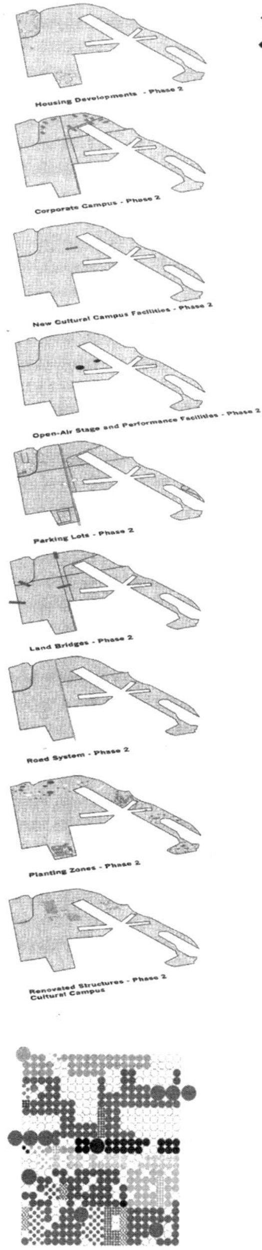


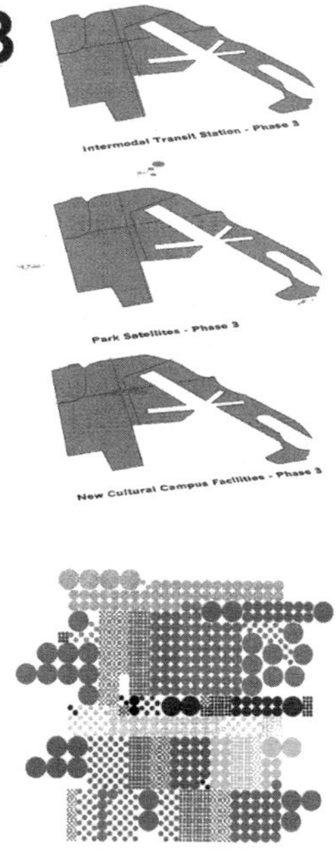


**Nature: A Planting Recipe**

This process will ensure that the park zones will be covered in a great, organic soil, full of micro-organisms and worms. It also means that you don't have to import soil. When you buy soil, it comes from sites being developed, where the topsoil has been scraped off. This soil is actually dead. The process kills the micro-organisms and the nutrients are lost, leaving only the minerals and anaerobic bacteria. This is not conducive to plant growth as it has none of the vital micro-organisms and worms and you would still have to introduce some other process to get this.

**Year One**

**1.** Do all grading, create berms and all physical changes to the site.
**2.** Do all hard landscaping, which includes walkways, washrooms, any pavilions, benches and other furniture.
**3.** Introduce a lot of coarse sandy material, concrete sand, mixed with as much well-rotten compost and manure as possible (this can be obtained from the city or other groups) and spread over all the areas that are to become park areas. You will need 55 tons per acre of this mix, this equals about a 3" layer of the mix over the area designated park.
**4.** In the driest month of the year, July or August, when the soil and the site are completely dry, go with a subsoiler (not just a usual farm plough which only creates a series of loose rows with compacted areas below and around them). The subsoiler vibrates the soil and ensures that all the soil layer is porous and broken up. The subsoiler must be used parallel to all the contours of the site. Go around the contours and not across them. You will end up spiralling around the hills.
**5.** After the subsoiler, then go in with a light cultivating tractor (25 horsepower), cultivate the soil and get rid of any ridges.
**6.** Seed the entire park with clover, and when it in full bloom, cultivate it under, mixing it into the soil. Clover will add nitrogen and green manure to the soil (nitrogen is collected from the air, and the green manure will act as organic material to enrich the soil.

**Year Two**

**7.** Seed another crop, preferably wheat or barley across all the park areas. Grow it to about a 10 inch height, and then cultivate it under, just as was done with the clover.

Now the site is ready to grow trees and bushes and flowers, and they will all grow to their full, healthy potential.

Downsview Park competition entry, phasing strategies.

an issue more readily associated with landscape design. Nevertheless, project descriptions by the architect and landscape architects reflect differing outlooks on the scheme, in accordance with their respective areas of expertise.

Their collaborative design emanated directly from the particular needs of the client, a high security electronics firm engaged in the research and manufacture of aircraft navigation systems for both civilian and military use. The company had sold its Paris factory, and for its new location chose a flat site in the urban periphery, which, according to Piano, lacked any distinguishing landscape character.—[3] The architectural program also lacked specificity, a factor that directly affected the building design and site layout. The client's needs were in a state of flux owing both to corporate reorganization, in which aspects of the manufacturing process were being delegated to subcontractors, and to the accelerating miniaturization of electronics, which implies progressively smaller and cleaner spaces devoted to manufacturing in relation to areas for research and administration. Thus, apart from the need for open space, a condition with which the architects were familiar, the allocation of functional divisions remained unpredictable, as did the eventual size of the facility. With only eighteen months to effect the company's relocation (including three months for the design competition), timing was crucial to the undertaking.

3 Renzo Piano, *Logbook* (New York: The Monacelli Press, 1997), 146. Similarly, Julia Czerniak remarks that the intricacies of the Downsview Park landscape were not readily apparent from her initial experience of the site. Julia Czerniak, "Appearance, Performance: Landscape at Downsview," in id., *CASE: Downsview Park Toronto*, 13.

The Renzo Piano Building Workshop responded to these criteria with an architectural kit of parts, elaborated as repetitive, narrow structural bays that admit natural light through north-facing clerestory windows and extend across the site in modules of varied lengths: a system that enables internal components to be rearranged as needs arise.—[4] The RPBW scheme evokes Rem Koolhaas's insight about OMA's Parc de la Villette proposal: "The underlying principle of programmatic indeterminacy as a basis of the formal concept allows any shift, modification, replacement, or substitutions to occur without damaging

4 The factory's 14.4-meter-wide structural bays are paired and separated by a 3.6-meter-wide zone accommodating circulation and services. The cladding system also comprises an adaptable kit of parts. Crowning the complex is a tower capped by a sphere, with aluminum elements that slide and fold to test the navigation devices.

the initial hypothesis."—[5] The linear bays of the RPBW factory buildings align in turn with alternating strips of parking and plantings that extend across the ground plane in a gridded layout, conferring a comparable flexibility on the broader site development. To the east of this open-ended system, a circular wall segment is bounded by mounds of earth obtained from excavating a pair of retention ponds. This earthen-banked wall, housing storage space and electrical substations and generators, enhances security by inhibiting site access and obstructing visibility from an adjoining roadway, while the ponds and associated plantings limit access at its southern limit, where entry to the facility is accommodated.

Fostering awareness of the temporal qualities of ambient nature through exposure to seasonal variation in planting appearance as well as hourly changes in light conditions, the building complex provides, in Piano's words, "pleasant working conditions" through the architect's propensity for direct access to natural light in combination with the "presence of greenery."—[6] Piano's approach to the factory landscape is more aesthetic than performative; it does not take into account such long-term temporal issues as social and ecological resilience—the capacity of a system to adapt or adjust to conditions of dynamic change—or to the operations of maintenance and development, all of which motivated Desvigne and Dalnoky's landscape scheme.—[7]

According to Piano, the geometry of the landscape design emanated directly from the architectural response:

> The landscape responds to the fluidity of the construction with the rigor of an orthogonal grid defined by lines of trees and other plants. Thus the buildings are given a logical setting by the "frame" of the vegetation, as if they were placed on a checkerboard. The integration of architecture and nature is based on a respect for the same formal rules: future enlargements will need to do no more than follow them.—[8]

5 Rem Koolhaas, "Congestion without Matter," *S, M, L, XL* (New York: Monacelli, 1999), 921.

6 Piano, *Logbook*, 146. Piano's interest in creating a pleasant working environment for the factory workers through proximity to elements of nature bears comparison with Le Corbusier's intentions for his Usine Verte (Green Factory) proposal of 1940–44.

7 For social and ecological resilience, see W. Neil Adger, "Social and ecological resilience: are they related?" *Progress in Human Geography*, 24, 3 (2000): 347–64; Cathy Wilkinson, "Social-ecological resilience: Insights and issues for planning theory," *Planning Theory*, 11 (2012): 148–69.

8 Piano, *Logbook*, 146.

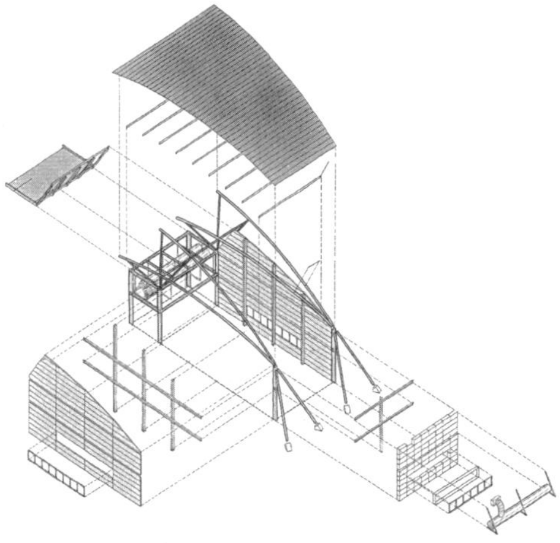

Renzo Piano Building Workshop, Thomson Optronics Factory, Saint-Quentin-en-Yvelines, France, 1988–91, building kit of parts.

Thomson Optronics Factory, process of parking lot construction, and agricultural environs.

Desvigne and Dalnoky, Thomson Optronics Factory, site plan representing intermediate state of landscape development.

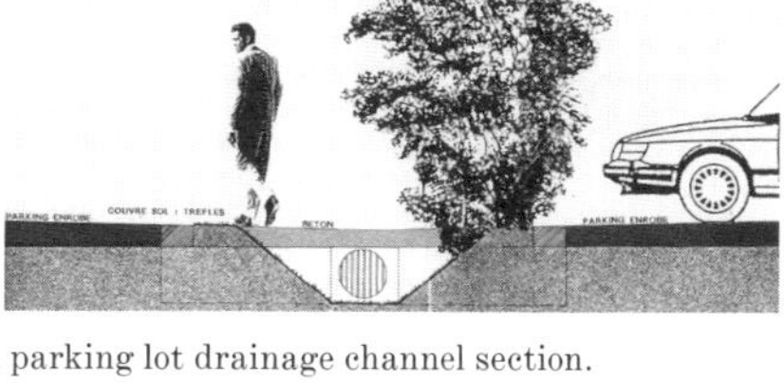


Thomson Optronics Factory, parking lot drainage channel section.

Architecture critic Peter Buchanan explains the site layout in related formal terms: "The site-planning strategy plays fixity against fluidity; these characteristics being marked by arcs of a circle and bands of straight lines respectively."—[9] Whereas fluidity in Piano's account emanates from the mutability of the architecture, Buchanan, like Desvigne and Dalnoky, also understands fluidity to encompass the temporality of landscape processes. Inverting this logic, however, Desvigne and Dalnoky rationalized the formal parallels of the respective designs by invoking a mechanical analogy: "the lines of the landscape continue the patterns of the construction, like the rails of a rolling gantry"—signifying a further, industrial source of temporal change.—[10]

Belying Piano's narrative concerning the imposition of a geometrical ordering system on a flat, featureless site is an alternate account. As might be expected, Desvigne and Dalnoky gleaned greater inspiration from the physical setting than did their architectural counterparts.—[11] As Manuel Delluc has observed with respect to the firm's practice: "the landscape designer is first of all the guarantor of the authenticity of the landscape on which he or she acts."—[12] This is a question not only of drawing upon the *genius loci*, but also of instilling a new legibility on the site. The geographical and historic attributes of the region and the site's potential as a cultural resource were thus essential starting points for the landscape proposal. Although depletion of the region's agricultural basis was providing opportunities for suburban residential enclaves and large-scale manufacturing facilities to be developed during this period, Desvigne and Dalnoky opted to challenge the area's incipient suburban sprawl in favor of an explicitly agrarian approach to the site, in effect conceptualizing this very private segment of land (due to the firm's internal security requirements) as a segment of a broader, more open, and quasi-public milieu. "To commandeer farming techniques and practices suddenly makes a place legible," argues Desvigne.—[13]

9 Peter Buchanan, *Renzo Piano Building Workshop*, Vol. 2 (London: Phaidon Press Ltd., 1995), 36.

10 "Desvigne and Dalnoky," in *Het Landschap/ The landscape: Vier Internationale Landschapsontwerpers. Four International Landscape Designers* (Antwerp: deSingel, 1995), 182.

11 Desvigne and Dalnoky, who worked together from 1983 to 1996, frequently collaborated with Piano, including on the following projects: Auvergne Regional Headquarters, Clermont-Ferrand, 1985 (with Michel Courajoud); Institute for Research into Light Metals, Novara, 1985–87 (only Desvigne); Jules Verne Amusement Park Competition, Amiens, 1987 (with Michel Courajoud); Sistiana Bay Renovation project, Trieste, 1987; San Nicola Stadium, Bari (only Desvigne), 1987–90; Bercy 2 Shopping Center, Paris, 1987–90; Rue de Meaux Housing, Paris, 1987–91 (with Philippe Convercey); Thomson Optronics Factory, Saint-Quentin en Yvelines, 1988–90 (with Philippe Convercey); Tjibaou Cultural Center competition, Noumea, New Caledonia, 1991. See Piano, *Logbook*, 270–73.

12 Manuel Delluc, "Michel Desvigne and Christine Dalnoky," in id.: *Desvigne and Dalnoky: The Return of Landscape* (New York: Whitney Library of Design, 1997), 14.

13 Michel Desvigne, "Introduction," in *Inter-mediate Natures: The Landscapes of Michel Desvigne*, by James Corner (Basel, Boston, Berlin: Birkhäuser, 2009), 11.

In these terms, their design tactic invokes the notion of *terroir*, which encompasses the interactions of a plant's genetic makeup with the local geography, geology, and climate as expressed in a region's agricultural products and thus comprises qualities that make a locale distinctive. The geometric logic of the Thomson Optronics landscape is thus agricultural as much as it is architectural or mechanical, an analogy that, together with the analogous temporal processes invoked in the overall design, contributes to the scheme's symbiosis of architecture and landscape.

While gleaning insights from the cultural history of the site, Desvigne and Dalnoky adopted a forward-looking approach, as Desvigne elaborates: "We draw inspiration and sustenance in the traces of society's activities. Above all, we aim to help this society envision other ways of occupying and constituting the area."—[14] To achieve this objective, they employed a process of material substitution; rather than attempting to reinstate the region's agricultural heritage directly, they introduced new plant materials as means to open the locale up to new uses, a process Desvigne associates with "the pleasure of combining, domesticating, and directing living systems."—[15] Cultivating the distinct attributes of the site by enhancing its legibility as a designed landscape and its connections to the broader terrain, Desvigne and Dalnoky endowed the project with a significance that transcends the limits of the problem as given. They invested the landscape with an identity that Piano found lacking in the site, a quality enhanced by the lightness of the RPBW building components, an architectural aesthetic that would ultimately yield to the visual dominance of landscape.

The factory landscape was to be developed in discrete phases, enabling Desvigne and Dalnoky to create a verdant expanse in this "forbidden plain," replete with a prevailing west wind and a dense clay soil that was prone to water stagnation.—[16] To make the site suitable for building, they initially created an earthen plateau inscribed with parallel drainage channels that correspond

14 Ibid., 13.

15 Ibid., 12.

16 "Genèse d'un paysage: Thomson CSF, Guyancourt, Saint-Quentin-en-Yvelines," in *L'Architecture d'Aujourd'hui* 402 (Juillet 1992), 92.

to the geometry of the anticipated building layout. Once the complex was in operation, these channels, which initially collected the excess water on the site and directed it to the retention ponds, would treat runoff from the intermediary parking surfaces to provide nourishment for the rows of willows planted between the parking strips, which in turn stabilize the banks and compensate for evaporation. Extending across the terrain, the lines of willows are interspersed with erratic stands of poplars; these short-lived specimens have an anticipated viability of only a few decades, "corresponding," as Desvigne and Dalnoky elaborate, "to the lifespan of the average industrial park."—[17] They envisioned the factory garden in its optimal state as a "vast, rapidly growing poplar grove at the scale of the plateau [that] encompasses the factory buildings."—[18] Black pines and isolated conifers were added incrementally to these initial plantings, while longer-lived specimens such as beeches and oaks were to be planted in the future. The processes of landscape succession would ultimately begin to obscure the initial compositional devices, anticipating a day when this industrial site might be vacated and its landscape merge back into the plain of Saint-Quentin, reasserting its origins as an open, public domain: a borderless expanse of modulated textures envisioned in agricultural terms. For Desvigne, "This is architecture … on the geographical scale."—[19]

17 Delluc, *Desvigne and Dalnoky: The Return of Landscape*, 68.

18 Ibid., 70.

19 Michel Desvigne, "Introduction," in Corner, *Intermediate Natures*, 12.

Owing to the inverse temporality of architecture and landscape, Desvigne and Dalnoky anticipated an unpredictable future for the Thomson factory site. They accordingly created a setting that could be appropriated equally for other uses, including as a catalyst for urban development. While opposing the implied permanence of formal, compositional design methods, Desvigne seeks "to give back to a public space its character as a common ground, as a base on which the city is built."—[20] Toward that end, he distinguishes between permanent structures, which enable one "to circulate easily, to receive sunlight, to get one's bearings, to find shelter from the wind [such that] various

20 Ibid., 112.

occupancy scenarios can be planned, and can follow one after the other,"—[21] and the more provisional aspects of his firm's landscape designs, which he terms "intermediate natures." As he elaborates, this "cannot be a question of producing the negative of a site plan, but rather of giving the land an immediate status, maintaining it, and accepting its transformation. This falls in the category of management, maintenance, and respect, even though the qualities and uses are only temporary."—[22] If the drainage channels that facilitate water retention and oxygenate and filter rainwater runoff at the Thomson Optronics Factory constitute its permanent structures, then the initial plantings comprise its "intermediate" nature.

21 Ibid., 39.

22 Ibid., 38.

Planning for the temporal flux of both architecture and landscape, the designers of the Thomson facility sought to provide a flexible framework for future development. As with "Tree City," a concern with process over product yielded open-ended design tactics in which urban and regional were no longer viewed in opposition—with landscape serving as a palliative of the urban environment—but as complementary conditions. This convergence of ambitions at the Thomson Optronics Factory was undoubtedly due in part to the unpredictable nature of the client's spatial needs, yet discussion of the project has focused on either its landscape or its architecture; its intrinsic symbiosis of architecture and landscape has not been analyzed in depth.—[23]

As a catalyst for an emergent urbanism, Desvigne and Dalnoky's factory landscape suggests parallels with aspects of the Downsview Park competition brief, namely the requirement that the proposals "respond to the social and natural histories of the site while developing its potential as a new landscape—one capable of supporting new as well as old ecologies and an evolving array of public uses and events."—[24] Accordingly, "Tree City," a self-styled "campaign to *Grow the Park* beyond Downsview's boundaries and into the urban realm," purports to use landscape as a form of city making by infiltrating the

23 For a general exception to this focus on one aspect of a project over the other in general, see Anita Berrizbeitia and Linda Pollak, *Inside/Outside: Between Architecture and Landscape* (Gloucester: Rockport, 1999); nevertheless, this discussion of the Thomson Optronics Factory focuses primarily on its landscape.

24 Cited by Kristina Hill, "Urban Ecologies: Biodiversity and Urban Design," in Czerniak, *CASE: Downsview Park Toronto*, 92.

park's low-density suburban context with an expansionist program of tree planting.—25 Yet in comparison with the analogous approach at the Thomson Optronics factory, this gesture seems compensatory: more a vehicle for bridging differences between the park and its suburban milieu than a viable means of propagating an urban condition.

25 Ibid., 76 [emphasis in original].

Although Downsview Park and the Thomson Optronics Factory were both envisaged as phased landscape developments, lacking definitive site plans that would imply fixed formal solutions, the two projects differ in their respective modes of representation. For the "Tree City" competition submission, the team combined abstract diagrams of the general concept, the site, and its anticipated construction phases with circular perspective images in which the graphic circles of the program and phasing diagrams are transmuted into circular landscape forms. While the precise geometry of these forms emphasizes the park landscape as a human construct ("Manufacture Nature"), the perspective images suggest definitive results of the development process: concrete aesthetic objectives that contradict the team's understanding of the site as a field condition understood in fluid temporal terms. In contrast, Desvigne and Dalnoky represented their proposal for the Thomson factory landscape through a combination of aerial photographs of the broader region and a series of plans diagramming the site's phased development, which provide concrete means for initiating and managing its landscape succession.

Aerial photography is a prominent analytical tool for Desvigne and Dalnoky; it facilitates interpretation of the site's historic and cultural dynamics, its patterns and processes at the scale of the region as well as that of the site. Denis Cosgrove and William L. Fox summarize the attributes of aerial photography in related terms: "What aerial photography does best … is to capture a context for individual features on the ground, to place them in relationship to one another and to a broader topography, revealing patterns to the eye, or, we might say, to create geographies."—26 Such patterns emanate from processes that may

26 Denis Cosgrove and William L. Fox, *Photography and Flight* (London: Reaktion Books, 2010), 9.

be natural, but are fundamentally of human generation. This geographic understanding of the site gleaned from the aerial view complements Desvigne and Dalnoky's understanding of its surface qualities and subsurface conditions, its geology, hydrology, etc.: aspects that had little impact on the "Tree City" proposal, despite its focus on soil remediation. Nevertheless Desvigne cautions us concerning the limitations of aerial photography for landscape designers:

> One must be wary of a ready fascination with aerial photographs. The processes at work—erosion, parcel division and provision of services—are observable in these documents, and in diverse situations, in a way that is so obvious that it is almost a caricature. Shapes can also appear, seen from the sky; they are beautiful precisely because they are strange, and there too is a danger that should be avoided. However, these exercises in observation complete what we analyze on the ground. We need to build up our knowledge, to train our eye to grasp these devices. This "fieldwork," these "anatomies of landscapes in the planning stages" allow us to dissect complex situations in order to reach simple solutions. And that is why these aerial photographs are valuable.—[27]

27 Corner, *Intermediate Natures*, 176–77.

This resistance to the seductive "beauty" of an image from any particular vantage point—whether ground plan, perspective drawing, or photograph—is reflected in a representational means Desvigne and Dalnoky use to document their built work: composite photographic series that convey the textural mosaic of the projects and their intermediate status as processes set in motion. They impart less about the scenic instrumentality of effects in these landscapes and more about their temporal qualities.

While the future of these two sites remains in doubt, both are envisioned as part of a more "sustainable" future for their respective locales. In Saint-Quentin-en-Yvelines, only the first two phases of landscape construction were completed (in 1991 and 1992 respectively), before the firm merged with Thales Optronics and the landscape development was halted, its significance apparently overlooked by the new management.—[28] Although establishing parameters for the phased evolution of a project has become a

28 In 2008, Thales sought to vacate the property, providing an opportunity for the municipality to offer it as a possible site for the Louvre to locate a remote museum storage, art research and restoration facility, but this proposal was rejected in May 2009.

prevalent design tactic for landscape architects, and was a requirement of the Downsview competition guidelines, such proposals assume a degree of feedback and follow-through to achieve their longer-term objectives.

The fate of Downsview Park remains in limbo for both practical and political reasons. As the park website explains:

> An abstract diagram rather than a conventional master plan, Tree City was seen as visionary, setting out a range of opportunities that would evolve over time rather than a highly prescriptive set of fixed elements. Downsview Park's greatest challenge is to take this two-dimensional abstract concept and transform it in to [*sic*] a tangible, functioning three-dimensional space—"a great urban park."—[29]

29 http://www.downsviewpark.ca/content/past-present-future (accessed January 21, 2013).

A government mandate for the site improvements to be financially self-supporting led Parc Downsview Parc (PDP), the corporation responsible for its development, to issue "Sustainable Community Development Guidelines" for the area in December 2007, in which the site is envisioned as "a model of progressive sustainable urban development."—[30] According to the park website, this vision involves "environmental, social, and economic sustainability":

30 Downsview Park Sustainable Community Development Guidelines (December 2007), 3; http://downsviewpark.ca/sites/default/files/wysiwyg_content/corporate/SustainableGuidelines_Dec2007.pdf (accessed December 17, 2012). Parc Downsview Park was established in 1999, but was only granted administrative control over the area in 2006.

> Downsview Park is a model development demonstrating sustainable practices in its design, construction, operation and maintenance. It is intended to be a recreational, educational and cultural amenity for all Canadians; a diverse, healthy and livable community for its occupants, visitors and neighbours; and an educational demonstration project of international significance.—[31]

31 http://www.downsviewpark.ca/content/sustainable-development-0 (accessed December 19, 2012).

Toward these ends, PDP commissioned Cicada Design, an architecture and design firm that specializes in visualizing urban proposals for Toronto, to create a series of images of the park and its associated housing developments and commercial enterprises. The result resembles a conventional master plan, replete with the scenic values of nineteenth-century park designs, in stark contrast to the

Cicada Design, vision for Downsview Park site.

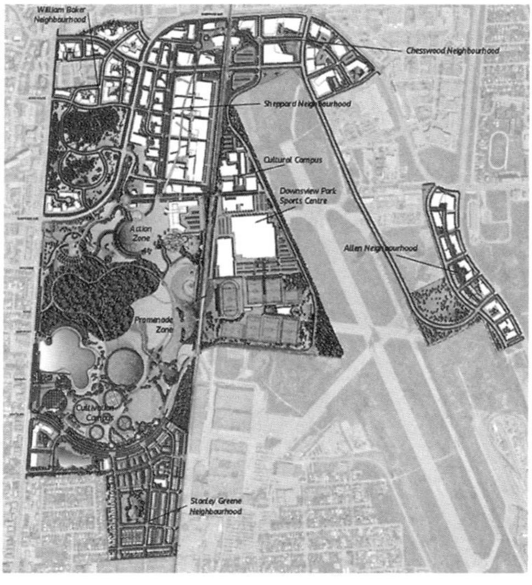


Downsview Park, Inc., master plan, 2011.

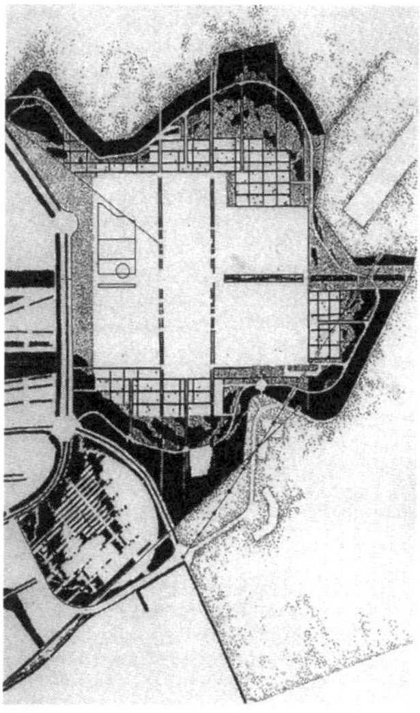

Desvigne and Dolnaky (with Valode and Pistre Architects), Renault Technical Facility, site plan (Thomson Optronics Factory in lower left), Saint-Quentin-en-Yvelines, France, 1991.

competition objectives as well as to those of the winning design team.—[32]

Roughly fifteen years have elapsed since the Downsview competition: the span of time originally allotted for the park's phased development. Although heralded as Canada's first urban national park, Downsview Park lacks the sort of landscape development that would indicate a meaningful response to such a provocative challenge. Whereas the PDP development guidelines appear to be primarily a marketing tool—a means to compensate for the limitations of the winning proposal and address the government edict that the site development be economically self-sustaining—the outlook of the local administration in Saint-Quentin derives from a more forward-looking perspective. There, the planning authority stipulated that the landscape approach used at the Thomson factory be extended to a neighboring site where a Renault technical facility was to be constructed, so that the broader landscape would be marked by gridded lines of trees thickening into woodlands between the major developments, but thinning as they approach the building complexes.—[33] This tactic would overcome the habitat fragmentation that typically accompanies suburban development by supplanting the existing isolated patches with a more continuous landscape mosaic. Moreover, according to a proposal from 2010 to transform Saint-Quentin-en-Yvelines into an eco-innovative city by 2030, the factory site is also part of a broader vision, one that aspires to engage the local citizenry in fostering ecological initiatives.—[34] As with Downsview Park, however, the viability of such a proposal would depend on economic and political circumstances, as well as on the complex issues associated with planning for sustainable development, a notion that prompts multiple interpretations among practitioners of both disciplines. For sustainable development remains a problematic concept, the meaning of which depends on the vantage point from which it is proffered; what is sustainable from one perspective may not be sustainable from another.

32 Casting further doubt on the park's ability to fulfill the competition guidelines, administration of Downsview Park was transferred in late November 2012 from Parc Downsview Park, Inc., to Canada Lands Co., the Crown property management arm whose mandate is to obtain the greatest economic yield from the management and/or sale of government properties. In the interim, the park website continues to report progress on landscape improvements on the site. See Peter Edwards, "Downsview Park taken over by federal land management agency," (Toronto: November 29, 2012); http://www.thestar.com/news/gta/crime/article/1295581-downsview-park-taken-over-by-federal-land-management-agency (accessed December 19, 2012); Gayle McDonald, "The uncertain fate of Toronto's Downsview Park," in *The Globe and Mail* (Toronto: December 8, 2012), downloaded December 19, 2012; http://www.theglobeandmail.com/news/toronto/the-uncertain-fate-of-torontos-downsview-park/article-6117677/ (accessed December 19, 2012).

33 Buchanan, *Renzo Piano Building Workshop*, Vol. 2, 37; "Desvigne and Dalnoky," in *Het Landschap*, 184. Desvigne collaborated with Valode and Pistre Architects on the winning competition proposal for the Renault technical facility (1991). Alain Provost developed the scheme and carried out the landscape realization (1992–2000).

34 http://www.slideshare.net/JosephIturbide/become-an-ecoinnovative-city-by-2030#btnNext (accessed Jan 28, 2013).

Piano addresses sustainability in multiple ways, ranging from physical considerations (conserving natural resources through the use of local and recycled materials and climate responsive skins, as well as capitalizing on natural light and the immediate presence of landscape elements) to the cultural aspects of each problem. "Sustainability consists in building while thinking of the future," he argues, "not only taking the physical resistance of a building into account, but also thinking of its stylistic resistance, of its future use and of the resistance of the planet itself and its energy resources."—[35] Stressing the need for open, flexible solutions, he continues, "instead of diminishing the poetic potential of a building, a sustainable approach must add to it by intensifying aspects like transparency, light, the relation to the land …"—[36] John Ehrenfeld characterizes such tactics as efforts to reduce unsustainability rather than to address sustainability, which he understands as a more complex phenomenon: "a call to reexamine the foundations of our society once again, and understand and correct the ways in which our modern culture perpetuates the problems it creates."—[37]

Although sustainability discourse has undoubtedly contributed to the contemporary prominence of landscape design as a cultural medium, Desvigne does not engage directly in this controversial concept. In several respects, his firm's philosophy parallels that of Piano, particularly in its respect for local cultural values and openness to change. However, in contrast to the capitalist model of economic viability operating in suburban Toronto or Piano's focus on ensuring the cultural longevity of a project, Desvigne's approach derives from the more substantive concept of *durability*—the capacity to respond to present-day needs without compromising the capacity of future generations to respond to theirs—and its inherent concern for social equity in terms of the complex ecological, economic, and cultural issues at play.—[38] By anticipating possible futures for the Thomson factory site, Desvigne and Dalnoky nurtured options for a range of activities, both anticipated

35 Anatxu Zabalbeascoa, "Interview [with Renzo Piano]," in *Renzo Piano: Sustainable architectures*, ed. Anatxu Zabalbeascoa and Javier Rodríguez Marcos (Barcelona: Editorial Gustavo Gili, 1998), 56.

36 Ibid., 57.

37 John R. Ehrenfeld and Andrew J. Hoffman, *Flourishing: A Frank Conversation about Sustainability* (Stanford, CA: Stanford University Press, 2013), 36.

38 Durability is a central tenet of *Our Common Future*, the Bruntland Commission report developed from 1983 under the chairmanship of Gro Harlem Bruntland, former Norwegian prime minister, and published in 1987 by the United Nations World Commission on Environment and Development.

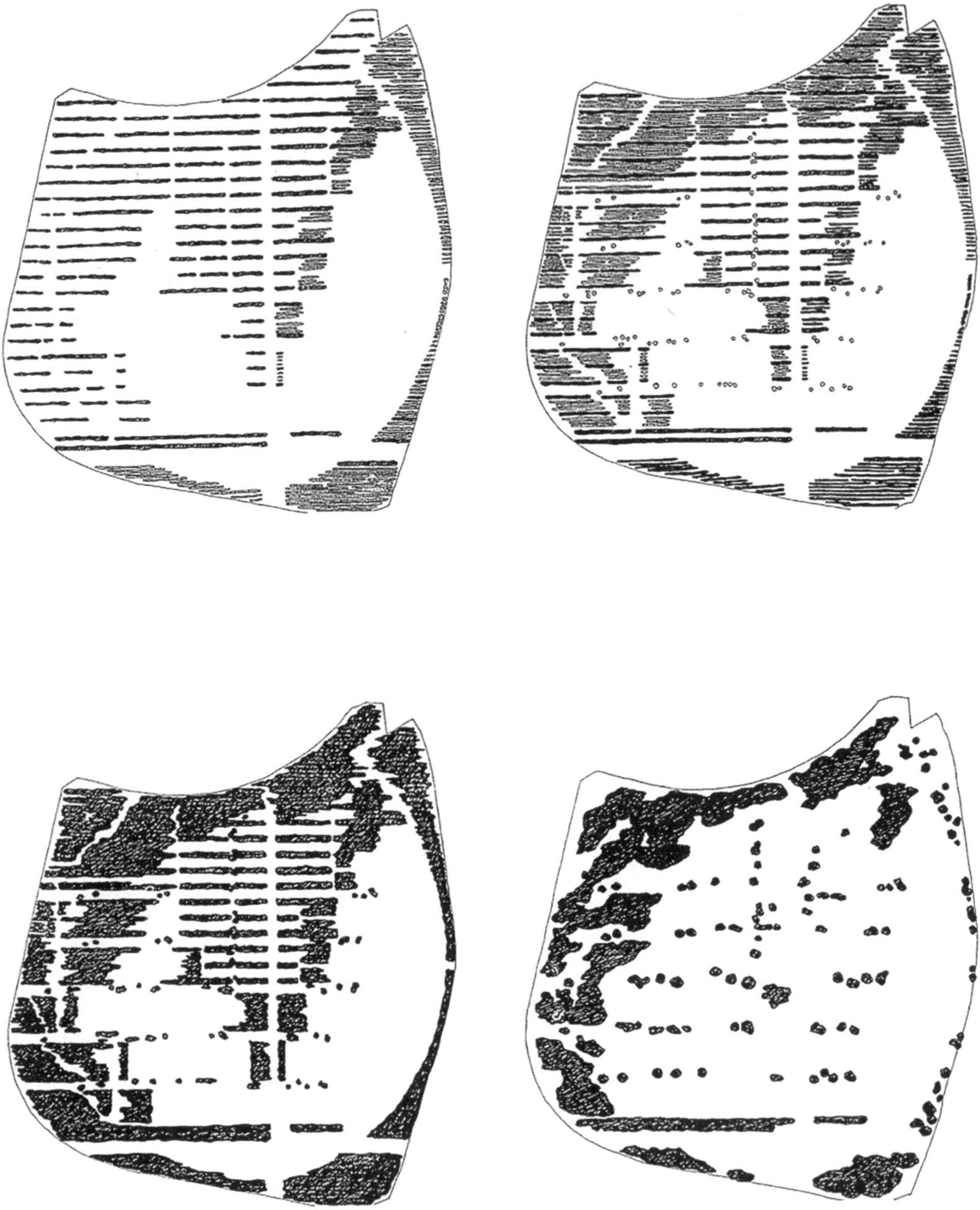

Thomson Optronics Factory, planting succesion diagrams.

and unanticipated, thereby prompting ongoing dialogue concerning the appropriate means to positively effect the quality of life on this planet.

As we have seen, differences in disciplinary approaches by the designers of the Thomson Optronics Factory resulted in a serendipitous synergy of architecture and landscape, whereas a more limited, literal understanding of landscape concepts on the part of the Downsview Park competitors contributed to their inability to meet the aesthetic, cultural, and environmental challenges posed by the competition guidelines. They reduced the temporal aspect of ecological emergence to graphic abstraction. At the Thomson facility, such emergence was given form through agricultural and mechanical analogies, while the architecture was motivated by related geometric and programmatic logics; form and process are inextricably intertwined.

To effect more productive dialogue within and across disciplines, architects and landscape architects need to strive for greater clarity in the use of concepts and terms inherent to their respective areas of expertise. When architects appropriate concepts inherent to landscape architecture, however, awareness of such distinctions is often lost. Although a broad range of disciplines—including planning, engineering, the physical and social sciences, and politics, as well as architecture and landscape architeture—must be engaged in order to have a significant effect on the built environment, greater disciplinary empowerment can result only when architects and landscape architects understand and respect their distinct values, modes of operation, areas of expertise, as well as their potential spheres of convergence and overlap, and work collaboratively with the aim of engaging the cultural imaginary and augmenting their disciplinary efficacy.

page 20: John Szarkowski, *The Idea of Louis Sullivan* (Minneapolis: University of Minnesota Press, 1956), 115
pages 26, 38: Photographs by Marko Pogacnik, Venice
page 32: Alfred Brehm, *Das Tierleben*, volume 2, *Die Vielfüßler, Insekten und Spinnenkerfe* (Leipzig and Vienna: Bibliographisches Institut, 1915), 460; volume 4, *Die Lurche und die Kriechtiere* (1920), 376
pages 44, 46, 56, 63: J. Paul Getty Trust; digitized in 2010–12 with support from the ARTstor Digital Library
page 69 bottom: Bibliothèque de la Ville de La Chaux-de-Fonds, Cabinet des arts graphiques, Fonds cartes postales
pages 69 top, 77 top and bottom left, 78: Fondation Le Corbusier, Paris/2017, ProLitteris, Zurich
page 70: Bibliothèque de la Ville de La Chaux-de-Fonds, Fonds spéciaux, Fonds Le Corbusier
page 77 bottom right: Bibliothèque de la Ville de La Chaux-de-Fonds, Fonds spéciaux, Fonds Charles L'Eplattenier
pages 87–96: Photographs by Richard Weston, Cardiff
pages 102–118: Archive David Leatherbarrow, Philadelphia
page 120: Wikimedia Commons
pages 124, 132 bottom right: Baukunst Archiv der Akademie der Künste, Berlin
page 132 top: Kunimoto Kawakami, *Kyoto-Gosho-Rikyu-Zushu*, 1929
page 132 bottom: Bildarchiv Foto Marburg
page 138: Manuscript illustrations and photographs from Bruno Taut, *Ein Wohnhaus* (Stuttgart: Franckh'sche Buchhandlung, 1927), 15, 100, 38
page 147: Archive Manfred Speidel, Aachen
pages 148–166: Photographs by Fritz Tugendhat from Wolf Tegethoff, Daniela Hammer-Tugendhat, *Tugendhat House. Ludwig Mies van der Rohe: New edition* (Basel: Birkhäuser, 2014), 65, 38, 43, 29, 67. Archive Daniela Hammer-Tugendhat, Vienna
page 168: Canadian Centre for Architecture, DR1983:1090
pape 171: Courtesy Art Institute of Chicago, Ryerson and Burnham Library Archives, Ludwig Hilberseimer Papers, Y36980
page 172 top: Courtesy Art Institute of Chicago, Ryerson and Burnham Library Archives, Ludwig Hilberseimer Papers, Y36980. Manuscript illustration from Ludwig Hilberseimer, *The New City: Principles of Planning* (Chicago: Paul Theobald, 1944), 121, fig. 92
page 172 bottom: Courtesy Art Institute of Chicago, Ryerson and Burnham Library Archives, Ludwig Hilberseimer Papers, Y36980. Manuscript illustration from Ludwig Hilberseimer, *The New Regional Pattern: Industries and Gardens, Workshops and Farms* (Chicago: Paul Theobald, 1949), 169, fig. 111
page 177: Courtesy Art Institute of Chicago, Ryerson and Burnham Library Archives, Ludwig Hilberseimer Papers, Y36980. Manuscript illustrations from Ludwig Hilberseimer, *The New Regional Pattern* (Chicago: Paul Theobald, 1949), 163, fig. 107 and 142, fig. 93
pages 178, 181: Chicago History Museum, Hedrich Blessing Archive
pages 190, 194, 196, 206, 208, 209, 213: Archive Álvaro Siza, Porto
pages 192 left, 200, 201: Photographs by Alessandra Chemollo, Venice
pages 192 right, 193: Photographs by Thorsten Hümpel, Hennef
pages 198, 202, 203: Photographs by Duarte Belo, Lisbon
page 210: Photograph by Fernando Guerra, Lisbon
pages 218, 219: Julia Czerniak, *CASE: Downsview Park Toronto* (Cambridge / MA: Prestel and Harvard Graduate School of Design, 2001), 75, 76, 79
page 222 top: http://srt251ddz.blogspot.com/2007_04_01_archive.html
page 222 center: http://www.rpbw.com/project/30/thomson-optronics-factory/#. Photograph by Michel Denancé
pages 222 bottom, 223 bottom: Michel Desvigne, Christine Dalnoky, *The Return of Landscape* (New York: Whitney Library of Design, 1997), 68, 69, 73
pages 223 top, 234: Peter Buchanan, *Renzo Piano Building Workshop*, Vol. 2 (London: Phaidon Press Ltd., 1995), 36
page 231 top: http://www.cicadadesign.ca/portfolio/downsviewpark.html
page 231 center: www.downsviewpark.ca/content/neighbourhoods-0
page 231 bottom: *Het Landschap/The landscape: Vier Internationale Landschapsontwerpers. Four International Landscape Designers* (Antwerp: deSingel, 1995), 185

The editors and publisher would like to thank image rights holders who have kindly given their permission for publication. Every effort has been made to identify all rights holders before publication. We would ask any rights holders we did not manage to contact to get in touch with the editors.

## EDITORS

CHRISTOPHE GIROT is Professor and Chair of Landscape Architecture at ETH Zurich. He received his Master of Architecture and Master of Landscape Architecture degrees from the University of California, Berkeley, and served as Director of the École Nationale Supérieure de Paysage in Versailles. His teaching and research interests range from new topological methods in landscape design, perception, analysis, and new media, to contemporary theory and the history of landscape architecture. His most recent publication, *The Course of Landscape Architecture* (2016), reviews the history of design in the natural world from prehistory to the present. His professional practice, Atelier Girot, focuses on large-scale landscape projects using advanced techniques in 3D-modeling and GIS-mapping, which contribute to the design of more sustainable landscape environments, such as the Sigirino Alptransit Depot and the Third Rhône River Correction in the canton of Valais.

ALBERT KIRCHENGAST is an architectural theoretician. He has worked in Christophe Girot's Theory Lab at ETH Zurich since 2010, and as a Senior Researcher since 2015. He was a Research Fellow at Harvard GSD and at the Institute for Human Sciences in Vienna. He has received research grants from the Canadian Center of Architecture and the Swiss National Science Foundation. His PhD thesis, "Das unvollständige Haus. Mies van der Rohe und die Landschaft der Moderne," was completed in 2017. He is contributor to the *Neue Zürcher Zeitung* and has been published in various architectural journals. His books include *Experiments—Architecture between Sciences and the Arts* (coedited with Ákos Moravánszky), *Mies als Gärtner*, *Archaische Moderne* (with Norbert Lehner), *Landschaft im Gespräch*, *Franz Riepl—Über Architektur* (with Hans Kolb), *Landschaft und Lebenssinn* (coedited with Erwin Frohmann).

## AUTHORS

CAROLINE CONSTANT is an architect, Professor Emerita of Architecture at the University of Michigan, a visiting scholar at the Harvard Graduate School of Design, and a Fellow of the American Academy in Rome. She studied architecture at Princeton University and taught at Harvard University, the University of Florida, and the University of Michigan, with visiting appointments at Rice University and the University of Minnesota, among other institutions. She is author of *The Palladio Guide* (1985), *The Woodland Cemetery: Toward a Spiritual Landscape* (1994), *Eileen Gray* (2000), *The Modern Architectural Landscape* (2012), as well as numerous essays. She is working on a new book, "Cambridge Modern: Architecture and Landscape, 1930–1970," which probes the disciplinary contributions of professionals associated with three Cambridge institutions: MIT, Harvard, and the Cambridge School of Architecture and Landscape Architecture for Women.

PIERRE-ALAIN CROSET was born 1957 in Geneva and trained as an architect at the Swiss Federal Institute of Technology of Lausanne, graduating in 1982. Assistant editor of the architectural international magazine *Casabella* (Milan) from 1982 to 1996, he published many critical works on modern and contemporary architecture. From 1985 to 1993, he worked with Luigi Snozzi, first as an academic assistant at the Swiss Federal Institute of Technology of Lausanne and later as an architect in the Locarno office. From 1995, he has worked as a professional architect in Brescia (Italy). He was a visiting professor at Columbia University (New York) in 1994 and in 1997 he became a Full Professor in architecture at the Technical University of Graz, where he served as Dean of the Faculty of Architecture from 2001 to 2002. In 2002, he was appointed Professor for Architectural and Urban Design and Director of the College of Architecture at the Polytechnic School of Turin. He has been Professor for Architecture and Head of the Department of Architecture at Xi'an Jiatong-Liverpool University in Suzhou, China since 2015.

PATRICK DÜBLIN is an art historian whose research focuses on architecture, urbanism, and landscape. He received a Master's degree in Art History and Philosophy from the University of Basel. In addition to working as a research associate at the Chair of Professor Christophe Girot at the ETH Zurich, he is an assistant curator to Director Josef Helfenstein at the Kunstmuseum Basel.

SANDY ISENSTADT teaches the history of modern architecture at the University of Delaware. His writings range from postwar reformulations of modern architecture by émigré architects to topics such as picture windows, refrigerators, automobile headlights, landscape views, and real estate appraisal. He addresses spatial perception in the built environment in his book *The Modern American House: Spaciousness and Middle Class Identity*, published by Cambridge University Press and recipient of the 2009 Spiro Kostof Book Award from the Society of Architectural Historians. He has co-edited two volumes:

*Modernism and the Middle East: Politics of the Built Environment* (2008), the first book-length treatment of modern architecture in the Middle East; and *Cities of Light: Two Centuries of Urban Illumination* (2015), the first global history of urban lighting. His current book project, "The Architecture of Artificial Light," examines the novel, luminous spaces introduced by electric lighting. His work has been recognized with fellowships from the National Endowment for the Humanities, the Graham Foundation for Advanced Studies in the Fine Arts, the Center for Advanced Study in the Visual Arts, and the Institute for Advanced Study, in Princeton, New Jersey.

DAVID LEATHERBARROW is Professor of Architecture and Chair of the Graduate Group in Architecture at the University of Pennsylvania School of Design, Philadelphia. Previously he taught theory and design at Cambridge University and at the Polytechnic of Central London (now: University of Westminster). He has lectured throughout the world and has held guest professorships in the United Kingdom, Denmark, and China. Questions of how architecture appears, how architecture is constructed and sited, and how topography shapes architecture direct his research. He was taught by Dalibor Vesely and Joseph Rykwert, and has collaborated with numerous scholars in the field of architectural phenomenology and history. Among Leatherbarrow's ten books are: *Three Cultural Ecologies* (with Richard Wesley); *Companion to Modern Architectural History*; *Architecture Oriented Otherwise*; *Topographical Stories: Studies in Landscape and Architecture*; *Uncommon Ground: Architecture, Technology, and Topography*; *Surface Architecture* (with M. Mostafavi); *On Weathering: The Life Buildings in Time* (with M. Mostafavi); and *The Roots of Architectural Invention: Site, Enclosure, Materials*.

MARKO POGACNIK is currently Associate Professor for the History of Architecture at the Università Iuav di Venezia. He was DAAD Guest Professor at the Faculty of Architecture of the Fachhochschule Potsdam, and visiting professor in Dortmund, Innsbruck, and Kaiserslautern. He has held lectures and seminars in many European universities: TU Graz, RWTU Aachen, Academy of Architecture, Mendrisio, University of Geneva, ETH Zurich, University of Applied Arts in Vienna, Faculty of Architecture of Cottbus, ILEK in Stuttgart, TU Munich, TU Berlin, and TU Delft. In September 2007, he was jury chairman for the Jurkovic Prize, Bratislava and in March 2008, he delivered the Schinkel lecture in Potsdam. Invited by the National Museum of Contemporary Art of Seoul, he sat on the jury for the competition for the new MOCA Seoul in January 2010. He has published work on Adolf Loos, Karl Friedrich Schinkel, Adalberto Libera, Carlo Scarpa, Mies van der Rohe, Le Corbusier, Camillo Sitte, Theodor Fischer, Claude-Nicolas Ledoux, Friedrich Gilly, and Gottfried Semper. In 2011 he was curator of the exhibition *Adolf Loos und Wien* (Vienna), and in 2014 of the exhibition *Details: Architecture Seen in Section* in the *Biennale Architettura* (see www.detailsinsection.org).

MANFRED SPEIDEL was born in 1938. He studied architecture in Stuttgart and from 1966 to 1975 with Prof. T. Yoshizaka at Waseda University, Tokyo. In 1973, he completed his doctoral thesis entitled "Semiotic Considerations on Man-made Environment." From 1975 to 2003, he was Professor for Theory of Architecture at Aachen University with a strong focus on the history of traditional and modern architecture in Europe and Asia, and architectural anthropology. Since 1988, he has conducted research on the works of Bruno Taut and has edited his writings, especially those on Japan, in conjunction with exhibitions on Bruno Taut in Japan and Germany.

CHARLES WALDHEIM is a Canadian-American architect, urbanist, and educator. His research examines the relations between landscape, ecology, and contemporary urbanism. He is the author, editor, or co-editor of numerous books on these subjects, and his work has been published and translated internationally. Waldheim is the John E. Irving Professor and director of the Office for Urbanization at Harvard Graduate School of Design. He has lectured internationally and taught at Rice University, University of Toronto, University of Pennsylvania, and the University of Michigan. Waldheim received the Rome Prize Fellowship from the American Academy in Rome, the Visiting Scholar Research Fellowship at the Canadian Centre for Architecture, the Cullinan Chair at Rice University, and the Sanders Fellowship at the University of Michigan.

RICHARD WESTON is an architect, writer, and former Professor of Architecture at the Welsh School of Architecture, Cardiff University. Previously head of the University of Portsmouth School of Architecture, he has also taught at De Montfort University. Weston is the Director of Richard Weston Studio Ltd and Molly's World Ltd and has received several prizes for his design work. An authority on the architecture of Finland in general, and the work of Alvar Aalto in particular, he has led several architectural tours to Finland. His monograph, *Alvar Aalto* (1995), won the Sir Banister Fletcher Prize, and *Modernism* (1996) received the International Book Award of the American Institute of Architects. Other books include *Schools of Thought: Hampshire Architecture 1974–1991*, *Villa Mairea*, *Town Hall, Säynätsalo*, *Alvar Aalto, Materials, Form and Architecture*, and *100 Ideas that Changed Architecture*. In addition, he has contributed numerous articles to architectural journals. Since taking early retirement in 2013, he has been pursuing his fascination for minerals, which led to the development of "Weston scarves" for Liberty London and "Molly's World," a creative/educational app for children.

IMPRINT



Editing and Layout: Albert Kirchengast
Translations: Elena Carlini (Italian/English: Pogacnik), Steve Piccolo (Italian/English: Croset), Inez Templeton (German/English: Speidel and Pogacnik), First Edition
Translations: Laila Friese/edited by James Stedman (German/English: Foreword by Kirchengast) and Rae Walter/edited by Robert Anderson (German/English: Kirchengast)
Proofreading: Inez Templeton

Graphic design: Willi Schmid & Radim Peško
Lithography: Bild1Druck, Berlin
Typefaces: Landscript Condensed (radimpesko.com), DeVinne
Paper: Surbalin board, 350 g/m$^2$ (cover) and Amber Graphic, 115 g/m$^2$
Printed in the European Union.

Bibliographic information published by the Deutsche Nationalbibliothek
The Deutsche Nationalbibliothek lists this publication in the Deutsche Nationalbibliografie; detailed bibliographic data are available on the Internet at http://dnb.d-nb.de

jovis Verlag GmbH
Kurfürstenstrasse 15/16
10785 Berlin

www.jovis.de

ISBN 978-3-86859-213-9